Competition Law in China and the EU

This book presents a comprehensive review of the Chinese and European responses to the abuse of market dominance, with a focus on the impact of antitrust institutional dynamics on enforcement decisions.

It uses the methods of functional comparison and case analysis to investigate how theories of harm relating to specific types of abuse differ within and across competition law regimes due to institutional dynamics. The Chinese and EU competition law regimes serve as excellent examples for this investigation because they have similar substantive laws on paper but vastly different institutional settings. The book examines—first individually and then comparatively—how the distinct institutional dynamics in the Chinese and EU regimes shape the development of theories of harm.

This volume will appeal to competition law scholars, students, and practitioners seeking a more nuanced understanding of how competition law works in the EU and China. It will also interest scholars trying to approach the Chinese legal system from an engaging rather than alienating standpoint.

Xingyu Yan obtained his doctorate from University of Groningen and is currently Assistant Professor of competition law at School of Law, Xiamen University. His research interests lie primarily in digital markets regulation, competition law and sustainability, and antitrust institutional studies, with an emphasis on comparative perspectives. He has published in journals such as *Journal of Competition Law & Economics*, *Computer Law & Security Review*, *and Journal of Antitrust Enforcement*. He is a member of the Academic Society for Competition Law (ASCOLA) and was the winner of the ASCOLA Best Junior Paper Award in 2021.

Routledge Research in Competition Law

Competition and Regulation in the Airline Industry
Puppets in Chaos
Steven Truxal

Merger Control in Post-Communist Countries
EC Merger Regulation in Small Market Economies
Jurgita Malinauskaite

Merger Control in Europe
The Gap in the ECMR and National Merger Legislations
Ioannis Kokkoris

Harmonising Regulatory and Antitrust Regimes for International Air Transport
Jan Walulik

Collective Redress and EU Competition Law
Eda Sahin

Competition Policy and Network Industries
Structural Separation in the Telecommunications Sector
Pierluigi Congedo

Competition Laws, National Interests and International Relations
Ko Unoki

Private Law and Competition Regulation
A Comparative Study
Alberto Brown

Competition Law in China and the EU
Institutional Dynamics and Theories of Harm
Xingyu Yan

Competition Law in China and the EU

Institutional Dynamics and Theories of Harm

Xingyu Yan

Routledge
Taylor & Francis Group
LONDON AND NEW YORK

First published 2025
by Routledge
4 Park Square, Milton Park, Abingdon, Oxon OX14 4RN

and by Routledge
605 Third Avenue, New York, NY 10158

Routledge is an imprint of the Taylor & Francis Group, an informa business

British Library Cataloguing-in-Publication Data
A catalogue record for this book is available from the British Library

ISBN: 978-1-032-74015-7 (hbk)
ISBN: 978-1-032-76656-0 (pbk)
ISBN: 978-1-003-47943-7 (ebk)

DOI: 10.4324/9781003479437

Typeset in Times New Roman
by Apex CoVantage, LLC

To my loving parents

献给我的父母

Contents

	List of tables	*viii*
1	Introduction	1
2	Antitrust institutional dynamics	11
3	Theory of harm: An antitrust concept	30
4	The centralized EU supranational regime	53
5	The federated Chinese Anti-Monopoly Law regime	70
6	Development of theories of harm in the centralized EU regime	99
7	Development of theories of harm in the federated Chinese regime	147
8	Comparisons and conclusions	185
	Appendices	*195*
	Index	*215*

Tables

5.1 AML enforcement announcements issued by the SAIC from 2013 to 2018 80
5.2 AML enforcement decisions issued by the NDRC from 2008 to 2018 83
5.3 Intervention by the SAMR against abuses of administrative power that restrict competition from 2018 to 2023 85
5.4 Conditional clearance and prohibition decisions by the SAMR in reviewing concentrations of undertakings from 2018 to 2023 85
5.5 Enforcement by the SAMR against anticompetitive agreements, abuses of dominance, and other AML infringements from 2018 to 2023 85
5.6 AML administrative suits by 31 December 2023 89
5.7 AML civil cases filed each year from 2008 to 2015 94
7.1 Excessive pricing cases of the SAMR and AMRs by 31 December 2023 153
7.2 Court cases concerning excessive pricing by 31 December 2023 154
7.3 Court cases concerning tying and the imposition of unfair trading conditions by 31 December 2023 162

1 Introduction

Institutional difference between the Chinese and EU competition laws and the implication

EU competition law is a leading model of law on how to regulate market failures resulting from market power, and it has been successfully exported to China. In 2007, the Chinese central legislators adopted the Anti-Monopoly Law (AML), whose substantive rules display a high level of consistency with their EU counterparts.[1] Besides influencing the AML legislation, EU competition law also serves as a major source of inspiration for the enforcement agencies and courts seeking to develop secondary legislation and case precedents.[2]

Substantive law aside, however, the AML has a quite peculiar institutional design. First, it is a dual-track system comprising public enforcement by administrative agencies on the one hand and private enforcement through civil litigations on the other. This is a common design for competition law regimes around the world, but what makes the AML regime peculiar is the largely perfunctory judicial supervision on administrative agencies.[3] The background to this peculiarity is that although enforcement decisions by administrative agencies have become judicially reviewable since the adoption of the Administrative Litigation Law in 1989, subjecting administrative powers to courts' constraints remains a sensitive matter,[4] and the AML enforcement is no exception. As a result, Chinese courts' role

1 The consistency is shown in, e.g., the block exemptions for certain agreements, the factors considered for determination of the existence of dominant market position, and the rebuttable presumptions of dominant position. See Giacomo Di Federico, 'The New Anti-Monopoly Law in China from a European Perspective', *World Competition* 32, no. 2 (2009): 252–63; Xiaoye Wang, 'Highlights of China's New Anti-Monopoly Law', *Antitrust Law Journal* 75, no. 1 (2008): 134.

2 An example is the AML agencies' approach to analysing horizontal price-fixing agreements, which draws heavily on the EU's analytical framework for cartels. See Yichen Yang, 'Price-Related Cartels under the Chinese Anti-Monopoly Law Regime: The Need to Clarify Four Substantive and Procedural Issues', *World Competition* 39, no. 3 (2016): 497.

3 Angela Huyue Zhang, 'Taming the Chinese Leviathan: Is Antitrust Regulation a False Hope', *Stanford Journal of International Law* 51, no. 2 (2015): 211–12.

4 Haibo He, 'Litigations without a Ruling: The Predicament of Administrative Law in China', *Tsinghua China Law Review* 3 (2011): 262–6.

DOI: 10.4324/9781003479437-1

in applying the AML is largely limited to the private enforcement track, thereby becoming *de facto* 'competitors' to the public enforcement agencies in developing antitrust decisional law. Second, the AML originally adopted a tripartite structure for public enforcement, with three central administrative agencies sharing the AML enforcement responsibilities: the National Development and Reform Commission (NDRC) and the State Administration for Industry and Commerce (SAIC) were responsible for tackling price-related and non-price-related monopolization conduct, respectively, while the Ministry of Commerce (MOFCOM) was responsible for reviewing concentrations of undertakings. To be sure, this tripartite structure was abandoned in the government restructuring in 2018, but it still has a long-lasting impact in the sense that many enforcement decisions made during this era still hold high precedential value.

These two aspects of peculiarity make the institutional structure of the AML stand in contrast with that of EU competition law, where the European Commission (hereinafter, the Commission) assumes a central role in the Union-wide enforcement network and is placed under judicial supervision of the Court of Justice of the European Union (CJEU). Unlike the three AML agencies, the Commission does not share the public enforcement power with anyone at the Union level, and its decisions are often carefully scrutinized by the CJEU.[5] Meanwhile, the CJEU is tasked with not only adjudicating administrative suits at the Union level but also interpreting EU competition rules in civil cases at the Member States level through preliminary rulings.

In that light, a key variance emerges between the institutional structures of the two regimes: the presence or the lack of judicial supervision. This variance persists even now that the AML tripartite design has been consolidated, and it leads to two contrasting modes of institutional function allocation—and two contrasting sets of institutional dynamics—between the administration and the judiciary: in the EU competition law context, the judiciary supervises the administration, whereas in the Chinese AML context, the judiciary competes with the administration for enforcement authority.

This contrasting pair raises some interesting questions under the 'principal-agent relationship'. Specifically, one might wonder how the AML enforcement agencies are controlled if not through judicial supervision, and how the courts are controlled when they are functionally parallel to the enforcement agencies. After all, enforcement agencies are supposed to carry out their responsibilities under the delegation of their principal, i.e., the legislators; to prevent the delegated agents from disobedience, the principal needs monitoring and control through (political) hierarchical control, obedience-internalization with the agent, or third-party (judicial) supervision.[6] So if the legislators are using the courts as agents as opposed to third-party

5 Loannis Lianos and Arianna Andreangeli, 'The European Union: The Competition Law System and the Union's Norms', in *The Design of Competition Law Institutions: Global Norms, Local Choices*, ed. Eleanor M. Fox and Michael J. Trebilcock (Oxford: Oxford University Press, 2012), 390–1, 399–402.

6 Tom Ginsburg, 'Administrative Law and the Judicial Control of Agents in Authoritarian Regimes', in *Rule by Law: The Politics of Courts in Authoritarian Regimes*, ed. Tom Ginsburg and Tamir Moustafa (New York: Cambridge University Press, 2008), 61–2.

supervisors, they would have to resort to other ways to control enforcement agencies, and they would need to find a way to properly supervise the courts as well.[7]

Addressing these questions is a meaningful endeavour because first, it provides a critical account of how institutional dynamics shape substantive decisions in competition law, thereby contributing to the scholarship on antitrust epistemology from an institutional perspective. For instance, there could be a positive, complementary dynamic between the AML administrative agencies and courts in tackling anticompetitive practices,[8] but at the same time, there could also be inconsistent and erroneous law enforcement since the decision-making of the administrative agencies is not properly checked and the courts only deal with AML cases in civil proceedings and on a contingent basis.[9] Second, addressing these questions entails a comparative analysis of the EU and Chinese competition law regimes, which could help us gain a deeper understanding of these two regimes and promote global competition law convergence in necessary aspects.[10]

Addressing these questions is also feasible. First, after almost 16 years of enforcement, there have been considerable AML cases to serve as samples for analysing how the structurally enabled 'institutional competition' dynamic has affected the substantive decision outcomes. Second, it is also feasible to analyse how the 'supervisor-supervisee' dynamic has shaped the substantive decision outcomes on the EU side because of the abundance of EU case precedents. To be sure, the *substantive decision outcomes* of the Chinese and EU competition laws may entail too many cases and substantive aspects to be sufficiently analysed in a single book, so this monograph narrows the scope to the Chinese and EU laws on *abuse of dominance* and retains the focus on *theories of harm*, which play the key role of explaining the unlawfulness of the disputed practices in individual case decisions.

Research questions and background premises

This book asks a central research question: How do institutional dynamics affect substantive antitrust law enforcement, specifically the development of theories of harm in abuse of dominance cases? It seeks answers by analysing the EU and Chinese regimes, whose institutional dynamics pose an interesting contrast. This central question can be developed into the following sub-questions: (1) How are the institutional dynamics of the EU and Chinese laws on abuse of dominance?

7 Matthew C. Stephenson, 'Legislative Allocation of Delegated Power: Uncertainty, Risk, and the Choice between Agencies and Courts', *Harvard Law Review* 119, no. 4 (2006): 1042–5.

8 Xiaoye Wang and Adrian Emch, 'Five Years of Implementation of China's Anti-Monopoly Law—Achievements and Challenges', *Journal of Antitrust Enforcement* 1, no. 2 (1 October 2013): 263.

9 Qian Hao, 'An Overview of the Administrative Enforcement of China's Competition Law: Origin and Evolution', in *Procedural Rights in Competition Law in the EU and China*, ed. Caroline Cauffman and Qian Hao (Berlin, Heidelberg: Springer Berlin Heidelberg, 2016), 57.

10 Eleanor Fox, John Fingleton, and Sophie Mitchell, 'The Past and Future of International Antitrust: Gaps, Overlaps and the Institutional Challenge', in *Building New Competition Law Regimes*, ed. David Lewis (Edward Elgar Publishing, 2013), 178–80.

(2) What are the theories of harm developed by decision-makers in the EU and Chinese regimes, and to what extent can the development be attributed to the institutional dynamics? And (3) based on these within-regime analyses, what insights can be drawn from a cross-regime comparison?

These research questions are backdropped by the following premises. First, all institutional actors want to expand their institutional powers, thereby justifying treating the EU and Chinese regimes as comparable samples in answering the posed research questions. This book does not address the convergence or divergence of the EU and Chinese regimes *per se*; rather, it seeks to examine the causal relationship between institutional dynamics and the development of antitrust theories of harm through a comparative approach (i.e., by looking inside one regime while using the other regime as a reference point). It is indisputable that the EU and Chinese regimes are quite different in many broader aspects such as economic ideology and policy objectives and many micro aspects like the specific wordings of rules, but for answering the posed research questions, we can largely set aside these differences and treat the two regimes as comparable samples. This is because irrespective of the broader and micro regime differences, institutional actors in these two regimes are uniformly incentivized to expand their institutional powers, and they are invariably given the opportunity to do so when being tasked to apply the open-textured antitrust provisions in individual cases and produce a convincing narrative of competitive harm.

Second, every abuse of dominance law enforcement decision has at least one theory of harm. In the context of competition law, a theory of harm is essentially an explanation of how a business practice has caused actual or potential anticompetitive effects and therefore deserves to be outlawed. Legislated antitrust rules tend to be highly abstract in determining the unlawfulness of suspected abuse of dominance practices, so it falls largely on courts and administrative agencies to prove the applicability of the rules and the illegality of conduct in specific case circumstances. In other words, courts and agencies would have to supply a theory of harm when they want to outlaw a practice as an abuse of dominance. Such a theory of harm could be elaborate or concise, convincing or controversial, but it would always be there. To outline it, we could start with identifying the allegations of competitive harm, then summarizing the decision-maker's reasoning on how that harm came about. To analyse it, we need to start with the recognition that different types of abuses have more or less different theories of harm (depending on where and how they cause competitive harms) and that abuses of the same type may also entail certain differences (due to the varying case circumstances). For instance, the theories of harm underlying predatory pricing and refusal to deal are quite different because the former restricts competition in the dominant firm's market through below-cost prices while the latter restricts competition in an adjacent market through input or output-foreclosure; meanwhile, refusal to deal and margin squeeze have more similar theories of harm, as they both cause competitive harm in an adjacent market, although the means to that end are somewhat different; also, predatory pricing practices in different cases likely have varied theories of harm because there are different definitions of 'below-cost' suited for different case circumstances.

Third, we can assess the quality of a theory of harm in an objective or relative manner and in turn evaluate the performance of the decision-maker. A high-quality theory of harm is expected to be logically coherent and in conformity with general economic principles and theories, and it is supposed to show no less merit when compared to a theory of harm made by another authority on the same type of conduct. By assessing the logical consistency and economic sense of a theory of harm against industrial economic theories and similar case precedents, one could appraise the quality of substantive analyses in that case decision, which reflects the decision-maker's performance. On that basis, one could analyse whether and how the underlying institutional structure and dynamics have affected the performance. In short, after identifying a theory of harm in a case, we can critically analyse it—from an institutional perspective—as to why it is the way it is when it *should* have been another way (according to economic theories) or when it *could* have been another way (compared to a theory of harm produced by another authority on the same type of conduct).

Research methods

This book follows to a large extent the so-called doctrinal approach, in the sense that it focuses on analysing the content of case law.[11] It looks closely at the abuse of dominance case law of the EU and Chinese regimes and critically describes the theories of harm developed therein. The doctrinal approach is also used in describing the legal frameworks and the institutional structures of the two regimes, in order to understand what the laws are from a normative perspective.

This book also adopts the methods of literature review and historical analysis. First, it reviews the literature to supplement the doctrinal analyses of institutional dynamics and theories of harm. Particularly, it reviews law and economics literature to introduce the economic theories underpinning the development of theories of harm. Second, the book refers to the existing literature in selecting and categorizing the to-be-analysed cases. Although all abuse of dominance cases of the EU and China until recently are covered by this book, not all of them will be given primary attention nor all of them will necessarily appear in the final text. This is because these case precedents have varying degrees of relevance to the subject of this book: while some are 'landmark' cases with unmistakable precedential importance, some others contribute only marginally to the development of theories of harm. To determine which cases should get more attention and how they should be grouped, this book refers to well-recognized textbooks and journal articles concerning EU competition case law and Chinese AML enforcement. Third, this book relies on historical official documents and relevant research literature to describe the legislative and institutional developments over time in the EU and Chinese regimes.

11 Ian Dobinson and Francis Johns, 'Legal Research as Qualitative Research', in *Research Methods for Law*, ed. Michael McConville and Wing Hong Chui, Research Methods for the Arts and Humanities (Edinburgh: Edinburgh University Press, 2007), 25–6.

Last but not least, this book adopts the functional comparison method. Following epistemological functionalism's focus on the interrelations of elements (instead of the nature of each element),[12] this research focuses on the relationship between 'the structurally induced institutional dynamics' and 'the development of theories of harm' and compares the EU and Chinese regimes for their differences pertaining to that relationship. The purpose of the comparison is two-fold: first, using the EU regime as a benchmark for appraising the impact of the Chinese AML institutional structure on the production of theories of harm and, second, drawing lessons from the EU regime analyses for the Chinese regime and vice versa. After all, we have no perfect knowledge to solve all market power problems, so a useful way to improve antitrust enforcement is to reflect upon the past and draw lessons from one another.[13]

Structure

This book consists of eight chapters. Chapter 1 is the introduction. Chapters 2 and 3 establish the theoretical framework by discussing antitrust institutional dynamics and antitrust theories of harm, respectively. Chapters 4 and 5 describe the institutional structures and dynamics in the EU and Chinese abuse of dominance regulation regimes. Chapters 6 and 7 analyse the development of theories of harm in the EU and Chinese regimes. Chapter 8 is the conclusion.

Specifically, Chapter 2 frames institutional dynamics as an impact factor on substantive antitrust outcomes. It posits a 'political power game' where antitrust agencies and adjudicating courts are institutionally committed to enforcing competition law and are incentivized by the specific institutional structures to behave strategically in carrying out that commitment. It is in this game setting that institutional dynamics come into being and shape substantive enforcement outcomes. Institutional dynamics may stabilize over time in the forms of, *inter alia*, agency discretionary power and judicial deference. The key point is that driven by the desire to expand its powers, an antitrust agency or a court may develop theories of harm in individual cases in a strategic manner, which could cost the validity of these case decisions.

Chapter 3 spotlights the concept of theory of harm, which is commonly used in antitrust commentaries but is rarely examined systematically. This chapter first describes the narrating function and key attributes of theories of harm in abuse of dominance cases. Second, it identifies industrial economic theories as the main component of theories of harm and describes how the economic theories have evolved over the past century. Third, it constructs a layered analytical framework

12 Ralf Michaels, 'The Functional Method of Comparative Law', in *The Oxford Handbook of Comparative Law*, ed. Mathias Reimann and Reinhard Zimmermann (Oxford: Oxford University Press, 2006), 339–82, 355.

13 William E. Kovacic, 'Achieving Better Practices in the Design of Competition Policy Institutions', *Antitrust Bulletin* 50, no. 3 (2005): 516.

for delineating and appraising the theories of harm in actual individual case decisions.

Chapter 4 first examines the components of EU law on abuse of dominance, which includes Article 102 TFEU and other relevant Treaty provisions, secondary legislation, soft law, and CJEU case law. Subsequently, it dissects the interrelationships of the Court of Justice, the Commission, national courts of the Member States, and national competition agencies and characterizes the institutional structure for enforcing Article 102 at the supranational level as hierarchical.

Similarly structured as Chapter 4, Chapter 5 describes the legal framework and institutional structure of the AML. It highlights three features of the AML enforcement regime: (1) the tripartite public enforcement regime before the State Administration of Market Regulation (SAMR) consolidated the enforcement powers in 2018, (2) the uneasy relationship between the State Administration of Market Regulation (SAMR) and sector-specific regulators when it comes to regulating digital market competition, and (3) the close-to-zero judicial supervision upon national competition and sector-specific regulators. On this basis, this chapter characterizes the institutional structure for enforcing the AML as federated.

Chapter 6 delves into the development of theories of harm at the EU supranational level by the Commission and the Court of Justice. It first looks at the market integration mandate, which is the idiosyncratic component of the EU substantive law on abuse of dominance. Then it selects and analyses a number of case precedents from annulment proceedings and preliminary rulings about various types of abusive conduct. The endgame is to examine how, if at all, different institutional actors deliver different theories of harm and why. Summarizing observations are presented at the end.

Chapter 7 looks at (1) the development of theories of harm by the AML enforcers. It selects and analyses a sizable number of abuse of dominance cases by the AML enforcement agencies and adjudicating courts. The endgame, like that of Chapter 6, is to understand how different antitrust institutional actors deliver different theories of harm and why. Summarizing observations are presented after the analyses.

Chapter 8 consists of five parts. The first one summarizes and compares the institutional structures of the EU and Chinese laws on abuse of dominance. The second part summarizes the findings from Chapters 6 and 7 concerning the development of theories of harm in these two regimes. The third part discusses how the different theories of harm of the two regimes could be attributed to the different institutional structures and their implications. On that basis, the fourth part provides summary answers to the research question, and the fifth part points out directions for further research.

Notably, Chapters 5, 6, and 7 contain topics that were also addressed in previous publications by the author. In that regard, references to those publications are provided and direct or indirect repetition is omitted.

Limitations

This book has several limitations. First, regarding the substantive scope, it is limited to the law on abuse of dominance. 'Abuse of dominance' is a segment of competition law where the open texture and wording of the law necessitates greater conceptual clarity in the application, including more elaborate and more clearly defined theories of harm. Other segments of competition law (most notably anti-competitive agreements regulation and merger control) are equally worthy of discussion, and they are saved for further research.

Second, its perspectives are limited. By focusing on the link between institutional structures and the production of theories of harm, this book refrains from scrutinizing the more fundamental impact factors such as economic theories and policy objectives. Thoroughly discussing those factors would be too extensive for the scope of this research. Moreover, this book discusses only the impact of institutional dynamics on the development of theories of harm, while fully aware that institutional influences extend far beyond this area. For instance, the effect of institutional power dynamics on competition law enforcement manifests perhaps more saliently in what kind of cases are being pursued and dropped than in the development of theories of harm. After all, if a case has reached the illegality assessment stage, it implies that there has been a relatively high level of political consensus among the relevant institutional actors; otherwise, the case would not have gone this far. Lastly, this book makes an effort to construct the concept of theory of harm, but this construction is not in any way complete; it is open for discussions and criticisms.

Thirdly, pertaining to the Chinese part of this book, the case samples are comprised of the existing online-available enforcement decisions and judgments. They are analysed from a doctrinal perspective, with the incorporated theories of harm critically described in terms of their internal consistency of logic and the extent to which they are compatible with established economic theories. This book fully acknowledges but chooses not to focus on a more imminent issue vis-à-vis the AML: inadequate enforcement. Addressing this issue would require more than just legal doctrinal analyses of the existing case records; it would be beyond the scope of this book and is thus saved for further research.

A terminological clarification

Before proceeding with subsequent chapters, it is necessary to clarify the use of three expressions in this book: 'competition law', 'anti-monopoly law', 'antitrust law', and 'antitrust'.

To a certain extent, these first three expressions are just contextually different terms referring to the same substance. The expression 'competition law' is predominantly used in the EU context, referring to the overall enterprise of EU competition law and also to the equivalent enterprises of other jurisdictions when compared to the EU. Meanwhile, the expression 'antitrust law' is commonly adopted in the US context. Accordingly, the equivalent enterprises of other jurisdictions could be referred to as antitrust laws when compared to the US. Lastly, the expression 'anti-monopoly law' is used typically in China-related discussion contexts to refer to the AML, although it can also be seen in other contexts. For instance, in a neo-Brandeisian discussion context, it is meant as a more value-laden alternative to 'antitrust law'.[14]

Outside the US antitrust law context, 'antitrust' as a standalone term is also used in EU competition law to refer to the first two pillars of competition law—anticompetitive agreements regulation and abuse of dominance regulation. For example, the Commission consistently characterized Articles 81 and 82 of the EC Treaty (now Articles 101 and 102 TFEU) as 'antitrust rules' in its preparatory work for the Damages Directive.[15] Another example is the headings of the internal units of DG Comp of the Commission. However, it seems that the Commission and the EU legislature prefer to use the expression of 'antitrust' only outside formal legislations; for instance, the expression of 'antitrust' is nowhere to be found in the 2014 Directive on antitrust damage actions.[16]

This book focuses on the abuse of dominance regimes of the EU and China, so it uses the expressions of 'competition law' and 'anti-monopoly law' within their respective contexts, with the term 'antitrust law' being used only when the US regime enters the discussion. The word 'antitrust' is used occasionally (e.g., antitrust enforcement, antitrust institutional structures, and antitrust theories of harm), either as a reference to anticompetitive agreements regulation and abuse of dominance regulation combined or as a shorthand for abuse of dominance regulation—but only when the discussion contexts have made anticompetitive agreements regulation irrelevant.

Reference list

Di Federico, Giacomo. 'The New Anti-Monopoly Law in China from a European Perspective'. *World Competition* 32, no. 2 (2009): 249–70.

Dobinson, Ian, and Francis Johns. 'Legal Research as Qualitative Research'. In *Research Methods for Law*, edited by Michael McConville and Wing Hong Chui, 18–47. Research Methods for the Arts and Humanities. Edinburgh: Edinburgh University Press, 2007.

14 Lina Khan, 'The New Brandeis Movement: America's Antimonopoly Debate', *Journal of European Competition Law & Practice* 9, no. 3 (1 March 2018): 131–2.

15 See Green Paper—Damages Actions for Breach of the EU Antitrust Rules, COM(2008) 165 final, https://eur-lex.europa.eu/legal-content/EN/TXT/?uri=CELEX%3A52005DC0672 (accessed 6 April 2024), 3; White Paper on Damages Actions for Breach of the EC Antitrust Rules, COM(2008) 165 final, https://eur-lex.europa.eu/legal-content/EN/ALL/?uri=CELEX%3A52008DC0165 (accessed 6 April 2024), 2; Proposal for a Directive of the European Parliament and of the Council on certain rules governing actions for damages under national law for infringements of the competition law provisions of the Member States and of the European Union, COM(2013) 404 final, https://eur-lex.europa.eu/LexUriServ/LexUriServ.do?uri=COM:2013:0404:FIN:EN:PDF (accessed 6 April 2024), 3, 11.

16 Directive 2014/104/EU of the European Parliament and of the Council of 26 November 2014 on certain rules governing actions for damages under national law for infringements of the competition law provisions of the Member States and of the European Union [5 December 2014] OJ L 349, 1–19.

Fox, Eleanor, John Fingleton, and Sophie Mitchell. 'The Past and Future of International Antitrust: Gaps, Overlaps and the Institutional Challenge'. In *Building New Competition Law Regimes*, edited by David Lewis, 163–82. Edward Elgar Publishing, 2013.

Ginsburg, Tom. 'Administrative Law and the Judicial Control of Agents in Authoritarian Regimes'. In *Rule by Law: The Politics of Courts in Authoritarian Regimes*, edited by Tom Ginsburg and Tamir Moustafa, 58–72. New York: Cambridge University Press, 2008.

Hao, Qian. 'An Overview of the Administrative Enforcement of China's Competition Law: Origin and Evolution'. In *Procedural Rights in Competition Law in the EU and China*, edited by Caroline Cauffman and Qian Hao, 39–57. Berlin, Heidelberg: Springer Berlin Heidelberg, 2016. https://doi.org/10.1007/978-3-662-48735-8_3.

He, Haibo. 'Litigations without a Ruling: The Predicament of Administrative Law in China'. *Tsinghua China Law Review* 3 (2011): 257–81.

Khan, Lina. 'The New Brandeis Movement: America's Antimonopoly Debate'. *Journal of European Competition Law & Practice* 9, no. 3 (1 March 2018): 131–2. https://doi.org/10.1093/jeclap/lpy020.

Kovacic, William E. 'Achieving Better Practices in the Design of Competition Policy Institutions'. *Antitrust Bulletin* 50, no. 3 (2005): 511–18.

Lianos, Loannis, and Arianna Andreangeli. 'The European Union: The Competition Law System and the Union's Norms'. In *The Design of Competition Law Institutions: Global Norms, Local Choices*, edited by Eleanor M. Fox and Michael J. Trebilcock, 384–443. Oxford: Oxford University Press, 2012.

Michaels, Ralf. 'The Functional Method of Comparative Law'. In *The Oxford Handbook of Comparative Law*, edited by Mathias Reimann and Reinhard Zimmermann, 339–82. Oxford: Oxford University Press, 2006.

Stephenson, Matthew C. 'Legislative Allocation of Delegated Power: Uncertainty, Risk, and the Choice between Agencies and Courts'. *Harvard Law Review* 119, no. 4 (2006): 1035–70. https://doi.org/10.2307/4093481.

Wang, Xiaoye. 'Highlights of China's New Anti-Monopoly Law'. *Antitrust Law Journal* 75, no. 1 (2008): 133–50.

Wang, Xiaoye, and Adrian Emch. 'Five Years of Implementation of China's Anti-Monopoly Law—Achievements and Challenges'. *Journal of Antitrust Enforcement* 1, no. 2 (1 October 2013): 247–71. https://doi.org/10.1093/jaenfo/jnt010.

Yang, Yichen. 'Price-Related Cartels under the Chinese Anti-Monopoly Law Regime: The Need to Clarify Four Substantive and Procedural Issues'. *World Competition* 39, no. 3 (2016): 479–512.

Zhang, Angela Huyue. 'Taming the Chinese Leviathan: Is Antitrust Regulation a False Hope'. *Stanford Journal of International Law* 51, no. 2 (2015): 195–228.

2 Antitrust institutional dynamics

Institutional dynamics as an impact factor on antitrust substantive law

The meaning of institutions

'Institution' is a term that could accommodate a wide range of conceptions. As Clague (1997) stated:

> [Institutions] can be organizations or sets of rules within organizations. They can be markets or particular rules about the way a market operates. They can refer to the set of property rights and rules governing exchanges in a society. . . . They may include cultural norms of behavior.[1]

But normally, institutions are understood as the sets of rules within organizations, such as training systems, legal systems, political systems, and educational systems.[2] For example, Nobel laureate Douglass C. North defined institutions as 'the humanly devised constraints that structure human interaction' to achieve efficient outcomes for those with the power to make rules, consisting of 'formal constraints (e.g., rules, laws, constitutions), informal constraints (e.g., norms of behavior, conventions, self-imposed codes of conduct), and their enforcement characteristics'.[3]

In light of the previous discussion, 'institutions' in the context of competition law could be understood flexibly. For example, when studying the institutions of the US antitrust regime, Crane (2011) observed that on the one hand, a broad economic definition of institutions could 'cover the entire spectrum of substantive legal norms, procedural rules, and informal mechanisms that comprise the antitrust

1 Christopher Clague, 'The New Institutional Economics and Economic Development', in *Institutions and Economic Development: Growth and Governance in Less-Developed and Post-Socialist Countries*, ed. Christopher Clague (Johns Hopkins University Press, 1997), 18.

2 Glenn Morgan et al., 'Introduction', in *The Oxford Handbook of Comparative Institutional Analysis*, ed. Glenn Morgan et al., Oxford Handbooks (Oxford: Oxford University Press, 2010), 3.

3 Douglass C. North, 'Economic Performance Through Time', *The American Economic Review* 84, no. 3 (1994): 360.

DOI: 10.4324/9781003479437-2

enterprise', but on the other hand, a narrower definition would simply be 'formally established governmental bodies'.[4] Eventually, Crane adopted a definition of institutions that includes both formally and informally established norms that contribute to (and also those that exert countervailing forces to) the application of substantive antitrust norms, and he distinguished antitrust institutions from substantive procedural antitrust rules.[5]

This book adopts a definition of institutions that builds on the one by Crane. Since the subject is the impact of institutional dynamics on the development of theories of harm, this book construes the institutions of a competition law regime as including the following two groups of actors: (1) administrative agencies entrusted with the public antitrust enforcement responsibilities; (2) courts that have the competence to adjudicate private antitrust suits and the ones that have the judicial competence to supervise the public enforcement agencies.

Interdependence and equilibration of the institutional actors

These two groups of institutional actors—enforcement agencies and adjudicating courts—are interrelated in a constant process of equilibration, much like animals in an ecosystem.[6] On that basis, they give rise to various types of institutional dynamics, in the sense that actions taken by one actor can be accentuated or offset by those of another.[7]

The concept of equilibration was originally brought to antitrust law by Calkin (1986), who suggested that, as changes occur in a legal system, 'the equilibrium position will depend both on the initial action and on the legal system's reaction'.[8] In the case of treble damages in US antitrust law, he found that this perceivably harsh standard of liability had induced courts' reluctance to impose sanctions and consequently restrained the reach of antitrust law in private litigations.[9]

The study of antitrust institutional interdependence and equilibration is premised on the relatively high level of confidence in state intervention as a supplement to the invisible hand of the market.[10] In other words, there is a normative dimension to the study: the interdependence and equilibration of antitrust institutional actors—along with the resulting institutional dynamics—is supposed to be working to ensure that the various operations taken by these actors are indeed addressing market failures

4 Daniel A. Crane, *The Institutional Structure of Antitrust Enforcement* (Oxford: Oxford University Press, 2011), xii.

5 Crane, *The Institutional Structure of Antitrust Enforcement*, xii–xiii; Daniel A. Crane, 'A Neo-Chicago Perspective on Antitrust Institutions', *Antitrust Law Journal* 78, no. 1 (2012): 49.

6 D. Daniel Sokol, 'Antitrust, Institutions, and Merger Control', *George Mason Law Review* 17 (2010): 1055.

7 William E. Kovacic, 'The Institutions of Antitrust Law: How Structure Shapes Substance', *Michigan Law Review* 110, no. 6 (2012): 1026.

8 Stephen Calkins, 'Summary Judgment, Motions to Dismiss, and Other Examples of Equilibrating Tendencies in the Antitrust System', *Georgetown Law Journal* 74 (1986): 1066.

9 Calkins, 'Summary Judgment, Motions to Dismiss', 1083.

10 Crane, 'A Neo-Chicago Perspective on Antitrust Institutions', 48–9.

and not creating government failures. To verify whether that is the case in reality, a promising approach is to explore how the institutional dynamics have shaped the development of antitrust substantive law.

The development of antitrust law and the underlying institutional dynamics

A law exists on the basis of its own structure while exerting an impact on society through its application.[11] This raises questions as to (1) how the law will develop and (2) what factors contribute to its development. These questions are especially relevant when the law is compared to a law of the same kind in a different jurisdiction.

To question (1), there is a spectrum of potential answers between two ends: one is function-determinist, arguing that all laws, as long as they serve the same functions or have the same teleology, evolve towards the same ideal template; the other one is context-based, suggesting that there is more contingency and individuality regarding the path of each law's development.[12] The law on abuse of dominance is somewhere in between. On the one hand, the law on abuse of dominance of a particular jurisdiction follows—or ought to follow—some principles that transcend jurisdictional boundaries because they are sustained by contemporary economic theories.[13] This underpins the global proliferation of competition laws and prompts the need for convergence, especially on the substantive part.[14] On the other hand, the law on abuse of dominance of a jurisdiction would most definitely have its individuality, as reflected in e.g., its regime-specific legal objectives. It would, therefore, be ignorant to say that there exists a 'one-size-fits-all' solution for all jurisdictions without the need to consider their respective contexts such as the stages of economic development,[15] and naive to say that policy agendas and political influences play no part in the law application.[16]

In that light, the development of an abuse of dominance law can be assessed with two criteria: horizontal coherence and vertical consistency. The first criterion

11 Glenn Morgan and Sigrid Quack, 'Law as a Governing Institution', in *The Oxford Handbook of Comparative Institutional Analysis*, ed. Glenn Morgan et al., Oxford Handbooks (Oxford: Oxford University Press, 2010), 277.

12 Morgan and Quack, 'Law as a Governing Institution', 279–82.

13 Ariel Ezrachi, 'Sponge', *Journal of Antitrust Enforcement* 5, no. 1 (2017): 59–60.

14 Eleanor M. Fox and Michael J. Trebilcock, 'Introduction', in *The Design of Competition Law Institutions: Global Norms, Local Choices*, ed. Eleanor M. Fox and Michael J. Trebilcock (Oxford: Oxford University Press, 2012), 45–6.

15 Umut Aydin and Tim Büthe, 'Competition Law & Policy in Developing Countries: Explaining Variations in Outcomes; Exploring Possibilities and Limits', *Law and Contemporary Problems* 79, no. 4 (2016): 15–26.

16 For some exemplifications of how wider policies and politics influence the application of competition laws, see generally, William E. Kovacic, 'Politics and Partisanship in U.S. Federal Antitrust Enforcement', *Antitrust Law Journal* 79, no. 2 (2014): 687–711. Angela Huyue Zhang, 'Bureaucratic Politics and China's Anti-Monopoly Law', *Cornell International Law Journal* 47, no. 3 (2014): 671–708.

responds to the need of the law to maintain a certain level of conformity with the neutral and universally applicable objectives and principles.[17] It entails a certain degree of similarity of abuse of dominance laws across jurisdictions, primarily in substance but also in procedural and institutional aspects.[18] The second criterion derives from the requirements of accountability and legitimacy in administrative law,[19] and it entails a property of continuity and cumulativeness of antitrust law enforcement.[20] For studies on the development of a competition law, the implication is that we need to look at how the law is evolving on a more substantive level and in a wider timeframe, rather than obsessing with superficial and shorter-term changes such as staff appointments.[21] This book adopts these two criteria and devises a study in which it first analyses how antitrust theories of harm have developed in the EU and China for their respective vertical consistencies and then compares them for their horizontal coherence.

To question (2), institutional dynamics are definitely an impact factor. After all, when a substantive law is applied and interpreted, it is never a simple deduction of legal text; instead, it is a complex process contextualized and effectuated by the institutional settings.[22] Discussing institutional dynamics is therefore crucial, which entails analysing the ways 'by which each part of the interconnected institutional system works together smoothly'.[23] Multiple subtopics could be formulated in this discussion, including but not limited to the capabilities of administrative agencies and courts in carrying out their enforcement responsibilities and the role of institutional self-interest in their decision-making.[24]

A political power game

The previous section overviews the role of institutional dynamics in shaping antitrust substantive law. To explain how the shaping takes place, this section introduces a 'political power game' featuring two assumptions regarding the institutional commitment of antitrust agencies and courts to enforcing competition law and their strategic behaviour to gain more power for that commitment, respectively.

17 Kent Roach, 'What's New and Old about the Legal Process Review Article', *University of Toronto Law Journal* 47 (1997): 373 (introducing the concepts of horizontal coherence and vertical coherence and referring to the former as the consistency with 'contemporary materials and values').

18 Fox and Trebilcock, 'Introduction', 2–4.

19 Fox and Trebilcock, 'Introduction', 1.

20 William E. Kovacic, 'The Modern Evolution of U.S. Competition Policy Enforcement Norms', *Antitrust Law Journal* 71, no. 2 (2003): 381.

21 Kovacic, 'The Modern Evolution of U.S. Competition Policy Enforcement Norms', 394 (criticizing the pendulum narrative for understanding the US antitrust evolution and introducing the concept of constrained continuity).

22 William N. Eskridge and Philip P. Frickey, 'The Making of "The Legal Process"', *Harvard Law Review* 107, no. 8 (1994): 2043–5, 2053.

23 Eskridge and Frickey, 'The Making of "The Legal Process"', 2044–5.

24 Roach, 'What's New and Old about the Legal Process', 386, 390.

Institutional commitment to enforcing competition law

The first assumption is that if we hold constant the variable of enforcement costs, antitrust agencies and adjudicating courts of a competition law regime would be institutionally committed to enforcing the competition law. Consequently, we should expect them to make high-quality enforcement decisions. This can be explained from a cost-benefit perspective: administrative agencies and courts can be seen as the 'agents' tasked by competition policymakers and legislators—the 'principals'—to operationalize competition law; accordingly, their commitment to this task depends on what they can gain and what they have to pay.

On the one hand, they would be institutionally committed to enforcing competition law because they can gain bureaucratic 'benefits' that are preset by their principals within the constitutional framework in general and the antitrust institutional structure in particular. After all, the coming into force of a competition law requires the designated agencies and courts to be sufficiently incentivized and accountable to assume the law enforcement responsibilities coming their way.

That being said, vis-à-vis competition law enforcement *in particular industries*, the principals may not have set the attainable benefits at an optimal level because they have counterbalancing policy considerations in those industries (e.g., establishing national champions and protecting national strategic interests). It is only when the counterbalancing interests diminish that they will increase the attainable benefits for the agencies and courts to induce more intense competition law enforcement. For example, antitrust agencies and courts in China had refrained from applying the Anti-Monopoly Law to the digital platform industry for over a decade because the central government had adopted a laissez-faire 'tolerant and cautious' policy stance; but circa 2020–2021, the central government suddenly changed to a hardened 'preventing disorderly capital expansion' policy stance, prompting a series of ground-breaking antitrust actions being quickly taken in the Chinese digital platform industry.[25] Furthermore, vis-à-vis competition law enforcement *in particular cases*, the attainable benefits may not have been set at an optimal level because the institutional structure is ill-prepared for the potential conflicts of interest between different principals. For example, when dealing with a case where a local champion firm is accused of wrongdoing, a local agency or court may be incentivized by the central government to strictly enforce competition law, while also pressured by the local government to relax enforcement. Unless the institutional structure resolves this central-local conflict of interest beforehand, the local agency or court's commitment to enforcing competition law will likely be undermined. This is exemplified in the *Qihoo v Tencent* case, in which the motive to protect a local champion from being labelled as a dominant firm drove the first-instance court to define an overly broad relevant market. This case is analysed in Chapter 7. In

25 Thomas F. Remington, Jiwei Qian, and Svetlana Avdasheva, 'Regulating Competition in the Digital Platform Economy: Russia and China Compared', *Problems of Post-Communism* 71, no. 1 (2 January 2024): 18; Angela Huyue Zhang, 'Agility Over Stability: China's Great Reversal in Regulating the Platform Economy', *Harvard International Law Journal* 63, no. 2 (2022): 487.

any event, when designated by competition policymakers and legislators to enforce competition law, administrative agencies and courts would be committed to this task, at least to the extent that the policymakers and legislators want them to be.

On the other hand, by committing to competition law enforcement, agencies and courts incur 'costs' to the government resources allocated to them such as staff and budget. After all, committing to competition law enforcement entails, among others, diligently taking on cases and reducing (false positive and false negative) enforcement errors in individual cases as much as possible. But first, government resources tend to be scarce,[26] which means agencies and courts can only take on a limited number of cases within a given timeframe without compromising the decision-making quality in each case. Agencies usually have a system to pick and prioritize cases,[27] whereas courts have less discretion in turning away or playing favourites with the cases brought before them, but given limited resources, they may try to unload cases to settlement procedures. Second, agencies and courts have to deal with varying levels of imperfect information in individual cases. The more informationally disadvantaged they are in individual circumstances, the more costly it is to achieve precise findings of unlawful conduct (i.e., to reduce enforcement errors).[28] The upshot is that as enforcement costs increase while the bureaucratic benefits remain unchanged, the commitment of agencies and courts to enforcing competition law would diminish. Put differently, agencies and courts' commitment to enforcing competition law would remain at a certain level if we hold constant enforcement costs—by, for example, increasing bureaucratic benefits proportionally when enforcement costs rise.

Incentive and possibility to take strategic actions for more power

The second assumption is that administrative agencies and courts committed to enforcing competition law would behave strategically within the bounds of the encompassing institutional structure. Their behaviour is strategic in the sense that it is to achieve an objective outside of themselves—i.e., to gain more competition law enforcement power than they already have. They are incentivized to take strategic actions because having more power would allow them to deliver better enforcement outcomes (i.e., processing more cases and making fewer enforcement errors) while spending a given amount of government resources, which in turn allows them to gain more bureaucratic benefits without raising enforcement costs.

26 C. Frederick Beckner and Steven C. Salop, 'Decision Theory and Antitrust Rules', *Antitrust Law Journal* 67, no. 1 (1999): 42.

27 Or Brook and Katalin J. Cseres, 'Priority Setting as the Blind Spot of Administrative Law Enforcement: A Theoretical, Conceptual, and Empirical Study of Competition Authorities in Europe', *The Modern Law Review* (17 April 2024): 25, https://doi.org/10.1111/1468-2230.12881; Wouter P. J. Wils, 'Discretion and Prioritisation in Public Antitrust Enforcement, in Particular EU Antitrust Enforcement', *World Competition* 34, no. 3 (2011): 357.

28 Isaac Ehrlich and Richard A. Posner, 'An Economic Analysis of Legal Rulemaking', *The Journal of Legal Studies* 3, no. 1 (1974): 268–70.

The specific institutional settings and arrangements make various strategic actions possible. In other words, agencies and courts resort to different power-grabbing strategies based on how they are institutionally empowered and constrained. For example, if the decisions made by an antitrust agency are subject to substantive scrutiny by courts, the agency is likely to invoke administrative agency discretion to loosen judicial control.[29] Meanwhile, when the development of a market brings forward new regulatory issues, an antitrust agency may use its generalist competition-protection mandate to race with the specific sector regulator for authority over such issues. Also, when interacting with their principals, agencies and courts may try to bargain and willingly give up certain things (e.g., public fanfare) in exchange for greater independence in enforcing competition law.[30]

To sum up at this point, committing to competition law enforcement makes agencies and courts act strategically for more enforcement power, and the specific strategic actions they take may vary according to the circumstances. The underlying concern is that driven by the desire to expand its power, an antitrust agency or a court may develop theories of harm in individual cases in a strategic manner, which could cost the validity of those case decisions and skew the substantive development of the law. To further understand the strategic-action dynamics, the following subsection takes a closer look at the two groups of strategic action-takers.

Players of the game: enforcement agencies and adjudicating courts

Enforcement agencies

Establishing a new agency or designating an existing agency for enforcement?

Public antitrust enforcement responsibilities could be assigned either to a new establishment or to an existing institution within the executive branch. This is a significant choice because either the enforcement agency would have a single mandate, or it would need to accommodate the antitrust responsibilities into a multi-folded mandate portfolio.[31] If it is the former, the agency would gain more independence and, therefore, a more solid basis for delivering consistent enforcement outcomes and developing the necessary technocracy.[32] But if it is the latter, the agency would be more susceptible to policy influences and external constraints, as exemplified by how the Nixon government used the Antitrust Division of the US Department of Justice for political ends.[33]

29 Michael S. McFalls, 'Institutional Design and Federal Antitrust Enforcement Agencies: Renovation or Revolution?', *Competition Policy International* 10, no. 1 (2014): 161.

30 Daniel A. Crane, 'Technocracy and Antitrust', *Texas Law Review* 86, no. 6 (2008): 1181.

31 Crane, 'A Neo-Chicago Perspective on Antitrust Institutions', 56.

32 Sokol, 'Antitrust, Institutions, and Merger Control', 1074–5; Crane, 'Technocracy and Antitrust', 1181.

33 Maurice E. Stucke, 'Does the Rule of Reason Violate the Rule of Law', *U.C. Davis Law Review* 42 (2009): 1448–50.

The different implications of an agency having singular or multiple mandates are exemplified in the US antitrust institutional structure, where the Antitrust Division of the Department of Justice (DOJ) (an agency in the executive branch) and the Federal Trade Commission (FTC) (an independent administrative agency) share antitrust enforcement responsibilities. It was observed that, in the field of merger control where the two agencies had overlapping authority, the FTC tended to be more aggressive in preserving competition while the DOJ was more laissez-faire.[34] The US institutional structure differs from the situations of the EU competition law regime and the Chinese Anti-Monopoly Law (AML) regime, as the DG Comp of the European Commission and the Chinese enforcement agencies are set within their respective executive branches.

Agency discretionary power

When a specific agency is designated to enforce competition law, a key question is how much discretionary power, or autonomy, should be conferred to it. The answer to that question depends essentially on how difficult it is for legislators to precisely identify unlawful conduct and provide remedies in varying circumstances at the legislation stage. If the difficulty is relatively small, the legislators would be able to formulate the law with a high level of specification, thus leaving little room for agencies and courts to interpret it alternatively. But if the difficulty is rather great, the legislators would probably need to formulate the law with more flexibility so as to leave the nitty-gritty of identifying unlawful conduct and devising remedies in individual cases to agencies with growing experience on the matter. These two types of legislative approaches result in law in the forms of 'rules' and 'standards', respectively. Generally speaking, rules refer to the type of legislation that specifies the solution to a societal problem and leaves only room for the determination of facts, whereas standards are the type of legislation that gives only general instruction and delegates the formation of solutions to particular institutions because the legislature is not sure how to proceed with a societal problem.[35] In short, what matters is to achieve a certain level of enforcement precision with a minimum amount of enforcement costs,[36] and in many situations, that entails legislators delegating the power to concretize the law to administrative agencies.

Besides the level of legislative specification, another determinant of agency discretionary power is the clarity of the legal objectives, which the agencies are expected to honour. Clearly explained objectives help align the enforcement focus in terms of both setting priorities and handling particular cases, while broad and

34 Rachel E. Barkow and Peter W. Huber, 'A Tale of Two Agencies: A Comparative Analysis of FCC and DOJ Review of Telecommunications Mergers Antitrust in the Information Age', *University of Chicago Legal Forum* 2000 (2000): 81–2.

35 Franziska Weber, 'European Integration Assessed in the Light of the "Rules vs. Standards Debate"', *European Journal of Law and Economics* 35, no. 2 (2013): 189–91.

36 See generally, Louis Kaplow, 'Rules versus Standards: An Economic Analysis', *Duke Law Journal* 42, no. 3 (1992): 557–629, https://doi.org/10.2307/1372840.

vague objectives create opportunities for agency discretion.[37] It was suggested that the ambiguity and plurality of competition law objectives necessitated a considerable margin of enforcement agency discretion.[38] A crucial aspect of such discretion is prosecutorial discretion, which enables an enforcement agency to prioritize the kinds of infringements to pursue and to determine the degrees of sanction.[39]

Premised under rational decision-making, discretionary power entails that an agency has the freedom and authority to make certain decisions and that those decisions are to be received with deference by other institutions.[40] In that light, exercising discretionary power also means reining it, both internally and externally. Internally, the exercise of discretionary power is guided by an agency's self-imposed norms, i.e., the 'customs or standards that members of a group develop voluntarily and apply to themselves'.[41] These norms evolve on the basis of experimentation, *ex post* self-evaluation, and changes in institutional design. Externally, judicial supervision is a crucial mechanism to ensure that agencies exercise their discretionary power properly.[42] Although, by creating an opposition of stance between the courts and the administrative agencies, this mechanism raises questions about whether generalist courts are capable of assessing the economic complexity prevalent in antitrust cases better than antitrust agencies.[43] Another important external mechanism is congressional control or any other form of principal control. But this mechanism raises questions as to how it should be carried out and whether this political and often populism-driven kind of control is compatible with the technocratic nature of antitrust enforcement.[44]

Ideological mindset

To fulfill their public antitrust enforcement responsibilities, administrative agencies need to engage intensively in the assessment of complex economic facts as well as the application of highly abstract legal standards. This requires the agencies to possess a high level of antitrust economics expertise. But there are various antitrust schools of thought, and they have varied influences on antitrust agencies in different times and different regions. Consequently, antitrust agencies may display

37 Fox and Trebilcock, 'Introduction', 7.

38 Albert A. Foer, 'The Politics of Antitrust in the United States: Public Choice and Public Choices', *University of Pittsburgh Law Review* 62, no. 3 (2001): 477.

39 Wils, 'Discretion and Prioritisation', 357–64.

40 D. J. Galligan, *Discretionary Powers: A Legal Study of Official Discretion* (Oxford: Oxford University Press, 1990), 7–9, 12–13.

41 Kovacic, 'Modern Evolution of U.S. Competition Policy', 395.

42 See generally, Martin Shapiro, *Who Guards the Guardians?: Judicial Control of Administration* (Athens, GA: University of Georgia Press, 1988).

43 Michael R. Baye and Joshua D. Wright, 'Is Antitrust Too Complicated for Generalist Judges? The Impact of Economic Complexity and Judicial Training on Appeals', *The Journal of Law & Economics* 54, no. 1 (2011): 20.

44 Rachel E. Barkow, 'Overseeing Agency Enforcement (Foreword)', *George Washington Law Review* 84, no. 5 (2016): 1170–80; Crane, 'Technocracy and Antitrust', 1162, 1181.

distinct ideological mindsets.[45] It was observed that the ideological mindsets of antitrust decision-makers had a wide range of substantive implications, from the balancing of different objectives at a fundamental level to the perception of facts at a more superficial level.[46] Similarly, courts may also exhibit a tendency of following certain economic schools of thought. For example, it was suggested that the US courts had been fundamentally influenced by the Chicago/Harvard double helix; particularly, the Chicago School prevailed in the US Supreme Court, although the Harvard School occasionally rose to dominance.[47] But of course, these observed 'ideological mindsets' of the institutions are composed of the political and economic preferences of the individuals inside those institutions.[48]

There are several notable points. First, an ideological mindset cannot be a premeditated design choice; rather, it can only appear through an inclusive and progressive process where different ways of legal and economic thinking can interact and merge.[49] Usually, the more diverse the staff's backgrounds are, the less rigid the mindset would be.[50] In that light, to grasp the dominant mindset of an agency, one is advised to look at the recently made decisions, as some scholars have already done.[51] Second, different ideological mindsets do not necessarily result in different stances on a specific issue. For example, it was observed that although the Chicago School and the Harvard School disagree with each other on many issues, they share a common distrust of non-court antitrust institutions.[52] Third, the level of independence of an institution tends to relate positively to the strength of its mindset. This partly explains why many studies on antitrust ideological mindsets have been focused on court judgments and legislative documents,[53] as the courts

45 Daniel A. Crane, 'Chicago, Post-Chicago, and Neo-Chicago (Reviewing How the Chicago School Overshot the Mark: The Effect of Conservative Economic Analysis on U.S. Antitrust by Robert Pitofsky)', *The University of Chicago Law Review* 76, no. 4 (2009): 1912; Kovacic, 'Modern Evolution of U.S. Competition Policy', 401.

46 John J. Flynn, 'Antitrust Jurisprudence: A Symposium on the Economic, Political and Social Goals of Antitrust Policy: Introduction', *University of Pennsylvania Law Review* 125, no. 6 (1977): 1183, 1187–8.

47 William E. Kovacic, 'The Intellectual DNA of Modern U.S. Competition Law for Dominant Firm Conduct: The Chicago/Harvard Double Helix', *Columbia Business Law Review* 1, no. 1 (2007): 14–15; Crane, 'Chicago, Post-Chicago, and Neo-Chicago', 1918–20.

48 Kovacic, 'Modern Evolution of U.S. Competition Policy', 394.

49 McFalls, 'Institutional Design and Federal Antitrust Enforcement Agencies', 162.

50 Sigrid Quack, 'Legal Professionals and Transnational Law-Making: A Case of Distributed Agency', *Organization* 14, no. 5 (1 September 2007): 645–6.

51 See generally, Einer R. Elhauge, 'Harvard, Not Chicago: Which Antitrust School Drives Recent U.S. Supreme Court Decisions?', *Competition Policy International* 3, no. 2 (2007): 59–77. Kovacic, 'The Intellectual DNA of Modern U.S. Competition Law for Dominant Firm Conduct'.

52 Daniel A. Crane, 'linkLine's Institutional Suspicions', *Cato Supreme Court Review* 2008–2009 (2009): 123.

53 See for example, Kovacic, 'The Intellectual DNA of Modern U.S. Competition Law for Dominant Firm Conduct'. Pinar Akman, 'Searching for the Long-Lost Soul of Article 82EC', *Oxford Journal of Legal Studies* 29, no. 2 (2009): 267–303.

and legislative bodies generally face fewer institutional constraints compared to administrative agencies.

Different ideological mindsets are likely to fall at various points on a continuum with respect to their levels of confidence in the market's self-correction ability. More specifically, different mindsets answer differently to this question: Which is more costly from an institutional standpoint, false positive errors (over-enforcement) or false negative errors (under-enforcement)?[54] This question is expanded on in the next chapter, which describes the underlying rationales of antitrust decision-making from a law and economics perspective.

Adjudicating courts

Supervising public enforcement: bases and limit

The separation of powers is the first and foremost basis for courts to supervise public antitrust enforcement by administrative agencies. As described in the previous subsection, legislators confer on administrative agencies a certain amount of discretionary power to enforce competition law. Therein lies a principal-agent relationship: much as these agencies have discretionary power, they as the law enforcers are subordinate to and functionally separate from the lawmakers. Consequently, these agencies' exercise of discretionary power must adhere to the scope and conditions as laid down by the legislators to be constitutionally justified.[55] This constraint is grounded on the belief that the exercise of discretionary power needs to be consistent with 'political values that are considered to be sufficiently important within a community to extend to all varieties of government actions'.[56] Responding to the need for supervising discretionary agencies, the idea that institutions with different functions could check and balance against each other was formulated on the basis of the separation of powers, and subsequently, the idea of the judiciary as the supervisor on the other branches of power began to develop in practice, initially in US constitutional law.[57]

But there is still one piece missing: in a democratic regime, the legislature holds the political supremacy because it is democratically established; the administrative agencies are empowered by the legislature to enforce laws and, therefore, are accountable to it; but the judiciary as an institution is also created and generally empowered by the legislature.[58] In that light, the separation of powers alone cannot

54 Sokol, 'Antitrust, Institutions, and Merger Control', 1062.

55 Galligan, *Discretionary Powers*, 208, 228.

56 Galligan, *Discretionary Powers*, 209.

57 Galligan, *Discretionary Powers*, 228–9. See also, Roger Alford, 'Deputy Assistant Attorney General Roger Alford Delivers Remarks at the University of Pennsylvania/UIBE Conference: Due Process in Antitrust Enforcement: China, Europe, and the United States', www.justice.gov/opa/speech/deputy-assistant-attorney-general-roger-alford-delivers-remarks-university.

58 Tom Zwart, 'Overseeing the Executive: Is the Legislature Reclaiming Lost Territory from the Courts?', in *Comparative Administrative Law*, ed. Susan Rose-Ackerman and Peter Lindseth (Edward Elgar Publishing, 2010), 148–9, 159–60.

justify why the judiciary should interfere with the accountability chain between the authority-delegating legislature and the directly delegated administration. This gives rise to another and more essential basis for judicial review: there are certain fundamental values and principles that override the delegation of discretionary power and perhaps even democracy, and the judiciary is considered to be the most suitable institution to guard those values and principles.[59]

These bases for judicial supervision also place a limit on it: normally, courts are not supposed to scrutinize substantive issues with the purpose of replacing agencies' discretionary choices with their own. In other words, there are certain administrative actions deemed not—or at least less—suitable for adjudication because, for example, they involve quantitative measurement rather than qualitative determination. The underlying concern is that if these actions become overly exposed to judicial scrutiny, the effectiveness of these decision-making processes would be jeopardized, therefore, increasing social costs.[60]

In other words, when supervising enforcement agencies, courts should show certain levels of deference to these agencies' decision-making. Such deference is required by the discretionary power of these agencies, and it limits the reach of judicial supervision because, under the functional separation of the judiciary and the administration, certain administrative actions cannot be viewed as right or wrong; they are merely subjective judgment calls that the agencies are entitled to make. This judicial deference is commonly observable in the field of competition law, where antitrust agencies often need to engage in highly technical economic assessments.[61] Overall, judicial supervision, accompanied by a certain extent of deference (usually to the findings of fact), has proved to be an effective institutional setting to improve antitrust agency performance.[62]

Judicial deference and agency technocracy

Populism has been rising in competition law in recent years. It is observable in the intellectual discourse and policy development of US antitrust law;[63] it has also pushed EU competition law towards emphasizing the value of fairness.[64] But despite these recent populist trends, competition law has been developing steadily

59 Galligan, *Discretionary Powers*, 233–6; John Hart Ely, *Democracy and Distrust: A Theory of Judicial Review* (Cambridge, MA: Harvard University Press, 1980), 88, 135–6.

60 Galligan, *Discretionary Powers*, 245–6; Zwart, 'Overseeing the Executive', 150–1.

61 José Carlos Laguna de Paz, 'Understanding the Limits of Judicial Review in European Competition Law', *Journal of Antitrust Enforcement* 2, no. 1 (2014): 204, 217; Marc Jaeger, 'The Standard of Review in Competition Cases Involving Complex Economic Assessments: Towards the Marginalisation of the Marginal Review?', *Journal of European Competition Law & Practice* 2, no. 4 (2011): 308.

62 McFalls, 'Institutional Design and Federal Antitrust Enforcement Agencies', 164.

63 Leon B. Greenfield, Perry A. Lange, and Nicole Callan, 'Antitrust Populism and the Consumer Welfare Standard: What Are We Actually Debating?', *Antitrust Law Journal* 83, no. 2 (2020): 395.

64 Niamh Dunne, 'Fairness and the Challenge of Making Markets Work Better', *The Modern Law Review* 84, no. 2 (March 2021): 261.

towards more technocracy in a wider timeframe.[65] Against this backdrop, disputes arise as to how much deference the courts should give to the agencies. On the one hand, more deference would seem desirable to accommodate the increasing level of technocracy. But on the other hand, there are short- and long-term concerns about giving too much deference: in the short term, the agencies' development towards technocracy could outrun the generalist courts' capability in reviewing new and complex competition law issues, resulting in a *de facto* expansion of the discretionary scope; in the long term, the development towards technocracy could reach a stage of redefining the institutional relationship between the courts and the agencies, eventually making the technocratic agencies institutionally more independent from the supervising courts.[66]

Here, it is important to clarify the connotation of technocracy. The notion of 'technocracy' is meant to be the opposite of 'populism', much like 'specialist' is the opposite of 'generalist'. As Crane (2008) observed when studying the development of US antitrust law towards technocracy, federal antitrust enforcement 'has become increasingly separated from popular politics, insulated from direct democratic pressures, delegated to industrial policy specialists, and compartmentalized as a regulatory discipline'.[67] Accordingly, technocracy does not necessarily entail a non-interventionist policy stance. This is contrary to the argument of some people that technocracy is attached to an overly laissez-faire ideology and, therefore, more democracy in antitrust is desirable.[68] The choice between populism and technocracy and the choice among different policy preferences are two separate issues: the former is a choice of 'means' whereas the latter is a choice of 'end'. Although it may be true that on many occasions technocracy comes with a laissez-faire ideology, there is no solid basis for assuming they are always associated and, therefore, discrediting technocracy.

Therefore, to approach the issue of how much deference the supervising courts should give to technocratic agencies, we need to first identify where technocracy appears to be necessary or where populism is desirable. Normally, populism is welcome where 'there are conflicts between the values perceived and the wisdom of the choices made', and therefore, inputs from various sources are needed.[69] In that light, it seems that technocracy should generally prevail in the field of competition law since there are no longer many major disagreements regarding fundamental issues that require populist inputs nor are there many explicit trade-offs between the interests of different social classes. Another argument for technocracy in competition law is that technocracy is more likely to improve enforcer performance than

65 Crane, 'Technocracy and Antitrust', 1165–74; Jaeger, 'The Standard of Review in Competition Cases Involving Complex Economic Assessments', 305–9.

66 Cheng-Yi Huang, 'Judicial Deference to Legislative Delegation and Administrative Discretion in New Democracies: Recent Evidence from Poland, Taiwan, and South Africa', in *Comparative Administrative Law*, ed. Susan Rose-Ackerman and Peter Lindseth (Edward Elgar Publishing, 2010), 468.

67 Crane, 'Technocracy and Antitrust', 1160.

68 Harry First and Spencer Weber Waller, 'The Goals of Antitrust', *Fordham Law Review* 81 (2013): 2567–8.

69 Flynn, 'Antitrust Jurisprudence', 1189.

populism, as generalist enforcers (mostly courts) tend to be unable or unwilling to handle cases involving complex economics.[70]

By raising the issue of how much judicial deference is ideal, the increase of technocracy in competition law has served as a catalyst for dynamics shifting between the supervising courts and the supervised agencies. For example, in EU competition law, there have been heated discussions about the CJEU's (particularly the General Court's) deference to the Commission's competition enforcement decisions. On the one hand, commentators criticize that the CJEU's reluctance to conduct vigorous reviews, coupled with the formalistic and out-of-touch legal standards, has insulated the Commission decisions from judicial scrutiny.[71] Moreover, there are concerns that the CJEU's disproportionately deferential attitude could be interpreted as a waiver of the unlimited jurisdiction of review as the increasingly large fines border on criminal penalties, consequently impeding the right to a fair trial as provided in Art 6(1) of the ECHR.[72] But on the other hand, there are arguments that the General Court's allegedly low standard of review on the Commission's competition decisions involving complex economic assessments is a conscious choice for respecting the Commission's margin of discretion; it is not a sign of supervisory negligence but an indication of effective judicial review.[73]

In short, the relationship between the enforcement agencies and the supervising courts is essentially about balancing agency discretionary power against judicial control. Although the rising technocracy adds variants to the 'agency-court' institutional dynamics, it does not change that essence. In the context of antitrust technocracy, the most relevant question is not how much deference should be given but whether such technocratic expertise has been translating into better agency performance. If the answer is no, the subsequent question would be what factors are hindering that translation. Only through answering these questions could we conclude whether the relationship between antitrust agencies and courts should be redefined. One aspect of an agency's performance (and also that of a court) is the quality of the theories of harm it delivers in individual cases. Useful criteria for evaluating that quality include a case decision's internal consistency of logic and the degree to which it makes economic sense. The case analyses in Chapters 6 and 7 generally adopt these criteria.

70 Crane, 'Technocracy and Antitrust', 1216–19; Christian Carlson, 'Antitrusting the Federal Trade Commission: Why Courts Should Defer to Federal Trade Commission Antitrust Decision Making', *DePaul Business and Commercial Law Journal* 12, no. 3 (2014): 370–2. Although, there are findings that technocratic agencies do not necessarily guarantee better performance than generalist courts. See Joshua D. Wright and Angela M. Diveley, 'Do Expert Agencies Outperform Generalist Judges? Some Preliminary Evidence from the Federal Trade Commission', *Journal of Antitrust Enforcement* 1, no. 1 (2013): 103.

71 Damien Geradin and Nicolas Petit, 'Judicial Review in European Union Competition Law: A Quantitative and Qualitative Assessment', *Discussion Paper, TILEC Discussion Paper* (Tilburg Law and Economics Center, 26 October 2010), 34–5.

72 Alexander Arabadjiev, 'Unlimited Jurisdiction: What Does It Mean Today?', in *Constitutionalising the EU Judicial System: Essays in Honour of Pernilla Lindh*, ed. Allan Rosas, Nils Wahl, and Pascal Cardonnel (Oxford: Hart Publishing, 2012), 216.

73 Jaeger, 'The Standard of Review in Competition Cases Involving Complex Economic Assessments', 300–3.

Adjudicating private enforcement

Most competition law regimes have installed private antitrust enforcement, which entails courts adjudicating not only antitrust administrative suits but also antitrust civil litigations. Nevertheless, the significance of private enforcement varies across jurisdictions. For example, it was observed that in the US, the ratio between private and public antitrust cases had 'stabilized in the 10–1 range' after the 1970s.[74] Meanwhile, in EU Member States, the number of private enforcement cases has been limited despite the recent boosting efforts.[75]

Private enforcement serves primarily the function of achieving corrective or restorative justice by rewarding damages to parties injured by anticompetitive conduct.[76] Additionally, it also supplements public enforcement and serves the function of deterrence.[77] There are two basic kinds of private enforcement: follow-on actions and standalone actions. The former refers to private litigations in which the claims are based on effectively rendered public enforcement decisions, and the latter refers to private litigations on their own initiatives.[78]

Public interest overarches a competition law regime; meanwhile, private interest is the main if not sole driver of private antitrust enforcement.[79] This needs not to be concerning, though, as the private interest in antitrust civil litigations does not necessarily clash with the public interest behind competition law. Rather, private enforcement presumably enhances public enforcement by fulfilling the restorative function that is less suited for public enforcement.[80] In that light, a dual-track system incorporating both private and public enforcement appears desirable, as the two tracks undertake different tasks that a competition law regime is supposed to perform simultaneously.[81]

Nevertheless, a dual-track system complicates substantive law development. In this system, courts interpret and apply the same set of substantive rules in both civil

74 Crane, *The Institutional Structure of Antitrust Enforcement*, 54. Note that in the US, the FTC and the Antitrust Division of the DOJ have to file cases before courts to carry out antitrust enforcement excluding merger control. So government litigation counts as public enforcement.

75 Niamh Dunne, 'The Role of Private Enforcement within EU Competition Law', *Cambridge Yearbook of European Legal Studies* 16 (2014): 149.

76 Assimakis P. Komninos, 'The Relationship between Public and Private Enforcement: Quod Dei Deo, Quod Caesaris Caesari', in *European Competition Law Annual 2011: Integrating Public and Private Enforcement—Implications for Courts and Agencies*, ed. Philip Lowe and Mel Marquis (Oxford: Hart Publishing, 2014), 141–2.

77 Wouter P. J. Wils, 'The Relationship between Public Antitrust Enforcement and Private Actions for Damages', *World Competition* 32, no. 1 (2009): 8.

78 Tim Reuter, 'Private Antitrust Enforcement and the Role of Harmed Parties in Public Enforcement', *European Journal of Law and Economics* 41, no. 3 (2016): 484.

79 Komninos, 'The Relationship between Public and Private Enforcement', 143–4.

80 Wils, 'The Relationship between Public Antitrust Enforcement and Private Actions for Damages', 12; Komninos, 'The Relationship between Public and Private Enforcement', 141.

81 For a brief analysis and literature review on how public enforcement and private enforcement exert mutual influence, see Abraham L. Wickelgren, 'Issues in Antitrust Enforcement', in *Research Handbook on the Economics of Antitrust Law*, ed. Einer Elhauge (Cheltenham: Edward Elgar Publishing, 2012), 269.

and administrative litigations. This means civil lawsuit judgments are an essential component of competition case law alongside administrative lawsuit judgments and antitrust agency decisions. In that light, a question arises as to how the courts' jurisprudence differs in private and public enforcement cases. Specifically, it is worth exploring how, in a dual-track setting, the courts' double roles have induced discrepant theories of harm. This exploration helps address the concern that substantive antitrust rules could be interpreted differently, especially considering that judges deciding on private cases need to weigh both public and private interests.[82] Admittedly, clarifying substantive law is not the primary function of private antitrust enforcement, and in competition law regimes dominated by public enforcement (e.g., the EU supranational regime), the courts' double roles may not result in many discrepancies anyway. Nevertheless, in regimes where the courts' role as civil case adjudicators significantly outweighs their role as public enforcement supervisors (e.g., the Chinese AML regime), there is a much greater risk of incoherent substantive law application by courts and administrative agencies because they are, to a certain extent, competitors in antitrust enforcement. Chapter 7 assesses this risk by comparing the theories of harm developed by the AML agencies and courts.

In sum, this chapter describes institutional dynamics as an impact factor on substantive antitrust outcomes. Two grounds of institutional actors—administrative agencies and courts—are presumably committed to enforcing competition law on the one hand and incentivized to take strategic actions within the bounds of the specific institutional structure to gain more power on the other. Their strategic actions and interactions result in institutional dynamics, which in turn shape substantive enforcement outcomes. As the first half of this book's theoretical framework, this chapter deals only with 'the cause', namely, institutional dynamics. It is the task of the next chapter to approach 'the result', namely, substantive antitrust outcomes—more specifically, antitrust theories of harm.

Reference list

Akman, Pinar. 'Searching for the Long-Lost Soul of Article 82EC'. *Oxford Journal of Legal Studies* 29, no. 2 (2009): 267–303.

Alford, Roger. 'Deputy Assistant Attorney General Roger Alford Delivers Remarks at the University of Pennsylvania/UIBE Conference: Due Process in Antitrust Enforcement: China, Europe, and the United States'. 30 June 2018. www.justice.gov/opa/speech/deputy-assistant-attorney-general-roger-alford-delivers-remarks-university.

Arabadjiev, Alexander. 'Unlimited Jurisdiction: What Does It Mean Today?'. In *Constitutionalising the EU Judicial System: Essays in Honour of Pernilla Lindh*, edited by Allan Rosas, Nils Wahl, and Pascal Cardonnel, 213–21. Oxford: Hart Publishing, 2012.

Aydin, Umut, and Tim Büthe. 'Competition Law & Policy in Developing Countries: Explaining Variations in Outcomes; Exploring Possibilities and Limits'. *Law and Contemporary Problems* 79, no. 4 (2016): 1–36.

Barkow, Rachel E. 'Overseeing Agency Enforcement (Foreword)'. *George Washington Law Review* 84, no. 5 (2016): 1129–86.

82 Komninos, 'The Relationship between Public and Private Enforcement', 143.

Barkow, Rachel E., and Peter W. Huber. 'A Tale of Two Agencies: A Comparative Analysis of FCC and DOJ Review of Telecommunications Mergers Antitrust in the Information Age'. *University of Chicago Legal Forum* 2000 (2000): 29–84.

Baye, Michael R., and Joshua D. Wright. 'Is Antitrust Too Complicated for Generalist Judges? The Impact of Economic Complexity and Judicial Training on Appeals'. *The Journal of Law & Economics* 54, no. 1 (2011): 1–24. https://doi.org/10.1086/652305.

Beckner, C. Frederick, and Steven C. Salop. 'Decision Theory and Antitrust Rules'. *Antitrust Law Journal* 67, no. 1 (1999): 41–76.

Brook, Or, and Katalin J. Cseres. 'Priority Setting as the Blind Spot of Administrative Law Enforcement: A Theoretical, Conceptual, and Empirical Study of Competition Authorities in Europe'. *The Modern Law Review* (17 April 2024). https://doi.org/10.1111/1468-2230.12881.

Calkins, Stephen. 'Summary Judgment, Motions to Dismiss, and Other Examples of Equilibrating Tendencies in the Antitrust System'. *Georgetown Law Journal* 74 (1986): 1065–162.

Carlson, Christian. 'Antitrusting the Federal Trade Commission: Why Courts Should Defer to Federal Trade Commission Antitrust Decision Making'. *DePaul Business and Commercial Law Journal* 12, no. 3 (2014): 361–86.

Clague, Christopher. 'The New Institutional Economics and Economic Development'. In *Institutions and Economic Development: Growth and Governance in Less-Developed and Post-Socialist Countries*, edited by Christopher Clague, 13. Johns Hopkins University Press, 1997.

Crane, Daniel A. 'Chicago, Post-Chicago, and Neo-Chicago (Reviewing How the Chicago School Overshot the Mark: The Effect of Conservative Economic Analysis on U.S. Antitrust by Robert Pitofsky)'. *The University of Chicago Law Review* 76, no. 4 (2009): 1911–34.

Crane, Daniel A. *The Institutional Structure of Antitrust Enforcement*. Oxford: Oxford University Press, 2011. https://doi.org/10.1093/acprof:oso/9780195372656.001.0001.

Crane, Daniel A. 'linkLine's Institutional Suspicions'. *Cato Supreme Court Review* 2008–2009 (2009): 111–32.

Crane, Daniel A. 'A Neo-Chicago Perspective on Antitrust Institutions'. *Antitrust Law Journal* 78, no. 1 (2012): 43–65.

Crane, Daniel A. 'Technocracy and Antitrust'. *Texas Law Review* 86, no. 6 (2008): 1159–222.

Dunne, Niamh. 'Fairness and the Challenge of Making Markets Work Better'. *The Modern Law Review* 84, no. 2 (March 2021): 230–64. https://doi.org/10.1111/1468-2230.12579.

Dunne, Niamh. 'The Role of Private Enforcement within EU Competition Law'. *Cambridge Yearbook of European Legal Studies* 16 (2014): 143–87. https://doi.org/10.1017/S1528887000002585.

Ehrlich, Isaac, and Richard A. Posner. 'An Economic Analysis of Legal Rulemaking'. *The Journal of Legal Studies* 3, no. 1 (1974): 257–86.

Elhauge, Einer R. 'Harvard, Not Chicago: Which Antitrust School Drives Recent U.S. Supreme Court Decisions?'. *Competition Policy International* 3, no. 2 (2007): 59–77.

Ely, John Hart. *Democracy and Distrust: A Theory of Judicial Review*. Cambridge, MA: Harvard University Press, 1980.

Eskridge, William N., and Philip P. Frickey. 'The Making of "The Legal Process"'. *Harvard Law Review* 107, no. 8 (1994): 2031–55. https://doi.org/10.2307/1341767.

Ezrachi, Ariel. 'Sponge'. *Journal of Antitrust Enforcement* 5, no. 1 (2017): 49–75. https://doi.org/10.1093/jaenfo/jnw011.

First, Harry, and Spencer Weber Waller. 'The Goals of Antitrust'. *Fordham Law Review* 81 (2013): 2543–74.

Flynn, John J. 'Antitrust Jurisprudence: A Symposium on the Economic, Political and Social Goals of Antitrust Policy: Introduction'. *University of Pennsylvania Law Review* 125, no. 6 (1977): 1182–90.

Foer, Albert A. 'The Politics of Antitrust in the United States: Public Choice and Public Choices'. *University of Pittsburgh Law Review* 62, no. 3 (2001): 475–502.
Fox, Eleanor M., and Michael J. Trebilcock. 'Introduction'. In *The Design of Competition Law Institutions: Global Norms, Local Choices*, edited by Eleanor M. Fox and Michael J. Trebilcock, 1–48. Oxford: Oxford University Press, 2012. https://doi.org/10.1093/acprof:oso/9780199670048.003.0001.
Galligan, D. J. *Discretionary Powers: A Legal Study of Official Discretion*. Oxford: Oxford University Press, 1990. https://doi.org/10.1093/acprof:oso/9780198256526.001.0001.
Geradin, Damien, and Nicolas Petit. 'Judicial Review in European Union Competition Law: A Quantitative and Qualitative Assessment'. *Discussion Paper. TILEC Discussion Paper*. Tilburg Law and Economics Center, 26 October 2010. https://papers.ssrn.com/abstract=1698342.
Greenfield, Leon B., Perry A. Lange, and Nicole Callan. 'Antitrust Populism and the Consumer Welfare Standard: What Are We Actually Debating?'. *Antitrust Law Journal* 83, no. 2 (2020): 393–428.
Huang, Cheng-Yi. 'Judicial Deference to Legislative Delegation and Administrative Discretion in New Democracies: Recent Evidence from Poland, Taiwan, and South Africa'. In *Comparative Administrative Law*, edited by Susan Rose-Ackerman and Peter Lindseth, 466–81. Edward Elgar Publishing, 2010. https://doi.org/10.4337/9781849808101.
Jaeger, Marc. 'The Standard of Review in Competition Cases Involving Complex Economic Assessments: Towards the Marginalisation of the Marginal Review?'. *Journal of European Competition Law & Practice* 2, no. 4 (2011): 295–314. https://doi.org/10.1093/jeclap/lpr049.
Kaplow, Louis. 'Rules versus Standards: An Economic Analysis'. *Duke Law Journal* 42, no. 3 (1992): 557–629. https://doi.org/10.2307/1372840.
Komninos, Assimakis P. 'The Relationship between Public and Private Enforcement: Quod Dei Deo, Quod Caesaris Caesari'. In *European Competition Law Annual 2011: Integrating Public and Private Enforcement—Implications for Courts and Agencies*, edited by Philip Lowe and Mel Marquis, 141–57. Oxford: Hart Publishing, 2014.
Kovacic, William E. 'The Institutions of Antitrust Law: How Structure Shapes Substance'. *Michigan Law Review* 110, no. 6 (2012): 1019–44.
Kovacic, William E. 'The Intellectual DNA of Modern U.S. Competition Law for Dominant Firm Conduct: The Chicago/Harvard Double Helix'. *Columbia Business Law Review* 1, no. 1 (2007): 1–81.
Kovacic, William E. 'The Modern Evolution of U.S. Competition Policy Enforcement Norms'. *Antitrust Law Journal* 71, no. 2 (2003): 377–478.
Kovacic, William E. 'Politics and Partisanship in U.S. Federal Antitrust Enforcement'. *Antitrust Law Journal* 79, no. 2 (2014): 687–711.
Laguna de Paz, José Carlos. 'Understanding the Limits of Judicial Review in European Competition Law'. *Journal of Antitrust Enforcement* 2, no. 1 (2014): 203–24. https://doi.org/10.1093/jaenfo/jnt014.
McFalls, Michael S. 'Institutional Design and Federal Antitrust Enforcement Agencies: Renovation or Revolution?'. *Competition Policy International* 10, no. 1 (2014): 160–79.
Morgan, Glenn, John L. Campbell, Colin Crouch, Ove Kaj Pedersen, and Richard Whitley. 'Introduction'. In *The Oxford Handbook of Comparative Institutional Analysis*, edited by Glenn Morgan, John L. Campbell, Colin Crouch, Ove Kaj Pedersen, and Richard Whitley, 2–12. Oxford Handbooks. Oxford: Oxford University Press, 2010.
Morgan, Glenn, and Sigrid Quack. 'Law as a Governing Institution'. In *The Oxford Handbook of Comparative Institutional Analysis*, edited by Glenn Morgan, John L. Campbell, Colin Crouch, Ove Kaj Pedersen, and Richard Whitley, 276–308. Oxford Handbooks. Oxford: Oxford University Press, 2010.
North, Douglass C. 'Economic Performance Through Time'. *The American Economic Review* 84, no. 3 (1994): 359–68.

Quack, Sigrid. 'Legal Professionals and Transnational Law-Making: A Case of Distributed Agency'. *Organization* 14, no. 5 (1 September 2007): 643–66. https://doi.org/10.1177/1350508407080313.

Remington, Thomas F., Jiwei Qian, and Svetlana Avdasheva. 'Regulating Competition in the Digital Platform Economy: Russia and China Compared'. *Problems of Post-Communism* 71, no. 1 (2 January 2024): 13–25. https://doi.org/10.1080/10758216.2022.2117199.

Reuter, Tim. 'Private Antitrust Enforcement and the Role of Harmed Parties in Public Enforcement'. *European Journal of Law and Economics* 41, no. 3 (2016): 479–507. https://doi.org/10.1007/s10657-015-9495-y.

Roach, Kent. 'What's New and Old about the Legal Process Review Article'. *University of Toronto Law Journal* 47 (1997): 363–94.

Shapiro, Martin. *Who Guards the Guardians?: Judicial Control of Administration*. Athens, GA: University of Georgia Press, 1988.

Sokol, D. Daniel. 'Antitrust, Institutions, and Merger Control'. *George Mason Law Review* 17 (2010): 1055–148.

Stucke, Maurice E. 'Does the Rule of Reason Violate the Rule of Law'. *U.C. Davis Law Review* 42 (2009): 1375–490.

Weber, Franziska. 'European Integration Assessed in the Light of the "Rules vs. Standards Debate"'. *European Journal of Law and Economics* 35, no. 2 (2013): 187–210. https://doi.org/10.1007/s10657-011-9259-2.

Wickelgren, Abraham L. 'Issues in Antitrust Enforcement'. In *Research Handbook on the Economics of Antitrust Law*, edited by Einer Elhauge, 267–82. Cheltenham: Edward Elgar Publishing, 2012. https://doi.org/10.4337/9780857938091.

Wils, Wouter P. J. 'Discretion and Prioritisation in Public Antitrust Enforcement, in Particular EU Antitrust Enforcement'. *World Competition* 34, no. 3 (2011): 353–82.

Wils, Wouter P. J. 'The Relationship between Public Antitrust Enforcement and Private Actions for Damages'. *World Competition* 32, no. 1 (2009): 3–26.

Wright, Joshua D., and Angela M. Diveley. 'Do Expert Agencies Outperform Generalist Judges? Some Preliminary Evidence from the Federal Trade Commission'. *Journal of Antitrust Enforcement* 1, no. 1 (2013): 82–103. https://doi.org/10.1093/jaenfo/jns007.

Zhang, Angela Huyue. 'Agility Over Stability: China's Great Reversal in Regulating the Platform Economy'. *Harvard International Law Journal* 63, no. 2 (2022): 457–514.

Zhang, Angela Huyue. 'Bureaucratic Politics and China's Anti-Monopoly Law'. *Cornell International Law Journal* 47, no. 3 (2014): 671–708.

Zwart, Tom. 'Overseeing the Executive: Is the Legislature Reclaiming Lost Territory from the Courts?'. In *Comparative Administrative Law*, edited by Susan Rose-Ackerman and Peter Lindseth, 148–60. Edward Elgar Publishing, 2010. www.elgaronline.com/view/9781848446359.xml.

3 Theory of harm

An antitrust concept

Competitive harm

Competitive harm as the qualifier of conduct illegality

The law on abuse of dominance condemns firms' conduct abusing their dominant positions, rather than their dominant positions as such. This leads to the question of what makes such conduct condemnable. The law in its statutory form tends to be evasive on that front. For instance, Article 102 of the Treaty on the Functioning of the European Union (TFEU) and Article 22 of the Anti-Monopoly Law (AML), which are the primary law on abuse of dominance of the EU and China, respectively, only contain a general statement proscribing abuse-of-dominance conduct and a non-exhaustive list describing the types of such conduct. Therefore, the task of concretizing the law is largely left to antitrust agencies and courts, which decide on individual cases under the guidance of legal standards and develop the law in a common law approach.[1]

When antitrust agencies and courts determine whether a given practice is unlawful, they refer to the concept of anticompetitiveness because, after all, the law on abuse of dominance pursues the direct objective of competition preservation.[2] In other words, anticompetitiveness is used to indicate the adverse impact of a unilateral practice by a dominant undertaking on competition, which the law is set out to preserve, and to qualify the unlawfulness of that practice. Under the direct objective of competition preservation, the concept of 'competitive harm' can also be introduced to explain how a unilateral practice by a dominant undertaking could be anticompetitive and, therefore, should be outlawed pursuant to the applicable legal standards.

1 Einer Elhauge, 'Defining Better Monopolization Standards', *Stanford Law Review* 56, no. 2 (2003): 255–6. Michael L. Katz and A. Douglas Melamed, 'Competition Law as Common Law: American Express and the Evolution of Antitrust', *University of Pennsylvania Law Review* 168 (2020): 2064.

2 Maurice E. Stucke, 'What Is Competition?', in *The Goals of Competition Law*, ed. Daniel Zimmer (Cheltenham: Edward Elgar, 2012), 29.

DOI: 10.4324/9781003479437-3

Outlining the concept of competitive harm

Two points are notable about the concept of competitive harm. First, although this concept is intuitively useful for assessing the lawfulness of unilateral conduct, there is no consensus on what kind of substance it should consist of. In other words, much as people may relate to 'the general idea that the investigated conduct needs to harm competition, or at least be likely to do so',[3] they may hesitate as to what is a harm to competition. For instance, one could say that a competitive harm is linked inherently to the objectives enshrined by each competition law regime, and therefore, its substance would vary according to the different legal contexts. As observed by the American Bar Association, 'While most jurisdictions maintain that their competition laws "preserve competition", the preservation of competition does not always mean the same thing in different jurisdictions and is sometimes only one of several objectives pursued under a country's antitrust laws'.[4] Even if the preservation of competition were construed homogeneously across jurisdictions, the law may still be unspecific as to what legal interests are at stake vis-à-vis a particular type of conduct. Consequently, the anticompetitiveness (or competitive harm) of that type of conduct can accommodate a wide range of legal interests so long as these interests do not explicitly contradict the objectives laid down in the law. This is exemplified by the EU regime: on some occasions, a type of conduct has been deemed abusive for causing a single set of competitive harm, which is competition foreclosure; but on some other occasions, the abusiveness of the same type of conduct derives from multiple competitive harms, which include but are not limited to fairness, discrimination, market structure, and market integration.[5] Two categories of competitive harms can be identified by looking at who is injured: harms borne by competitors and harms borne by counterparties in trade (including up- and downstream firms and consumers).[6] That being said, these two categories are not mutually exclusive, as a competitive harm could be injuring competitors and counterparties at the same time.

Second, it is not entirely settled as to how and to what extent competitive harms could be identified and elaborated. For example, one of the biggest discussions in competition law is how, if at all, one should choose between a form-based and effects-based analytical approach to assessing the anticompetitiveness of a given

3 Anne C. Witt, *The More Economic Approach to EU Antitrust Law*, Hart Studies in Competition Law, vol. 14 (Oxford: Hart Publishing, 2016), 110.

4 Section of Antitrust Law American Bar Association, 'Report on Antitrust Policy Objectives', 12 February 2003, www.americanbar.org/content/dam/aba/administrative/antitrust_law/v7/report_policyobjectives.pdf. See the text following footnote 4 for the quote.

5 Witt, *More Economic Approach*, 144–5. This is also shown in chapter 6.

6 Jan Broulík, 'Two Contexts for Economics in Competition Law: Deterrence Effects and Competitive Effects', in *New Developments in Competition Law and Economics*, ed. Klaus Mathis and Avishalom Tor, vol. 7, Economic Analysis of Law in European Legal Scholarship (Cham: Springer International Publishing, 2019), 37.

practice.[7] An effects-based approach has risen to dominance, thanks to the advancing understanding of competition economics.[8] In any event, much as these two approaches may diverge in their theoretical underpinnings and factual emphases,[9] they are both compatible with the conception of competitive harm. As Witt (2016) observed, 'Restriction of competition by object and restriction of competition by effect do not refer to different types of competitive harm. The distinction relates to different tests and a different standard of proof'.[10]

That being said, the concept of competitive harm is more aligned with the tenets of an effects-based approach. This is because an effects-based approach is more prone to establishing—as opposed to presuming—the actual or potential harms at stake. In other words, an effects-based approach is more aware of, and therefore puts more emphasis on, competitive harm analyses, while a form-based approach relies more on generalization and form-categorization. This alignment stems from that economic theories underpin the conception of competitive harm: for one thing, economic theories inform the law on abuse of dominance in establishing legal objectives, therefore laying the ground for conceptualizing competitive harms; for another, the development of economic theories shapes the ways to identify and elaborate competitive harms in actual cases. This next subsection discusses how economic theories shape competitive harm explanations in individual cases, while the subsection after it discusses how economic theories shape competition law objectives with the example of the EU.

Theories of harm

Narratives to bridge the law and the facts

A theory of harm is essentially a narrative to explain competitive harms in individual cases, with the endgame of helping a competition law regime generate 'substantively sound outcomes'.[11] Theories of harm are an invention of practicality:

7 Viktor J. Vanberg, 'Consumer Welfare, Total Welfare and Economic Freedom—On the Normative Foundations of Competition Policy', in *Competition Policy and the Economic Approach: Foundations and Limitations*, ed. Josef Drexl, Wolfgang Kerber, and Rupprecht Podszun (Cheltenham: Edward Elgar Publishing, 2011), 62–3; Justin Lindeboom, 'Formalism in Competition Law', *Journal of Competition Law & Economics* 18, no. 4 (26 December 2022): 856.

8 William J. Baer and David A. Balto, 'The Politics of Federal Antitrust Enforcement', *Harvard Journal of Law & Public Policy* 23, no. 1 (1999): 120 (describing an economics-driven shift in US antitrust enforcement from reliance on structural presumptions to reliance on the consumer welfare standard of anticompetitive harm).

9 Nicholas Economides and Ioannis Lianos, 'The Elusive Antitrust Standard on Bundling in Europe and in the United States at the Aftermath of the Microsoft Cases', *Antitrust Law Journal* 76, no. 2 (2009): 534–5 (describing the difference between a form-based approach and an effects-based one for assessing bundling practices).

10 Witt, *More Economic Approach*, 271.

11 William E. Kovacic and David A. Hyman, 'Competition Agency Design: What's on the Menu?', *European Competition Journal* 8, no. 3 (2012): 535.

because the application of the law is a practice of praxis and sense-making,[12] and because the law on abuse of dominance prohibits conduct that harms competition, it is necessary to demonstrate how the invariable legal provisions, along with their underlying legal objectives and principles, are applied or at least applicable to diverse factual scenarios. As Ibáñez Colomo (2016) suggested, 'Broad and vague prohibitions such as those found in Articles 101 and 102 TFEU have to be fleshed out and given an operational meaning in concrete factual scenarios'.[13] In other words, there is a pressing need for narratives in antitrust enforcement to explain exactly how a business practice could generate competitive harms and, therefore, should be outlawed;[14] this need is fulfilled by antitrust theories of harm.

Serving as a bridge between abstract legal objectives and concrete factual scenarios, a theory of harm consists of two necessary elements. The first one is *methods for establishing facts* from varying case circumstances. To find relevant facts, there is a need for the gathering and processing of information. Economics and econometrics methods are commonly used in that regard. But this process could be costly, and the outcome is likely imperfect, so a decision-maker may have to make factual presumptions at certain points.[15] The second element is *legal principles,* which are derived from existing law and are used to normatively evaluate the established (by proof or by presumption) facts. After making the relevant factual findings based on (imperfect) information gathering and processing, it would be time to determine what legal standards should be applied. In other words, post fact-finding, it is necessary to clarify what kind of facts have what kind of legal implications. For example, after determining the market share of an undertaking, we would come to the question of how much legal significance this particular number should have. Normally, a market share number matters to competition law only to the extent that it is a useful—but not the only—indicator of market power. This second element entails the construction of legal reasoning, which requires the making of judgment calls on the one hand and abiding by economic thinking on the other. After all, economic thinking underpins the sensibility, and ultimately, the legitimacy, of such legal reasoning.

Notably, serving as a bridge, a theory of harm merely provides an analytical framework. It is not able to predict the analytical outcome. Instead, the outcome

12 Sigrid Quack, 'Legal Professionals and Transnational Law-Making: A Case of Distributed Agency', *Organization* 14, no. 5 (1 September 2007): 647–8.

13 Pablo Ibáñez Colomo, 'Beyond the "More Economics-Based Approach": A Legal Perspective on Article 102 TFEU Case Law', *Common Market Law Review* 53, no. 3 (2016): 726.

14 Carles Esteva Mosso, 'The More Economic Approach Paradigm—An Effects-Based Approach to EU Competition Policy', in *Structure and Effects in EU Competition Law: Studies on Exclusionary Conduct and State Aid*, ed. Jürgen Basedow and Wolfgang Wurmnest, International Competition Law Series, vol. 47 (Alphen aan den Rijn: Kluwer Law International, 2011), 19.

15 C. Frederick Beckner and Steven C. Salop, 'Decision Theory and Antitrust Rules', *Antitrust Law Journal* 67, no. 1 (1999): 41–2; Cyril Ritter, 'Presumptions in EU Competition Law', *Journal of Antitrust Enforcement* 6, no. 2 (1 August 2018): 190–1 (introducing factual presumptions as one of the several types of presumptions).

largely depends on the individual case circumstances.[16] This is discussed in the immediately following subsection.

The conduct-specific and case-specific dimensions of a theory of harm

As mentioned earlier, theories of harm are a practical invention for operationalizing the law on abuse of dominance. They constitute a standalone concept, although they do not have any fixed forms. In practice, the narration of a theory of harm depends on two factors: the accused conduct at hand and the available findings of facts relating to that conduct. The result is that different theories of harm could be narrated in different case scenarios depending on two varying factors: (1) the type of conduct in question and (2) the factual scenario at hand.

First, different types of conduct entail (at least conceptually) different theories of harm. Under the premise that competitive harms stem from the implementation of a (potentially abusive) practice and that all dominance-abuse practices can be categorized (at a certain level) into different types, one could infer that a particular type of abuse generates one or more types of competitive harms. If two types of abuses generate the same competitive harms, these two abuse types could still have different mechanisms to realize such harms. For example, as two separate types of abuses, exclusive dealing requirements and most-favoured-nation clauses are both capable of foreclosing competition in a market dominated by the firm taking such actions, but exclusive dealing accomplishes the foreclosure by eliminating the possibility of the targeted competitor contracting with the dominant firm's customers, whereas most-favoured-nation clauses accomplish the foreclosure not by preventing a competitor from contracting customers but by making those customers contractually obligated not to give the competitor any edge. The upshot is that one should expect at least one theory of harm to be identifiable for each type of abuse. Such a theory of harm might concur, to a certain extent and in certain aspects, with the theory of harm of another type of abuse.

The second factor refers to the individual case circumstances. The point is that although we should in theory be able to narrate a theory of harm for a particular type of conduct, in practice, we could only attain some imperfect variations of that theory of harm. This is because the individual case circumstances inevitably result in discrepant findings of facts vis-à-vis the conduct in question. For example, predatory pricing is a particular type of abusive conduct whose theory of harm necessitates the finding of below-cost prices, but the practical challenge is that product costs can be very difficult to ascertain due to imperfect information in varying case circumstances. The circumstances of a current case may lack the key findings in previous cases that helped measure costs, and therefore, a new way to measure costs and establish anticompetitiveness would be necessary; alternatively, a current

16 Lars-Hendrik Röller, 'Economic Analysis and Competition Policy Enforcement in Europe', in *Modelling European Mergers: Theory, Competition Policy and Case Studies*, ed. Peter A. G. van Bergeijk and Erik Kloosterhuis (Cheltenham: Edward Elgar, 2005), 16.

case may bring forward new facts that help measure costs and were not present in previous cases, so the theory of harm in this case requires some departure from those in previous cases. In any event, the variation of case circumstances results in the development of different theories of harm.

The inter-temporal change and the counterbalancing need for coherence

A conduct- and case-specific theory of harm can change as economic theory advances. Namely, the same case concerning the same abusive conduct may yield different theories of harm in different times 'as understanding about the operation of the economy grows'.[17] After all, economic theory plays a crucial role in elaborating antitrust doctrines, and its development is a key driver of competition policy evolution. Advancing economic thinking has guided us in rethinking the classification of abusive conduct, thereby shaping the development of theories of harm at the conduct level.[18] It has also shaped the development of theories of harm at the case level by informing us on how to establish and normatively weigh economic facts.[19]

However, a theory of harm's inter-temporal change is constrained by the fact that it is based on past theories of harm. This constraint serves the need for decision-making coherence and in turn two more fundamental values: legal certainty and common law development.[20] First, undertakings rely on case decisions made by law enforcers to self-assess their business practices in the future. So a lack of decision-making coherence would make previous decisions unable to provide legal guidance, eventually undermining those decisions' precedential credibility in the long run.[21] Second, competition law displays a heavy common-law trait in the sense that much of it is fleshed out and updated through the making of case law. Consequently, as part of that case law, antitrust theories of harm must also be developed in a coherent manner that is neither too conservative to reflect the current level of economic learning and enforcement experience nor too progressive to stunt the future development of the law.[22]

In light of the tension between the possibility of change and the need for coherence, there are at least two pointers for agencies and courts when they try to come up with theories of harm in individual cases. First, as a narrative explaining the anticompetitiveness of a practice, a theory of harm should be *self-explanatory*. Second, it should be *replicable*, meaning that, technically, anyone who applies the

17 William E. Kovacic, 'The Modern Evolution of U.S. Competition Policy Enforcement Norms', *Antitrust Law Journal* 71, no. 2 (2003): 401.

18 Colomo, 'Beyond the "More Economics-Based Approach"', 727.

19 Jan Broulík, 'Relevant Generality of Antitrust Economics: Competitive Effects as Adjudicative and Legislative Facts', *Journal of Competition Law & Economics* 19, no. 3 (28 October 2023): 464.

20 D. Daniel Sokol, 'Antitrust, Institutions, and Merger Control', *George Mason Law Review* 17 (2010): 1061; Beckner and Salop, 'Decision Theory and Antitrust Rules', 51.

21 Jürgen Habermas, *Between Facts and Norms: Contributions to a Discourse Theory of Law and Democracy*, trans. William Rehg (Cambridge: Polity Press, 1996), 198–9.

22 Katz and Melamed, 'Competition Law as Common Law', 2067, 2015.

same logic to the same facts should be able to reach the same conclusion. The underlying consideration is that if the results of an analysis cannot be replicated, such results cannot be verified.[23] Accordingly, a theory of harm should be comprehensible and persuasive to stakeholders from all sides.

Economic theories as a foundation of theories of harm: the example of Article 102 TFEU

To further analyse the concept of theory of harm requires reviewing the various antitrust economic theories, which play a co-foundational role in the development of theories of harm. Namely, together with regime-specific policies and ideologies,[24] economic theories help define the goals and objectives overarching an abuse of dominance legal regime. Specifically, economic thinking helps rationalize political considerations and establish them as the legal interests to be protected by competition law.[25] This subsection exemplifies this co-foundational role of economic theories with the EU abuse of dominance law regime. For the sake of brevity, it describes the relevant economic theories at a rather general level based on the commonly established classification of antitrust schools of thought.

Ordoliberalism

The Freiburg School

Although different views exist as to which schools of thought supported the creation and the evolution of EU competition law,[26] the one school that has never been left out of the discussion is ordoliberalism, which originated from the Freiburg School on law and economics in the 1930s in Germany. Two primary points can be noted about ordoliberalism. First, it takes a sceptical stance against private economic power (private 'Macht'), claiming, among other things, that the uncontrolled existence of private power could collude with public power and lead to

23 Simon Bishop and Mike Walker, *The Economics of EC Competition Law: Concepts, Application and Measurement*, 3rd ed. (London: Sweet & Maxwell, 2010), 9–005.

24 John J. Flynn, 'Antitrust Jurisprudence: A Symposium on the Economic, Political and Social Goals of Antitrust Policy: Introduction', *University of Pennsylvania Law Review* 125, no. 6 (1977): 1183–5.

25 Ariel Ezrachi, 'Sponge', *Journal of Antitrust Enforcement* 5, no. 1 (2017): 60.

26 Sigfrido M. Ramírez Pérez and Sebastian van de Scheur, 'The Evolution of the Law on Articles 85 and 86 EEC [Articles 101 and 102 TFEU]', in *The Historical Foundations of EU Competition Law*, ed. Kiran Klaus Patel and Heike Schweitzer (Oxford: Oxford University Press, 2013), 19–20. See also, Frank Maier-Rigaud, 'On the Normative Foundations of Competition Law—Efficiency, Political Freedom and the Freedom to Compete', in *The Goals of Competition Law*, ed. Daniel Zimmer (Cheltenham: Edward Elgar, 2012), 139.

totalitarianism.[27] Second, to prevent the devastating eventuality of totalitarianism, ordoliberalism advocates embedding market supervision in a constitutional framework to protect the process of competition from distortions by private power.[28]

Born in the 1930s, ordoliberalism reflected the political and economic reality of that time: Germany was the land of cartels, where undertakings were being coerced to collude or otherwise forced out of competition.[29] Against this economic background and the political background of growing Nazism, a number of lawyers and economists gathered at the University of Freiburg and began rethinking the relationship between the economy and the political system, especially the relationship between economics and its legal foundations. Among those scholars were Franz Böhm and Walter Eucken. They thought that highly concentrated economic power—as they put it, 'monopoly'—should be prohibited as such because otherwise it would erode political democracy, and in turn, a totalitarian political system would destroy the liberal market economy.[30] According to Eucken, it was necessary to construct a well-functioning economic order if a society's political system were to function properly. To that end, he assigned a vital role to competition and suggested that the law must establish and maintain an order of competition, namely, a competitive process.[31]

Classical liberalism, as represented by Adam Smith, claimed that a process of free competition would contribute to enhancing the general welfare of society by serving as the 'invisible hand'.[32] Ordoliberalism agreed with this view but was distrustful of the presumed self-correction ability of the market.[33] It suggested that a process of free competition could be achieved only if it was embedded in a constitutional framework, the core of which was the supervision of competition through law.[34] In that sense, ordoliberalism had a particular conception of competition law: competition law was 'to translate the economic principles that govern markets into legal principles' to achieve the ultimate goal of protecting the economic and political freedom of

27 Giuliano Amato, *Antitrust and the Bounds of Power: The Dilemma of Liberal Democracy in the History of the Market* (Oxford: Hart Publishing, 1997), 99.

28 Doris Hildebrand, *The Role of Economic Analysis in the EC Competition Rules* (The Hague: Kluwer Law International, 2002), 10.

29 Amato, *Antitrust and the Bounds of Power*, 40.

30 Elias Deutscher and Stavros Makris, 'Exploring the Ordoliberal Paradigm: The Competition-Democracy Nexus', *The Competition Law Review* 11, no. 2 (2016): 186–8. See also, Roger van den Bergh, Peter D. Camesasca, and Andrea Giannaccari, *Comparative Competition Law and Economics* (Cheltenham: Edward Elgar Publishing, 2017), 31.

31 Damien Geradin, Anne Layne-Farrar, and Nicolas Petit, *EU Competition Law and Economics* (Oxford: Oxford University Press, 2012), 1.45.

32 Adam Smith, *Wealth of Nations* (Hoboken, NJ: Generic NL Freebook Publisher, n.d.), 400.

33 Norman P. Barry, 'Political and Economic Thought of German Neo-Liberals', in *German Neo-Liberals and the Social Market Economy*, ed. Alan Peacock and Hans Willgerodt (London: Palgrave Macmillan UK, 1989), 108.

34 Deutscher and Makris, 'Exploring the Ordoliberal Paradigm', 193.

individuals.[35] In other words, competition law was expected to construct and maintain the conditions under which competition would flourish and to prevent deviations from the competitive process.[36] Disempowering ('Entmachtung') private economic power would be the core task of competition law[37] because both the existence of such power and the exercise thereof were considered distortions of competition. Also, according to Eucken, effective competition should be fostered in all markets, and in the case of special markets that were not open to competition, policies should be installed to ensure that the market operators act 'as if' they were in a competitive situation.[38]

Böhm and Eucken represented the first wave of ordoliberalism, which gradually developed into the second wave. Absorbing thoughts from Hayek and represented by Hoppmann and Mestmäcker, the second wave of ordoliberalism took a fundamental turn from the first wave: it no longer advocated the abolishment of private power as such and instead thought that dominant undertakings should have the freedom to compete as well.[39] Scholars following the second wave suggested that it would be institutionally preferable to entrust the law enforcement responsibilities more to the judiciary and less to administrative agencies with discretionary powers. The underlying concern was that in the absence of adequate judicial control, policymakers and legislators may attempt to politicize competition law.[40]

Ordoliberal influence on EU competition law

Ordoliberalism was crafted into EU competition law through two channels. The first one was the making of the overarching competition law framework. When clarifying the legal objectives, Article 3(f) of the EEC Treaty (the Treaty of Rome) established the protection of the competition process as one of the two guiding principles for interpreting the EEC competition law (the other one being market integration). This Treaty provision provided that the Community should establish a system ensuring that competition in the internal market is not distorted. This objective corresponded with the second-wave ordoliberal view that the virtue of competition lay in competition being a rivalry process to protect individual economic freedom. As Behrens (2015) observed, originally, the Freiburg School ordoliberalism viewed competition as static and defined restraints to competition as deviations from perfect competition, but this view was abandoned in later ordoliberal developments, which perceived competition as a rivalry process and, therefore, recognized

35 Peter Behrens, 'The "Consumer Choice" Paradigm in German Ordoliberalism and Its Impact Upon EU Competition Law', *SSRN Electronic Journal* (2014): 12.

36 Deutscher and Makris, 'Exploring the Ordoliberal Paradigm', 194.

37 Amato, *Antitrust and the Bounds of Power*, 100.

38 Deutscher and Makris, 'Exploring the Ordoliberal Paradigm', 208. On the concept of 'as if' competition, see Bergh, Camesasca, and Giannaccari, *Comparative Competition Law and Economics*, 32.

39 René Joliet, *Monopolization and Abuse of Dominant Position: A Comparative Study of the American and European Approaches to the Control of Economic Power* (Liège: Facultè de droit, 1970), 248.

40 Heike Schweitzer and Kiran Klaus Patel, 'EU Competition Law in Historical Context: Continuity and Change', in *The Historical Foundations of EU Competition Law*, ed. Kiran Klaus Patel and Heike Schweitzer (Oxford: Oxford University Press, 2013), 211, 228.

the rationality of attaining market power.[41] Article 3(f) remained in place until the Treaty of Lisbon, in which it was rearranged as Protocol 27 with the same binding effect. After being established by EC legislators as an objective of EU competition law, the protection of the competitive process inevitably became a guiding doctrine of the CJEU's case ruling and a foundation of the development of EU competition law.[42] Besides the competitive-process protection objective, ordoliberalism was also reflected in the wording of Articles 85 and 86 of the EEC Treaty (now Articles 101 and 102 of the TFEU), which have been the primary source of EU competition law since 1958. It was observed that the insertion of these two provisions was mainly the result of the German efforts and that the substance drew heavily from the ordoliberal way of thinking that was dominant at the time in Germany.[43]

The second channel was the appointment of Community officials and staffing. At the top level, Walter Hallstein, Hans von der Groeben, and Alfred Müller-Armack, all of who embraced ordoliberal ideas,[44] were appointed as the first President of the European Commission, the first Commissioner for competition policy, and the German Secretary of State for European Affairs, respectively. As the Commission gained increasing autonomy and power after the adoption of Regulation 17/62,[45] the theoretical background and preference of these ordoliberal officials became even more influential, as exemplified by the visions and activities of the DG IV under the leadership of Hans von der Groeben.[46]

Disputes exist as to how important ordoliberalism has been in shaping EU competition policy and law. On the one hand, some scholars argued that ordoliberalism was never the theoretical foundation of Article 102 based on examining the *travaux préparatoires* of the EEC Treaty.[47] Some others took a less drastic stance, suggesting that although ordoliberalism had a strong influence in the beginning, it lost momentum in later stages because the protection of the competitive process did not offer a precise analytical framework and because protecting the competitive process could be easily confused with protecting the competitors.[48] Besides, in later stages, other economic schools of thought had come up with more feasible analytical frameworks and tests that were not available when ordoliberalism was originally brought forward, therefore overshadowing ordoliberal thinking.[49]

41 Peter Behrens, 'The Ordoliberal Concept of "Abuse" of a Dominant Position and Its Impact on Article 102 TFEU', *SSRN Scholarly Paper* (Rochester, NY: Social Science Research Network, 9 September 2015), 15–16.

42 Pérez and Scheur, 'The Evolution of the Law on Articles 85 and 86 EEC', 22; Deutscher and Makris, 'Exploring the Ordoliberal Paradigm', 196–9.

43 Behrens, 'The Ordoliberal Concept of "Abuse" of a Dominant Position', 26.

44 Pérez and Scheur, 'The Evolution of the Law on Articles 85 and 86 EEC', 23.

45 David Gerber, *Law and Competition in Twentieth-Century Europe: Protecting Prometheus* (Oxford: Oxford University Press, 2001), 349–52.

46 Pérez and Scheur, 'The Evolution of the Law on Articles 85 and 86 EEC', 24–5.

47 Pinar Akman, 'Searching for the Long-Lost Soul of Article 82EC', *Oxford Journal of Legal Studies* 29, no. 2 (2009): 277.

48 Hildebrand, *Role of Economic Analysis*, 162.

49 Schweitzer and Patel, 'EU Competition Law in Historical Context', 220.

On the other hand, some scholars argued that ordoliberalism has been consistently adaptive and therefore should not be diminished as referring only to the Freiburg School. On that basis, they defended ordoliberalism as the foundation of EU competition policy by demonstrating the connections of ordoliberal claims with Article 3(f) of the EEC Treaty, with the inscription of exclusionary abuses, and with certain CJEU landmark cases.[50]

The importance of ordoliberalism to the development of EU competition policy may be subject to dispute, but there is no dispute that ordoliberalism had no exclusive influence. For example, it was suggested that there were other mitigating forces at the same time of ordoliberalism's prevalence, such as neo-corporatism, which claimed that the competitive process should be compromised to achieve certain necessary economic and social interests.[51] Ordoliberal scholars themselves acknowledged this point. For example, they claimed that the stipulation of exploitative abuse in Article 86 was a concession to the French delegates' stance of promoting welfare through a more state-based interventionist approach.[52] In that light, it is necessary to continue examining other theoretical elements underpinning Article 102 as well as Article 101.

The Harvard School

Workable competition

John M. Clark, a pioneer of institutional economics, proposed the concept of workable competition, intending to provide a more feasible framework for the application of economic theories. He defined workable competition as 'the most desirable form of competition, selected from those that are practically possible, within the limits set by conditions which we cannot escape'.[53] Workable competition is a normative concept, as it judges whether a certain form of competition is good or bad and strives to create conditions that can foster such competition.[54] This concept is the starting point of the Harvard School: inspired by Clark's proposition, a number of publications began focusing on the structural elements of markets, thus forming the so-called Harvard School.

The S-C-P paradigm and the beginning of industrial organization

Edward S. Mason and Joe Bain, two prominent spokespersons for the Harvard School, came up with the structure-conduct-performance ('S-C-P') analytical

50 Behrens, 'The "Consumer Choice" Paradigm in German Ordoliberalism', 18, 24–5; Behrens, 'The Ordoliberal Concept of "Abuse" of a Dominant Position', 8, 11, 22–4.

51 Pérez and Scheur, 'The Evolution of the Law on Articles 85 and 86 EEC', 28.

52 Behrens, 'The Ordoliberal Concept of "Abuse" of a Dominant Position', 17.

53 J. M. Clark, 'Toward a Concept of Workable Competition', *The American Economic Review* 30, no. 2 (1940): 253.

54 Hildebrand, *Role of Economic Analysis*, 122.

paradigm.[55] This paradigm premises that there is a causative chain trickling down the three elements.[56] It pursues the maximization of market performance, or as referred to by Mason, 'the protection of public interests', which was understood as the maximized allocation of resources and stability of production.[57] To that end and based on the trickling-down causal link, Harvard scholars strived to construct and preserve healthy market structures through their economic analyses.[58]

Mason elaborated the 'structure' element as consisting of the following components: the product's economic characteristics, the firm's cost and production conditions, the numbers and sizes of upstream sellers and downstream buyers, demand conditions, and the nature of the distribution channels.[59] Harvard scholars claimed that these structural components could induce or influence various market practices, including collusion, discriminatory pricing, predatory pricing, and R&D planning.[60]

The S-C-P paradigm laid the ground for countless studies in the 1930s and 1940s that were aimed at outlining the economic roadmap of how market structure could impact conduct. The fruit of these studies is now referred to as industrial organization.[61] Since the very beginning, industrial organization has been focusing on empirical analysis to confirm the S-C-P link across various industries.[62] Supported by the outputs of industrial organization, the S-C-P paradigm became the mainstream antitrust theory from the 1940s to the late 1960s.[63]

Impact on EU competition law

Both the notion of workable competition and the S-C-P paradigm contributed to the development of EU competition law. The notion of workable competition caught the attention of the Community officials in the 1960s for its practicality, a virtue that the policymakers were seeking. This was evidenced by a working document prepared by the DG IV and several publications by Groeben in the 1960s.[64]

55 Herbert Hovenkamp, *The Opening of American Law: Neoclassical Legal Thought, 1870–1970* (Oxford: Oxford University Press, 2014), 214.

56 Luc Peeperkorn and Vincent Verouden, 'The Economics of Competition', in *The EU Law of Competition*, ed. Jonathan Faull and Ali Nikpay, 3rd ed. (Oxford: Oxford University Press, 2014), 6. See also, Bergh, Camesasca, and Giannaccari, *Comparative Competition Law and Economics*, 66.

57 Edward S. Mason, 'Monopoly in Law and Economics', *The Yale Law Journal* 47, no. 1 (1937): 49; Hildebrand, *Role of Economic Analysis*, 128.

58 Hildebrand, *Role of Economic Analysis*, 129.

59 Edward S. Mason, 'Price and Production Policies of Large-Scale Enterprise', *The American Economic Review* 29, no. 1 (1939): 69.

60 Hildebrand, *Role of Economic Analysis*, 127.

61 Lynne Pepall, Dan Richards, and George Norman, *Industrial Organization: Contemporary Theory and Empirical Applications*, 5th ed. (Hoboken, NJ: Wiley, 2014), 8.

62 Stephen Martin, *Industrial Economics: Economic Analysis and Public Policy*, 2nd ed. (New York: Maxwell Macmillan International, 1994), 8.

63 Dennis C. Mueller, 'Lessons from the United States's Antitrust History', *International Journal of Industrial Organization* 14, no. 4 (1996): 418.

64 Brigitte Leucht and Mel Marquis, 'American Influences on EEC Competition Law', in *The Historical Foundations of EU Competition Law*, ed. Kiran Klaus Patel and Heike Schweitzer (Oxford: Oxford University Press, 2013), 140.

The S-C-P paradigm has shaped EU competition law in two profound and yet subtle ways. First, it served as a tool for promoting market integration. With its focus on the preservation of an open and contestable market structure, this paradigm fitted seamlessly with the mandate of European market integration, which was prioritized as the core objective of EC competition law in the early years.[65] This was exemplified by the *Continental Can* case, in which the Court of Justice of the European Communities (hereinafter, 'the ECJ') accepted the Commission's argument that a merger could breach Article 86 by altering the competitive structure of the market in question.[66] Second, the S-C-P paradigm complemented the ordoliberal thinking. Aimed at guiding antitrust policy-making and assisting law enforcement,[67] the S-C-P paradigm shared with ordoliberalism the idea of integrating economic analyses into the legal order.[68] In that sense, this paradigm offered ordoliberalism a solution to the practical issue of how to carry out public intervention against private market power, as it proposed a rather clear and consistent framework in which the legality of various practices could be examined.[69] This solution was enriched by the booming empirical studies of industrial organization from the 1940s onwards, which were dedicated to empirically verifying the S-C-P links.[70]

Nevertheless, the S-C-P paradigm as an analytical framework did not manifest itself in EU competition law until 1971, when the Commission activated Article 86 of the EEC Treaty through the *Continental Can* case ruling. In this case, the Commission applied Article 86 to block a merger, and it applied an analytical model that focused on the preservation of market structure, as summarized in the ECJ's judgment.[71] The Commission was permitted to rely on this analytical model from there on since its reasoning in this case was not questioned by the ECJ.[72] In short, the S-C-P paradigm took root in EU competition law ever since the Commission began regulating abuse of dominance, if not since the regulation of anticompetitive agreements. As described in the following subsections, although the original conceptions concerning the S-C-P causal link have subsequently changed, the distinction of structure, conduct, and performance was passed on.

The Chicago School

Attacking the S-C-P paradigm

The Harvard School's original S-C-P proposition had its limitations. Empirical studies of Industrial Economics in the 1950s and 1960s set out to confirm this

65 Pérez and Scheur, 'The Evolution of the Law on Articles 85 and 86 EEC', 43, 53.
66 Case 6/72, *Europemballage Corp and Continental Can Co Inc v Commission of the European Communities* [1973] ECR 215, paras 26, 27 (hereinafter, '*Continental Can*').
67 Pepall, Richards, and Norman, *Industrial Organization*, 8–9.
68 Gerber, *Law and Competition in Twentieth-Century Europe*, 245.
69 Hildebrand, *Role of Economic Analysis*, 165.
70 Pepall, Richards, and Norman, *Industrial Organization*, 9.
71 *Continental Can*, paras 28–9.
72 Hildebrand, *Role of Economic Analysis*, 165.

proposition but found many inconsistent results instead, suggesting that the S-C-P paradigm had limited explanation power.[73] A major limitation was that the S-C-P paradigm treated structure 'as exogenous—a factor that determines firm behaviour but is not determined by it'.[74] This motivated a group of economists and lawyers to propose a different version of antitrust policy. This led to the Chicago School, which came onto the horizon in the 1960s and grew throughout the 1970s.[75] By the 1980s, the Chicago School had become the mainstream antitrust theory in the US.[76]

The Chicago School's antitrust ideas were based on its critiques of the Harvard School, and they could be summarized as follows. First, the Chicago School thought the goal of antitrust policy should only be the maximization of consumer welfare, and it understood consumer welfare as an equivalent of economic efficiency that included allocative efficiency and productive efficiency.[77] While equating consumer welfare with economic efficiency, the Chicago School never clarified how welfare should be distributed among different interest groups, so it could be inferred that by referring to consumer welfare, the Chicago School meant total welfare for the whole society.[78] On that basis, the Chicago School had a completely different take on the causal links around the 'conduct' element in the S-C-P paradigm. To begin with, the Chicago School rejected the Harvard idea that high concentration would necessarily lead to high prices and consequently poor market performance (economic inefficiency).[79] Rather, it argued that there was no clear evidence establishing a link between concentration and market performance and posited that competition among a few firms can be just as effective as competition among many.[80] Furthermore, the Chicago School reversed the S-C-P causal chain and argued that it was efficiency (performance) that determined concentration (structure), not the other way around.[81] Accordingly, it viewed concentration as a good thing, as it was a necessary means to achieve efficiency and it made collusion between competitors more detectable.[82]

Second, the Chicago School advocated a non-interventionist approach to antitrust policymaking. To an extreme, the Chicago School supported the view that no antitrust law was necessary and the only thing hindering competition was

73 W. Kip Viscusi, Joseph Emmett Harrington, and John M. Vernon, *Economics of Regulation and Antitrust*, 4th ed. (Cambridge, MA: MIT Press, 2005), 62.

74 Pepall, Richards, and Norman, *Industrial Organization*, 11.

75 Peeperkorn and Verouden, 'The Economics of Competition', 7.

76 Eleanor M. Fox, 'What Is Harm to Competition? Exclusionary Practices and Anticompetitive Effect', *Antitrust Law Journal* 70, no. 2 (2002): 378.

77 Robert H. Bork, *The Antitrust Paradox: A Policy at War with Itself* (New York: Basic Books, 1978), 51, 59.

78 Pinar Akman, *The Concept of Abuse in EU Competition Law: Law and Economic Approaches* (Oxford: Hart Publishing, 2012), 28–9.

79 William Lee Baldwin, *Market Power, Competition and Antitrust Policy*, Irwin Publications in Economics (Homewood, IL: Irwin, 1987), 306.

80 Hildebrand, *Role of Economic Analysis*, 146, 148.

81 Peeperkorn and Verouden, 'The Economics of Competition', 6–7.

82 Hildebrand, *Role of Economic Analysis*, 146.

government intervention. Less radically, though, it advised antitrust policy to focus only on cartel regulation and horizontal merger control.[83] The Chicago School viewed most unilateral conduct, such as refusal to deal and exclusive dealing, as *per se* legal or at least highly justifiable in efficiency, so it advised refraining from abuse of dominance regulation.[84] Even towards cartels, the Chicago School tended to be lenient because they thought cartel agreements were highly unstable and temporary.[85]

Theoretical confinement

Unlike the situation where the Harvard School was nourished by empirical studies of industrial organization, the Chicago School relied primarily on hypothetical assumptions and reasoning.[86] In fact, of all the schools of thought introduced in this section, the Chicago School stands out as the more 'ideologically charged' one, whereas the other schools of thought are more methodology-based. For example, the Chicago School adopted the neoclassical model of perfect competition as the theoretical basis for analysing industrial markets.[87] Also, it viewed competition as a dynamic process evolving towards the ever-changing equilibrium of perfect competition.[88] Under these premises, it confidently assumed the self-correction ability of the market and believed that unless there was sufficient evidence suggesting the market was being disturbed, what the market was offering now would be the best it could ever offer. Accordingly, it claimed that any market power generated during this dynamic competition process would only be transitory, as long as technological development and market entry are uninhibited.[89]

This was where the Chicago School incurred criticism. Namely, by using its own theoretical model as the benchmark to assess factual scenarios and to appraise all research, the Chicago School became highly fixated on its own assumptions and rather hostile to industrial organization studies[90] and consequently failed to accommodate empirical evidence that suggested alternative conclusions.[91] For example, empirical studies did not support the Chicago School's view that concentration was purely the result of efficiency; instead, they demonstrated that concentration could

83 Richard A. Posner, 'The Chicago School of Antitrust Analysis', *University of Pennsylvania Law Review* 127, no. 4 (1979): 928.

84 Herbert Hovenkamp, 'The Harvard and Chicago Schools and the Dominant Firm', in *How the Chicago School Overshot the Mark: The Effect of Conservative Economic Analysis on US Antitrust*, ed. Robert Pitofsky (Oxford: Oxford University Press, 2008), 110–11.

85 Posner, 'The Chicago School of Antitrust Analysis', 928.

86 Martin, *Industrial Economics*, 9.

87 George Joseph Stigler, *The Organization of Industry* (Chicago: University of Chicago Press, 1983), 5.

88 Hildebrand, *Role of Economic Analysis*, 144–5.

89 Melvin W. Reder, 'Chicago Economics: Permanence and Change', *Journal of Economic Literature* 20, no. 1 (1982): 12, 15.

90 Posner, 'The Chicago School of Antitrust Analysis', 928–9, 931.

91 Reder, 'Chicago Economics', 13.

be attributed to market power, which was not as harmless as Chicago presumed and was responsible for the lack of competition.[92]

The Post-Chicago School

Calibrating the Chicago School

As discussed earlier, both the S-C-P paradigm and the Chicago School had their theoretical weaknesses. It was against this backdrop that the Post-Chicago School began to grow in the 1980s. As the name suggested, the Post-Chicago School was based on the thoughts of the Chicago School, and it was dedicated to patching up the weaknesses of the Chicago School by appreciating the complexity of factual scenarios.[93]

The Post-Chicago School calibrated the Chicago School from two aspects. First, it strengthened the analytical approach. While the Chicago School adopted a deductive approach relying heavily on certain theoretical assumptions, the Post-Chicago approach was less ideologically driven and more open-ended. In other words, the Post-Chicago School strived to account for empirical evidence and formulate more particularized theoretical models, and it had little interest in aligning analytical models or controlling analytical outcomes.[94] Meanwhile, the Chicago School tended to disregard analytical outcomes that were inconsistent with its theoretical premise (i.e., price theory).[95]

Second, the Post-Chicago School reoriented the antitrust policy stance. It rejected the Chicago School's idea that consumer welfare equalled economic efficiency. Instead, looking more closely at the original intentions of US antitrust law, it argued that welfare fruits in the form of competitively priced goods should belong to consumers and not cartelists and that antitrust law should be concerned with not only efficiency but also wealth transfer.[96] In addition, by engaging with empirical findings, the Post-Chicago School saw more instances of market imperfections and barriers to entry than the Chicago School did and therefore advocated stricter antitrust policies.[97]

New developments of Industrial Economics

The prevalence of the Post-Chicago School was closely associated with the development of Industrial Organization Economics, as the latter complemented the

92 Hildebrand, *Role of Economic Analysis*, 148.
93 Herbert Hovenkamp, 'Post-Chicago Antitrust: A Review and Critique', *Columbia Business Law Review*, no. 2 (2001): 336.
94 Lawrence A. Sullivan, 'Post-Chicago Economics: Economists, Lawyers, Judges, and Enforcement Officials in a Less Determinate Theoretical World', *Antitrust Law Journal* 63, no. 2 (1995): 671, 673–4.
95 Reder, 'Chicago Economics', 13.
96 Hildebrand, *Role of Economic Analysis*, 150.
97 Hovenkamp, 'Post-Chicago Antitrust', 267.

Post-Chicago School by supplying a substantial amount of economic thoughts and findings. For a start, both Post-Chicago and Industrial Economics emphasized the importance of verifying economic theories.[98] Moreover, Post-Chicago relied on the fruits of Industrial Economics to refute the claims of the Chicago School.[99] This was especially the case after the development of Industrial Economics towards game theory and behavioural studies. Referred to as the new industrial organization ('new IO'), this development started in the late 1980s and focused on using game theory to examine strategic behaviour in contexts of imperfect competition such as oligopoly.[100] By using the new IO theory on oligopoly and exclusion, Post-Chicago scholars convincingly explained why vertical and conglomerate mergers could cause anticompetitive concerns.[101]

Nevertheless, compared to the success of the Post-Chicago School and the new IO in revolutionizing antitrust theories, their normative impacts are rather obscure. This issue stems from the fact that by emphasizing too much on diversified factual scenarios, the Post-Chicago School and the new IO did not provide enough testable hypotheses based on which consistent and repeatable conclusions could be produced. In other words, while striving to provide more accurate economic analyses, they also generated evidentiary complexities and uncertainties that were very difficult to reconcile with the manageability of evidence and the risk of Type I error (false positive).[102] In that light, the contributions of Post-Chicago and new IO to the development of EU competition law are limited mostly to less normative and ideological aspects, such as the shift of assessment approach (to a more case-by-case approach) and the advancement of empirical techniques.[103]

Two sides of consideration for applying economic theories

The risks of Type I (false positive) and Type II (false negative) errors are presumably prevalent in antitrust enforcement.[104] However, the risk of Type I error would be greater than that of Type II error if antitrust law enforcers (including both administrative agencies and courts) tend to 'view each business practice

98 Sullivan, 'Post-Chicago Economics', 670.

99 Hildebrand, *Role of Economic Analysis*, 152–3.

100 Richard Schmalensee, 'Industrial Economics: An Overview', *The Economic Journal* 98, no. 392 (1988): 660, 663.

101 See for example, Michael H. Riordan and Steven C. Salop, 'Evaluating Vertical Mergers: A Post-Chicago Approach', *Antitrust Law Journal* 63, no. 2 (1995): 513–68.

102 Michelle M. Burtis, 'Modern Industrial Oranization: A Comment', *George Mason Law Review* 12, no. 1 (2003): 42, 45. See also, Hovenkamp, 'Post-Chicago Antitrust', 269–73.

103 Peeperkorn and Verouden, 'The Economics of Competition', 8.

104 Thomas A. Lambert and Alden F. Abbott, 'Recognizing the Limits of Antitrust: The Roberts Court versus the Enforcement Agencies', *Journal of Competition Law & Economics* 11, no. 4 (2015): 796–7.

with suspicion, always wondering how firms are using it to harm consumers'.[105] The aforementioned economic theories help reduce antitrust enforcers' Type I and Type II error risks since they all strive to provide a better understanding of the anticompetitiveness of a business practice and more accurate ways to identify such anticompetitiveness in real scenarios. Nevertheless, these theories are only able to reduce the risks to a certain extent. Besides, they could generate their own false positive and negative errors because they all showed theoretical imperfections under the examination of later economic theorists. The upshot is that relying on economic theories could reduce but not eliminate the risks of Type I and Type II errors in real cases; antitrust enforcers should generally increase the use of economic theories, for it enhances the justifiability of their enforcement decisions.

That being said, there is another side that needs to be taken into consideration. First, the application of economic theories adds to the enforcement costs of an antitrust regime.[106] Second, the application of economic theories may sometimes be at odds with the law enforcers' responsibility of upholding legal certainty in their decision-making. As Areeda (1983) put it:

> the legal system inevitably operates in a world where the real facts are obscure and where only rough assessments are possible, and where relatively simple rules are necessary to guide private action and to permit courts to act with a modicum of consistency.[107]

Therefore, under the assumption that the application of economic theories is aimed at providing decision-making accuracy in individual cases, the question is how law enforcers should balance their pursuit of *decision-making accuracy* against the resulting *enforcement costs* plus the need to uphold *legal certainty* vis-à-vis competition decisional law.[108] To further complicate the situation, there is a possibility that economic theories and methods may not be as accurate as they are expected to be. As Heyer (2005) said, 'the new and improved economic tools, their high degree of sophistication, and emphasis on quantitative prediction risk leaving one with a false sense as to their accuracy and precision'.[109] Consequently, compromises may have to be made, in the sense that the application of economics

105 Frank H. Easterbrook, 'Limits of Antitrust', *Texas Law Review* 63, no. 1 (1984): 4; Frank H. Easterbrook, 'Does Antitrust Have a Comparative Advantage?', *Harvard Journal of Law & Public Policy* 23, no. 1 (1999): 8.

106 Easterbrook, 'Limits of Antitrust', 16. See also, Lambert and Abbott, 'Recognizing the Limits of Antitrust', 796–8.

107 Phillip Areeda, 'Introduction to Antitrust Economics', *Antitrust Law Journal* 52, no. 3 (1983): 534.

108 Emily Sherwin, 'Judges as Rulemakers', *The University of Chicago Law Review* 73, no. 3 (2006): 926–7.

109 Ken Heyer, 'A World of Uncertainty: Economics and the Globalization of Antitrust', *Antitrust Law Journal* 72, no. 2 (2005): 378–9.

within an established legal framework may have to be based on numerous presumptions, extensive analytical efforts, and decision-making with imperfect information.[110]

In the EU competition law context, these two sides of consideration are best exemplified in the ongoing discussion on how, if at all, we should accommodate a 'more economic approach' in the existing legal framework, a major part of which is the CJEU case law.[111] As described in the previous chapter, institutional actors (specifically antitrust agencies and adjudicating courts) generate institutional dynamics as they strive to carry out their competition law enforcement responsibilities and increase their institutional power at the same time. Such institutional dynamics shape substantive decision outcomes, which include but are not limited to the balancing of decision-making accuracy against enforcement costs and legal certainty. A key takeaway here is that in the EU competition law context, the Commission and the CJEU tend to balance these two sides somewhat differently. This is shown in the case analyses in Chapter 6.

A framework for evaluating theories of harm in individual cases

As this chapter has discussed so far, a theory of harm is essentially based on certain economic theories and it entails at least two aspects: the identification of competitive harms and the narration of how such harms have transpired. This section proposes a two-fold framework for outlining the theories of harm contained in individual case decisions and appraising their quality: First, with respect to the identification of competitive harms, we may approach a case decision by asking (1) how articulated are the competitive harms and (2) to what extent do the identified competitive harms make sense in light of relevant economic theories. Second, with respect to the narration of how such harms have transpired, we may ask (1) how presumptive are the narratives and (2) whether the presumptions are well founded in economic theories. Notably, appraising the quality of the existing theories of harm inevitably requires taking a normative stance on what is considered good and bad. To that end, this book adopts a neoclassical perspective centring on efficiency and welfare, which is consistently upheld by the different schools of thought described in this chapter.

Chapters 6 and 7 adopt this framework for analysing the selected cases from the EU competition law regime and the Chinese AML regime. The endgame is to describe the existing theories of harm at a more nuanced and critical level, to compare the theories of harm developed by different institutional actors and in (the two)

110 Anne-Lise Sibony, 'Limits of Imports from Economics into Competition Law', in *The Global Limits of Competition Law*, ed. D. Daniel Sokol and Ioannis Lianos (Stanford, CA: Stanford Law Books, 2012), 34–5.

111 Witt, *More Economic Approach*, 261, 296; Pablo Ibáñez Colomo, 'Whatever Happened to the "More Economics-Based Approach"?', *Journal of European Competition Law & Practice* 11, no. 9 (11 December 2020): 473.

different regimes, and to discuss how such difference could be attributed to institutional dynamics. But before diving into the case analyses in Chapters 6 and 7, this book needs to describe in more detail the institutional dynamics encompassing the EU competition law and the Chinese AML regimes. This is done in the following Chapters 4 and 5, respectively.

Reference list

Akman, Pinar. *The Concept of Abuse in EU Competition Law: Law and Economic Approaches*. Oxford: Hart Publishing, 2012.

Akman, Pinar. 'Searching for the Long-Lost Soul of Article 82EC'. *Oxford Journal of Legal Studies* 29, no. 2 (2009): 267–303.

Amato, Giuliano. *Antitrust and the Bounds of Power: The Dilemma of Liberal Democracy in the History of the Market*. Oxford: Hart Publishing, 1997.

American Bar Association, Section of Antitrust Law. 'Report on Antitrust Policy Objectives'. 12 February 2003. www.americanbar.org/content/dam/aba/administrative/antitrust_law/v7/report_policyobjectives.pdf.

Areeda, Phillip. 'Introduction to Antitrust Economics'. *Antitrust Law Journal* 52, no. 3 (1983): 523–37.

Baer, William J., and David A. Balto. 'The Politics of Federal Antitrust Enforcement'. *Harvard Journal of Law & Public Policy* 23, no. 1 (1999): 113–32.

Baldwin, William Lee. *Market Power, Competition and Antitrust Policy*. Irwin Publications in Economics. Homewood, IL: Irwin, 1987.

Barry, Norman P. 'Political and Economic Thought of German Neo-Liberals'. In *German Neo-Liberals and the Social Market Economy*, edited by Alan Peacock and Hans Willgerodt, 105–24. London: Palgrave Macmillan UK, 1989. https://doi.org/10.1007/978-1-349-20148-8.

Beckner, C. Frederick, and Steven C. Salop. 'Decision Theory and Antitrust Rules'. *Antitrust Law Journal* 67, no. 1 (1999): 41–76.

Behrens, Peter. 'The "Consumer Choice" Paradigm in German Ordoliberalism and Its Impact upon EU Competition Law'. *SSRN Electronic Journal* (2014). https://doi.org/10.2139/ssrn.2568304.

Behrens, Peter. 'The Ordoliberal Concept of "Abuse" of a Dominant Position and Its Impact on Article 102 TFEU'. *SSRN Scholarly Paper*. Rochester, NY: Social Science Research Network, 9 September 2015. https://papers.ssrn.com/abstract=2658045.

Bergh, Roger van den, Peter D. Camesasca, and Andrea Giannaccari. *Comparative Competition Law and Economics*. Cheltenham: Edward Elgar Publishing, 2017.

Bishop, Simon, and Mike Walker. *The Economics of EC Competition Law: Concepts, Application and Measurement*. 3rd ed. London: Sweet & Maxwell, 2010.

Bork, Robert H. *The Antitrust Paradox: A Policy at War with Itself*. New York: Basic Books, 1978.

Broulík, Jan. 'Relevant Generality of Antitrust Economics: Competitive Effects as Adjudicative and Legislative Facts'. *Journal of Competition Law & Economics* 19, no. 3 (28 October 2023): 444–65. https://doi.org/10.1093/joclec/nhad011.

Broulík, Jan. 'Two Contexts for Economics in Competition Law: Deterrence Effects and Competitive Effects'. In *New Developments in Competition Law and Economics*, edited by Klaus Mathis and Avishalom Tor, 7:27–49. Economic Analysis of Law in European Legal Scholarship. Cham: Springer International Publishing, 2019. https://doi.org/10.1007/978-3-030-11611-8_2.

Burtis, Michelle M. 'Modern Industrial Oranization: A Comment'. *George Mason Law Review* 12, no. 1 (2003): 39–46.

Clark, J. M. 'Toward a Concept of Workable Competition'. *The American Economic Review* 30, no. 2 (1940): 241–56.
Colomo, Pablo Ibáñez. 'Beyond the "More Economics-Based Approach": A Legal Perspective on Article 102 TFEU Case Law'. *Common Market Law Review* 53, no. 3 (2016): 709–40.
Colomo, Pablo Ibáñez. 'Whatever Happened to the "More Economics-Based Approach"?'. *Journal of European Competition Law & Practice* 11, no. 9 (11 December 2020): 473–4. https://doi.org/10.1093/jeclap/lpaa088.
Deutscher, Elias, and Stavros Makris. 'Exploring the Ordoliberal Paradigm: The Competition-Democracy Nexus'. *The Competition Law Review* 11, no. 2 (2016): 181–214.
Easterbrook, Frank H. 'Does Antitrust Have a Comparative Advantage?'. *Harvard Journal of Law & Public Policy* 23, no. 1 (1999): 5–10.
Easterbrook, Frank H. 'Limits of Antitrust'. *Texas Law Review* 63, no. 1 (1984): 1–40.
Economides, Nicholas, and Ioannis Lianos. 'The Elusive Antitrust Standard on Bundling in Europe and in the United States at the Aftermath of the Microsoft Cases'. *Antitrust Law Journal* 76, no. 2 (2009): 483–567.
Elhauge, Einer. 'Defining Better Monopolization Standards'. *Stanford Law Review* 56, no. 2 (2003): 253–344.
Ezrachi, Ariel. 'Sponge'. *Journal of Antitrust Enforcement* 5, no. 1 (2017): 49–75. https://doi.org/10.1093/jaenfo/jnw011.
Flynn, John J. 'Antitrust Jurisprudence: A Symposium on the Economic, Political and Social Goals of Antitrust Policy: Introduction'. *University of Pennsylvania Law Review* 125, no. 6 (1977): 1182–90.
Fox, Eleanor M. 'What Is Harm to Competition? Exclusionary Practices and Anticompetitive Effect'. *Antitrust Law Journal* 70, no. 2 (2002): 371–411.
Geradin, Damien, Anne Layne-Farrar, and Nicolas Petit. *EU Competition Law and Economics*. Oxford: Oxford University Press, 2012.
Gerber, David. *Law and Competition in Twentieth-Century Europe: Protecting Prometheus*. Oxford: Oxford University Press, 2001.
Habermas, Jürgen. *Between Facts and Norms: Contributions to a Discourse Theory of Law and Democracy*. Translated by William Rehg. Cambridge: Polity Press, 1996.
Heyer, Ken. 'A World of Uncertainty: Economics and the Globalization of Antitrust'. *Antitrust Law Journal* 72, no. 2 (2005): 375–422.
Hildebrand, Doris. *The Role of Economic Analysis in the EC Competition Rules*. The Hague: Kluwer Law International, 2002.
Hovenkamp, Herbert. 'The Harvard and Chicago Schools and the Dominant Firm'. In *How the Chicago School Overshot the Mark: The Effect of Conservative Economic Analysis on US Antitrust*, edited by Robert Pitofsky, 110–22. Oxford: Oxford University Press, 2008.
Hovenkamp, Herbert. *The Opening of American Law: Neoclassical Legal Thought, 1870–1970*. Oxford: Oxford University Press, 2014.
Hovenkamp, Herbert. 'Post-Chicago Antitrust: A Review and Critique'. *Columbia Business Law Review*, no. 2 (2001): 257–338.
Joliet, René. *Monopolization and Abuse of Dominant Position: A Comparative Study of the American and European Approaches to the Control of Economic Power*. Liège: Facultè de droit, 1970.
Katz, Michael L., and A. Douglas Melamed. 'Competition Law as Common Law: American Express and the Evolution of Antitrust'. *University of Pennsylvania Law Review* 168 (2020): 2061–106.
Kovacic, William E. 'The Modern Evolution of U.S. Competition Policy Enforcement Norms'. *Antitrust Law Journal* 71, no. 2 (2003): 377–478.
Kovacic, William E., and David A. Hyman. 'Competition Agency Design: What's on the Menu?'. *European Competition Journal* 8, no. 3 (2012): 527–38.

Lambert, Thomas A., and Alden F. Abbott. 'Recognizing the Limits of Antitrust: The Roberts Court versus the Enforcement Agencies'. *Journal of Competition Law & Economics* 11, no. 4 (2015): 791–853.

Leucht, Brigitte, and Mel Marquis. 'American Influences on EEC Competition Law'. In *The Historical Foundations of EU Competition Law*, edited by Kiran Klaus Patel and Heike Schweitzer, 125–61. Oxford: Oxford University Press, 2013. https://doi.org/10.1093/acprof:oso/9780199665358.003.0005.

Lindeboom, Justin. 'Formalism in Competition Law'. *Journal of Competition Law & Economics* 18, no. 4 (26 December 2022): 832–80. https://doi.org/10.1093/joclec/nhac003.

Maier-Rigaud, Frank. 'On the Normative Foundations of Competition Law—Efficiency, Political Freedom and the Freedom to Compete'. In *The Goals of Competition Law*, edited by Daniel Zimmer, 132–68. Cheltenham: Edward Elgar, 2012.

Martin, Stephen. *Industrial Economics: Economic Analysis and Public Policy.* 2nd ed. New York: Maxwell Macmillan International, 1994.

Mason, Edward S. 'Monopoly in Law and Economics'. *The Yale Law Journal* 47, no. 1 (1937): 34–49.

Mason, Edward S. 'Price and Production Policies of Large-Scale Enterprise'. *The American Economic Review* 29, no. 1 (1939): 61–74.

Mosso, Carles Esteva. 'The More Economic Approach Paradigm—An Effects-Based Approach to EU Competition Policy'. In *Structure and Effects in EU Competition Law: Studies on Exclusionary Conduct and State Aid*, edited by Jürgen Basedow and Wolfgang Wurmnest, 11–22. International Competition Law Series, vol. 47. Alphen aan den Rijn: Kluwer Law International, 2011.

Mueller, Dennis C. 'Lessons from the United States's Antitrust History'. *International Journal of Industrial Organization* 14, no. 4 (1996): 415–45. https://doi.org/10.1016/0167-7187(95)00490-4.

Peeperkorn, Luc, and Vincent Verouden. 'The Economics of Competition'. In *The EU Law of Competition*, edited by Jonathan Faull and Ali Nikpay. 3rd ed., 3–90. Oxford: Oxford University Press, 2014.

Pepall, Lynne, Dan Richards, and George Norman. *Industrial Organization: Contemporary Theory and Empirical Applications*. 5th ed. Hoboken, NJ: Wiley, 2014.

Pérez, Sigfrido M. Ramírez, and Sebastian van de Scheur. 'The Evolution of the Law on Articles 85 and 86 EEC [Articles 101 and 102 TFEU]'. In *The Historical Foundations of EU Competition Law*, edited by Kiran Klaus Patel and Heike Schweitzer, 19–53. Oxford: Oxford University Press, 2013.

Posner, Richard A. 'The Chicago School of Antitrust Analysis'. *University of Pennsylvania Law Review* 127, no. 4 (1979): 925–48.

Quack, Sigrid. 'Legal Professionals and Transnational Law-Making: A Case of Distributed Agency'. *Organization* 14, no. 5 (1 September 2007): 643–66. https://doi.org/10.1177/1350508407080313.

Reder, Melvin W. 'Chicago Economics: Permanence and Change'. *Journal of Economic Literature* 20, no. 1 (1982): 1–38.

Riordan, Michael H., and Steven C. Salop. 'Evaluating Vertical Mergers: A Post-Chicago Approach'. *Antitrust Law Journal* 63, no. 2 (1995): 513–68.

Ritter, Cyril. 'Presumptions in EU Competition Law'. *Journal of Antitrust Enforcement* 6, no. 2 (1 August 2018): 189–212. https://doi.org/10.1093/jaenfo/jny008.

Röller, Lars-Hendrik. 'Economic Analysis and Competition Policy Enforcement in Europe'. In *Modelling European Mergers: Theory, Competition Policy and Case Studies*, edited by Peter A. G. van Bergeijk and Erik Kloosterhuis, 11–24. Cheltenham: Edward Elgar, 2005.

Schmalensee, Richard. 'Industrial Economics: An Overview'. *The Economic Journal* 98, no. 392 (1988): 643–81. https://doi.org/10.2307/2233907.

Schweitzer, Heike, and Kiran Klaus Patel. 'EU Competition Law in Historical Context: Continuity and Change'. In *The Historical Foundations of EU Competition Law*, edited by Kiran Klaus Patel and Heike Schweitzer, 207–30. Oxford: Oxford University Press, 2013.
Sherwin, Emily. 'Judges as Rulemakers'. *The University of Chicago Law Review* 73, no. 3 (2006): 919–31.
Sibony, Anne-Lise. 'Limits of Imports from Economics into Competition Law'. In *The Global Limits of Competition Law*, edited by D. Daniel Sokol and Ioannis Lianos. Stanford, CA: Stanford Law Books, 2012.
Smith, Adam. *Wealth of Nations*. Hoboken, NJ: Generic NL Freebook Publisher, n.d.
Sokol, D. Daniel. 'Antitrust, Institutions, and Merger Control'. *George Mason Law Review* 17 (2010): 1055–148.
Stigler, George Joseph. *The Organization of Industry*. Chicago: University of Chicago Press, 1983.
Stucke, Maurice E. 'What Is Competition?'. In *The Goals of Competition Law*, edited by Daniel Zimmer, 27–52. Cheltenham: Edward Elgar, 2012.
Sullivan, Lawrence A. 'Post-Chicago Economics: Economists, Lawyers, Judges, and Enforcement Officials in a Less Determinate Theoretical World'. *Antitrust Law Journal* 63, no. 2 (1995): 669–81.
Vanberg, Viktor J. 'Consumer Welfare, Total Welfare and Economic Freedom—On the Normative Foundations of Competition Policy'. In *Competition Policy and the Economic Approach: Foundations and Limitations*, edited by Josef Drexl, Wolfgang Kerber, and Rupprecht Podszun, 44–71. Cheltenham: Edward Elgar Publishing, 2011.
Viscusi, W. Kip, Joseph Emmett Harrington, and John M. Vernon. *Economics of Regulation and Antitrust*. 4th ed. Cambridge, MA: MIT Press, 2005.
Witt, Anne C. *The More Economic Approach to EU Antitrust Law*. Hart Studies in Competition Law, vol. 14. Oxford: Hart Publishing, 2016.

4 The centralized EU supranational regime

Legal framework

Treaty provisions on competition protection

The founding Treaties drafted by the acceded and acceding Member States governments have been the primary legal source ever since the foundation of the European Coal and Steel Community. The current Treaty underpinning the EU is referred to as the Treaty of Lisbon, which consists of the Treaty on the European Union ('TEU') and the Treaty on the Functioning of the European Union ('TFEU').[1] They are equally binding and have been effective since 1 December 2009. The responsibility of ensuring uniform interpretations of these Treaties lies with the Court of Justice of the European Union ('CJEU').

From the Treaty of Rome to the Treaty of Nice, the founding Treaties had always reserved a provision under Article 3 to stress the essentiality of competition as a means to the objective of establishing a Common Market.[2] This legislative structure was changed in the Treaty of Lisbon: instead of identifying competition in Article 3 of the TEU along with several other activities and responsibilities as intermediaries for achieving the internal market objective, the Treaty of Lisbon adopted Protocol 27 to address the role of competition in the internal market. To be sure, this change does not officially undermine the role of competition as an intermediary objective for achieving the goal of an internal market since the protocols and the normal Treaty provisions are of equal binding force according to Article 51 TEU.[3]

1 Consolidated version of the Treaty of European Union [26 October 2012] OJ C 326, 13–390 (hereinafter, 'the TEU'); consolidated version of the Treaty on the Functioning of the European Union [26 October 2012] OJ C 326, 47–390 (hereinafter, 'the TFEU').

2 Article 3(f) of Treaty Establishing the European Economic Community, effective on January 1, 1958 (hereinafter, 'the Treaty of Rome' or 'the EEC Treaty'); Article 3(1)(g) of Treaty Establishing the European Community (Consolidated version 2002), [2002] OJ C 325, 33–184 (hereinafter, 'the Treaty of Nice' or 'the EC Treaty').

3 Article 51 of the TEU states that the 'Protocols and Annexes to the Treaties shall form an integral part thereof'.

DOI: 10.4324/9781003479437-4

The Treaty provisions on competition are the primary EU competition law, and despite the change in legislative structure, the content of these Treaty provisions has remained intact since the EEC Treaty became effective in 1958. These Treaty provisions are currently taking the form of Articles 101–9 of the TFEU, with Articles 101–6 regulating the conduct of undertakings while Articles 107–9 regulating state aid. Amongst them, the most relevant one to this book is Article 102, which lays down the principles and conditions for regulating abusive conduct by one or more undertakings of a dominant position that could be considered incompatible with the internal market. Besides Articles 101–9 TFEU, some other Treaty provisions also help clarify the role of competition law within the whole EU legal system. These provisions include Article 3(1)(b) of the TFEU, which stipulates the Union's exclusive competence (in relation to the Member State governments) in establishing competition rules necessary for the functioning of the internal market; Protocol No 27 of the TFEU, which emphasizes undistorted competition as an integral part of the internal market and stipulates the Union's responsibility to take actions necessary to achieve it; and Article 3(3) of the TEU, which lays down the mandate of establishing an internal market.

Secondary legislation

The types of legal instruments and the institutional actors at play

According to Article 288 of the TFEU, the types of legal instruments available for concretizing the Treaty provisions include the following. The first type is *regulations*, which shall be binding in their entirety and directly applicable in all Member States. This means competition rules adopted in the form of regulations will not only be applied by the Commission but also by the national competition authorities ('NCAs') and national courts. The second type is *directives*, which shall be binding as to the result to be achieved, but it is up to the authorities of each addressed Member State to choose the legislative form and methods. The third type is *decisions*, which shall be binding in their entirety. According to Article 288 TFEU, there are two types of decisions distinguished by whether they have specific addressees. If a decision specifies to whom it is addressed, it shall be binding only on them; otherwise, it shall be binding in general. The fourth type is *recommendations and opinions*, which do not have binding effects. Instruments of this type are often referred to as soft law. In practice, though, the scope of soft law is not limited to documents titled 'Recommendation' and 'Opinion'; it also includes 'Notices' and 'Guidelines'.

As the political organ representing the Member States, the Council is empowered by the Treaties to legislate. Article 103(1) of the TFEU stipulates that, based on proposals from the Commission and after consulting the European Parliament, the Council shall adopt regulations or directives to give effect to the principles set out in Articles 101 and 102. Three things should be noted about the Council's legislative power in the area of competition law. First, the Council follows the special legislative procedure where it enjoys exclusive legislative power. According to

Article 103(1) TFEU, the European Parliament is only to be consulted in legislative processes concerning matters of competition, instead of being a co-legislator with the Council in ordinary legislative procedures. As a result, most of the legislative acts on competition bear no signature of the European Parliament. That being said, there are exceptions. For example, the European Parliament retains a co-legislator authority in the area of agriculture and fisheries pursuant to Articles 42 and 43(2) of the TFEU, so to regulate competition in the agricultural and fishery area, the European Parliament and the Council have jointly adopted Regulation 1308/2013.[4] Another example is the Digital Markets Act, which, despite substantively converging to a large extent with EU law on abuse of dominance (i.e., Article 102 TFEU), is officially positioned as a sectoral regulation that complements EU competition law,[5] so its adoption has followed an ordinary legislative process with the European Parliament as a co-legislator. Second, the types of legal instruments that the Council can adopt include regulations and directives, both of which have binding effects across the Union. Third, as provided in Article 3(1)(b) of the TFEU, competition rulemaking falls within the exclusive competence of the Union. In that event and according to Article 2(1) of the TFEU, the Member States share no legislative power regarding matters of competition in the internal market unless authorized by the Council; they are to implement the legal instruments adopted by the Council.

The Commission is another essential institution in the Union's competition law-making. First, according to Article 103(1) of the TFEU, it holds the power to initiate a procedure of competition legislation, while the Council holds the power to adopt a legislative act on competition. In other words, the Council cannot adopt any legislative act on competition without a proposal from the Commission. Second, the Council can delegate the Commission to adopt certain legislative acts, as provided in Article 290 of the TFEU. For example, according to Article 105(3) of the TFEU, the Commission 'may adopt regulations relating to the categories of agreement in respect of which the Council has adopted a regulation or a directive pursuant to Article 103(2)(b)'. Third, by adopting individual decisions that are reviewable by the CJEU in annulment proceedings, the Commission contributes heavily to the CJEU's law-making in the form of case precedents. On that account, Chapter 5 of this dissertation selects and analyses a number of annulment cases.

Secondary legislation laying down Articles 101 and 102 TFEU

The very first piece of secondary legislation on competition was Council Regulation 17. Adopted in 1962 to implement Articles 85 and 86 of the EEC Treaty (now

4 Regulation (EU) No 1308/2013 of the European Parliament and of the Council of 17 December 2013 Establishing a Common Organisation of the Markets in Agricultural Products and Repealing Council Regulations (EEC) No 922/72, (EEC) No 234/79, (EC) No 1037/2001, and (EC) No 1234/2007 [20 December 2013] OJ L 347, 671–854.

5 Regulation (EU) 2022/1925 of the European Parliament and of the Council of 14 September 2022 on Contestable and Fair Markets in the Digital Sector and Amending Directives (EU) 2019/1937 and (EU) 2020/1828 (Digital Markets Act) [12 October 2022] OJ L 265, 1–66, Recitals 7, 10, 11.

Articles 101 and 102 of the TFEU), it established a centralized enforcement system of competition law.[6]

In 2003, the Council replaced Regulation 17/62 with Regulation 1/2003, which has since then been the cornerstone of the legal regime built upon Articles 101 and 102 of the TFEU.[7] Regulation 1/2003 launched a modernization reform of EU competition law, which can be described from two aspects. The first aspect is the revision of substantive rules. The changes made include, *inter alia*, the availability of leniency (Article 19 of Regulation 1/2003) and the increased amount of applicable fines (Article 23). The second aspect is the decentralization of the enforcement system. Regulation 1/2003, supplemented by Commission Regulation 773/2004 and several Commission Notices and Guidelines, abolished the old centralized system established by Regulation 17. In addition to Regulation 1/2003, the Council also adopted substantive rules for specific sectors. For example, Regulation 411/2004 replaced Regulations 3975/87 and 3976/87 applying to air transport. Regulation 1419/2006 replaced Regulation 4056/86 applying to maritime transport. Regulation 169/2009 replaced Regulation 1017/68 applying to transport by rail, road, and inland waterway (with the exception of Article 13(3) of Regulation 1017/68).

According to Articles 290 and 291 of the TFEU, the Commission can adopt delegated acts and implementation acts. In practice, delegated acts have been used by the Commission to enrich the substantive law while implementation acts have been used to construct the enforcement system. First, to implement Article 101(3), the Council issued several regulations, delegating the legislative power to the Commission to adopt 'block' exemption regulations ('BERs') that apply to certain categories of agreements. The Council also adopted several BERs regarding special sectors. Second, regarding implementation acts, so far, the most prominent one is Commission Regulation 773/2004, which lays down the main procedural rules concerning the application of Articles 101 and 102. Two later commission regulations amended Regulation 773/2004: Commission Regulation 622/2008 (concerning settlement procedures in cartel cases) and Commission Regulation 519/2013 (an adaptation for the accession of Croatia into the EU).

Directives are of general applicability, too, but they give the Member States certain discretion on implementation, in the sense that the Member States are allowed to adopt the forms of rules that are in line with their domestic contexts. Most of the directives are concerned with particular sectors and industries. Directives as a type of legal instrument are mainly used to establish institutional framework or to harmonize substantive rules.

6 EEC Council Regulation No 17: First Regulation Implementing Articles 85 and 86 of the Treaty [21 February 1962] OJ 13, 204–11 (English special edition: Series I Volume 1959–1962, 87–93) (hereinafter, 'Regulation 17').

7 Council Regulation (EC) No 1/2003 of 16 December 2002 on the Implementation of the Rules on Competition Laid Down in Articles 81 and 82 of the Treaty [4 January 2003] OJ L 1, 1–25.

A decision will have general binding effects if it does not have specific addressees. In practice, decisions of this kind are often used to enhance the institutional system or to clarify specific law-application issues.

Secondary legislation laying down the merger control system

The EEC Treaty did not contain any provisions on merger control. Some Member States were afraid that a cross-Europe merger control system would lead to over-regulation of domestic industries, so they strongly opposed writing merger control into the Treaty.[8] For this reason, subsequent Treaties, including the most recent Treaty of Lisbon, did not incorporate any provisions on merger control either. However, there remained the practical need to tackle mergers that benefited the merging parties at the expense of market competition and social welfare. So the lack of Treaty provisions on merger control eventually forced the Commission to invoke Article 86 of the EEC Treaty (on abuse of dominance) to control mergers in the *Continental Can* case.

It was not until the adoption of Council Regulation 4064/89 in 1989 that a merger control system was established. In 2004, the Council replaced Regulation 4064/89 with Regulation 139/2004. Supplemented by an implementation Regulation 802/2004 and several Commission Notices, this new council regulation modified the review standard from the 'dominance' test to a 'significant impediment to effective competition' test.[9]

Soft law

As a concept opposite to 'hard law', soft law refers to rules that do not have legally binding force but have the aim and consequence of producing a certain level of legal effect in practice.[10] It fulfils the function of clarifying secondary legislation, with its legitimacy stemming from the Treaties and the general principles of EU law. According to Article 288 of the TFEU, recommendations and opinions, as forms of soft law, can be adopted for exercising the Union's competences. But they have no binding force, meaning that soft law cannot be the legal basis of a Commission decision nor can a soft law document derogate from the existing statutory laws or the case law. Nevertheless, having no binding force does not necessarily mean having no legal effects. As established by the CJEU in its case law, whenever a soft law document is adopted and published by the Commission, it becomes binding upon the Commission itself. Such binding effects derive from the principle of legitimate expectations, along with five other Community law principles.[11]

8 Alison Jones and Brenda Sufrin, *EU Competition Law: Text, Cases, and Materials*, 5th ed. (Oxford and New York: Oxford University Press, 2014), 1134–5.

9 Article 2(2) of Council Regulation (EC) No 139/2004 of 20 January 2004 on the Control of Concentrations between Undertakings [2004] OJ L 24, 1–22.

10 Linda Senden, *Soft Law in European Community Law* (Oxford: Hart, 2004), 104.

11 Case T-23/99, *LR AF 1998 v Commission* [2002] ECR II 1705, para 245; Case T-31/99, *ABB Asea Brown Boveri v Commission* [2002] ECR II 1881, para 258; Joined Cases C-189/02 P, C-202/02 P,

However, the Commission could escape such binding effects if it was able to give explanations compatible with the principle of equal treatment.[12]

Soft law is a beneficial addition to primary and secondary EU competition legislation in at least two ways. First, by guiding with flexibility, it reconciles to a great extent the requirement of legal certainty and the complexity of economic assessments in competition law application. Second, by elaborating hard law, it helps ensure a uniform application of the Union's competition rules. That being said, soft law as a type of competition law instrument also raises potential concerns. For example, it could be used as a 'backdoor' for legislation, enabling quick adoption of laws without the necessary constitutional checks and balances.[13] Also, it might be short on procedural legitimacy in the sense that the rulemaking process of soft law could have inadequate participation and interest representation from the relevant stakeholders such as the European Parliament, the Member State governments, and the private parties.[14]

In practice, the Commission is the only producer of soft law on competition. The Commission's soft law takes various forms, ranging from the more commonly seen notices and guidelines to the less common comfort letters, communications, and recommendations.[15] The Commission's soft law clarifies, with flexibility, the open-textured Treaty provisions and secondary legislative acts, therefore providing more—albeit generic—guidance on the law. In that sense, it sometimes is an indicator of the direction that EU competition policymaking is potentially headed towards.

Rulings of the CJEU

A hierarchy between the CJEU and General Court rulings

Article 19 of the TEU stipulates that the CJEU consists of the Court of Justice ('ECJ'), the General Court ('GC', formerly named the Court of First Instance, 'CFI'), and specialized courts. There used to be one specialized court, the Civil Service Tribunal, but in December 2015, the Council adopted a regulation reforming the GC, which entailed dissolving the Civil Service Tribunal and transferring its seven judge posts to the GC in September 2016.[16] So currently, the CJEU consists of only the ECJ and the GC, with no specialized courts in place.

C-205/02 P to C-208/02 P and C-213/02 P, *Dansk Rørindustri and others v Commission* [2005] ECR I 5425, paras 82 and 88.

12 Joined Cases C-189/02 P, C-202/02 P, C-205/02 P to C-208/02 P and C-213/02 P, *Dansk Rørindustri and others v Commission* [2005] ECR I 5425, para 290.

13 Imelda Maher and Oana Stefan, 'Competition Law in Europe: The Challenge of a Network Constitution', in *The Regulatory State: Constitutional Implications*, ed. Dawn Oliver, Tony Prosser, and Richard Rawlings (Oxford: Oxford University Press, 2010), 194.

14 Herwig C. H. Hofmann, 'Negotiated and Non-Negotiated Administrative Rule-Making: The Example of EC Competition Policy', *Common Market Law Review* 43, no. 1 (2006): 171–3.

15 Oana Andreea Stefan, 'European Competition Soft Law in European Courts: A Matter of Hard Principles?', *European Law Journal* 14, no. 6 (2008): 755.

16 Council of the European Union, *Court of Justice of the EU: Council Adopts Reform of General Court*, 3 December 2015, www.consilium.europa.eu/en/press/press-releases/2015/12/03/

There is a hierarchical division of labour between the ECJ and the GC. According to Article 256 of the TFEU and Article 58 of the Statute of the CJEU, the main jurisdictional difference between the GC and the ECJ is that the GC reviews points of both law and facts, whereas the ECJ as the supreme judicial authority reviews only points of law.[17] Rulings of the GC on points of law could be reviewed and subsequently quashed by the ECJ. Specifically, Article 256 TFEU provides that the following types of GC judgments are subject to re-examination by the ECJ: (1) judgments on first-instance cases brought to the GC, (2) appeals against decisions of the specialized courts, and (3) preliminary rulings for questions submitted by Member State courts. The second type is irrelevant since there are no longer any specialized courts. The third type is not relevant either but for a different reason. Theoretically speaking, the GC has the power to give preliminary rulings according to Article 256(3) of the TFEU: 'The General Court shall have jurisdiction to hear and determine questions referred for a preliminary ruling under Article 267, in specific areas laid down by the Statute'. But the Statute never laid down any of such specific areas, so in reality, it has always been the ECJ who handles all the preliminary ruling cases.

As provided by Article 56 of the CJEU Statute, what triggers the ECJ's review of a GC judgment is an appeal brought by a Member State, an EU institution, or *inter alia*, a party of direct concern. The grounds for the ECJ's intervention include a lack of competence of the GC, a breach of the appellant's procedural rights, and an infringement of Union law by the GC. This is provided by Article 58 of the CJEU Statute. According to Article 61 of the CJEU Statute, the outcome of the ECJ's review is either a GC judgment being quashed or being upheld. If the ECJ decides to quash a GC judgment, it could either give a final judgment to replace that judgment or refer the case back to the GC for a retrial. When a case is referred back, the GC would be bound by the ECJ's rulings on points of law in making the retrial judgment.

Effects of the CJEU rulings

The effects of the CJEU rulings (including annulment case judgments and preliminary rulings) can be described from two aspects: (1) their binding effects as individual judgments and (2) their precedential effects as part of the case law.

As individual judgments, each CJEU ruling is binding in its entirety upon its addressees. This binding effect derives from the CJEU's role as the Union's judiciary, which hears cases involving not only private parties but also the Commission and the Member States. First, as Article 263 of the TFEU provides, the

eu-court-of-justice-general-court-reform/ (accessed 5 May 2018). For a more in-depth analysis on the Civil Service Tribunal, see Graham Butler, 'An Interim Post-Mortem: Specialised Courts in the EU Judicial Architecture after the Civil Service Tribunal', *International Organizations Law Review* 17, no. 3 (2020): 586–632, https://doi.org/10.1163/15723747-2019010.

17 Protocol on the Statute of the Court of Justice of the European Union [2016] OJ C 203, 72–95 (hereinafter, 'the CJEU Statute').

CJEU hears cases instituted by a natural or legal person against 'an act addressed to that person or which is of direct and individual concern to them, and against a regulatory act which is of direct concern to them and does not entail implementing measures'. In these proceedings, the CJEU has the power to review the legality of the acts adopted by EU institutions. Second, as Articles 17(1) and 19(1) of the TEU provide, the CJEU supervises the Commission in the interpretation and application of the Union law. Third, according to Article 267 of the TFEU, the CJEU also supervises the Member States regarding their application of EU law through making preliminary rulings. The upshot is that within the current EU legal framework, every GC judgment (unless being referred back to the GC or being re-adjudicated by the ECJ) and every ECJ judgment represents the ultimately authoritative interpretation of the existing EU rules in a particular factual context, and therefore must be followed by the addressees and the relevant parties of the judgment at hand.

As part of the case law, a CJEU ruling technically does not have binding effects on future cases. This is because first, there are no rules explicitly stating that the GC and the ECJ are bound by their own precedents or rules stating that the precedents established by the ECJ are generally binding upon the GC. Only in two exceptional scenarios does an ECJ ruling bind the GC: (1) when the ECJ quashes a GC judgment and refers it back to the GC, then the GC would be bound by the quash decision of the ECJ on points of law; and (2) when the ECJ finds a case falling under the GC's jurisdiction so it refers the case in question to the GC, then the GC would be bound by the ECJ's ruling on jurisdiction. These two scenarios are addressed by Articles 61 and 54 of the CJEU Statute respectively. Second, the ECJ's preliminary rulings are not strictly binding on future cases either. A qualified court of the Member States is allowed to ask questions on any issue, even if a particular issue has already been addressed by the ECJ in its previous rulings; meanwhile, the ECJ is not prevented from making, over time, more than one reference on the same issue.[18] That being said, judgments of the CJEU have significant precedential effects *de facto*. For preliminary rulings, their precedential effects are recognized by Article 99 of the Rules of Procedure of the Court of Justice, which states that where a preliminary question is identical to a question on which the Court has already ruled, or where the answer to such a question could be deducted from existing case law, the Court is allowed to give its reply by reasoned order.[19] For annulment case judgments, their precedential effects stem from the CJEU's self-restraint: to promote legal certainty, the CJEU is inclined to follow its previously delivered judgments unless the circumstances of the case at hand have changed or the relevant precedent appears to be wrongly decided.[20]

18 Anthony Arnull, 'Owning Up to Fallibility: Precedent and the Court of Justice', *Common Market Law Review* 30, no. 2 (1993): 249, 251–2.

19 Article 99 of the Rules of Procedure of the Court of Justice, [2012] OJ L 265, 1–42.

20 Arnull, 'Owning up to Fallibility', 251–2.

Institutional structure at the Union level

The Commission: the supranational centre of the enforcement regime

Responsibilities and composition

As an EU institution, the Commission assumes the general responsibilities of budget execution, program management, and other coordination, execution, and management tasks laid down in the Treaties. Externally, it represents the EU, except in the area of common foreign and security policy and other cases provided for in the Treaties. In the area of competition law, it has two main responsibilities: participating in competition legislation and undertaking public enforcement of the Union's competition law. First, the Commission plays an instrumental role in the Union's competition law-making, as it is the only competent institution that can submit a legislative proposal and it can adopt delegated acts. Second, the Commission undertakes public enforcement of EU competition law at the Union level. It has been given an extensive range of powers to carry out this responsibility. In the area of competition law—where the EU has exclusive competence vis-à-vis the Member State governments, the Commission is accountable to the Council and the European Parliament and is subject to the judicial review of the CJEU in individual enforcement cases. Known as 'the guardian of the Treaties', the Commission ensures the adherence of the Member States to the Treaties. For this task, Article 258 of the TFEU empowers the Commission to initiate infringement procedures against the Member States.

The Commission has 27 Commissioners, one from each Member State. Aside from the President of the Commission and seven Vice Presidents, each of the remaining 19 Commissioners has one or more portfolios. Since November 2014, the Commissioner chairing competition has been Margrethe Vestager from Denmark.

The Commission is administratively divided into a number of Directorate-Generals ('DGs') that preside over different policy areas. Each DG has a Director General as the leader. The DG dealing with competition is DG COMP, which had been DG IV until 1999. Notably, although the Commission delegates its competition law responsibilities to DG Comp, decisions are made on behalf of the Commission as a whole. The Director General of DG COMP has been Olivier Guersent since January 2020, and this position is assisted by three Deputy Director Generals and a Chief Economist. In 2023, DG COMP caused quite a stir when it announced its pick for the Chief Economist position to be US antitrust scholar Fiona Scott Morton. Some civil society groups and Member State politicians strongly objected to this staff appointment, alleging that it would cause a conflict of interest to hire an American citizen who had consulted American Big Tech companies to work for the EU on antitrust against those companies. Eventually, Scott Morton withdrew her application due to the political controversy, leaving many wonder to whether this incident was a sign of nationalism prevailing in the EU to the detriment of better competition policymaking.[21]

21 'A Spat in Brussels Pits an Open Vision of Europe against an Insular One', *The Economist*, 19 July 2023, www.economist.com/europe/2023/07/19/a-spat-in-brussels-pits-an-open-vision-of-europe-against-an-insular-one. Lionel Barber, 'French Rejection of Top American Economist

The general decision-making process of DG COMP in competition law enforcement can be described as the following steps. First, DG COMP opens an investigation or files a proceeding based on a notification by the addressees, a complaint from relevant parties, or its own initiative. The specific procedural rules governing the public enforcement by the Commission are laid down in Regulation 1/2003, Regulation 773/2004, and several Commission Notices. Second, a case team will be established to handle the case. If requested, a hearing will be held before a Hearing Officer, who acts independently from the DG COMP and reports only to the Commissioner for Competition, to clear out procedural issues, particularly the ones that might endanger the defendant's right of defence. The case team is responsible for producing the first draft of the decision. After the first draft is formulated, it will be sent to the Legal Service of DG COMP and the Advisory Committees for legal proofreading and peer review. After this, the Director General will present the draft decision to the Commissioner for Competition, who will further present the draft decision to the College of Commissioners, where the 27 Commissioners will collectively decide the adoption of this decision.

The decentralization reform and the entrenched centrality of the Commission

The Commission has been playing a vital role in enforcing the Union's competition law since the adoption of Regulation 17 in 1962. Regulation 17 established a centralized system in which the Commission had the exclusive power to grant exemptions (to allegedly anticompetitive agreements between undertakings) under Article 85(3) of the former EEC Treaty. The main objective of that centralization was to promote market integration and to foster a 'competition culture' within the European Community.[22] Regulation 17 made substantial progress in achieving that objective in its four decades of implementation. However, with the continuing expansion of the European Community, new challenges arose, including the increasingly overwhelming caseload of the Commission. To address these new challenges, a reform was brought to the agenda in the 1990s by the Council, leading to the adoption of Regulation 1/2003, which entailed a decentralization reform of the EU competition law enforcement regime.[23]

This decentralization reform resulted in two major changes. The first one was the diffusion of the Commission's exclusive power to exempt anticompetitive agreements under Article 85(3) of the EEC Treaty (now Article 101(3) of the TFEU). Set out to relieve the Commission's overwhelming caseload, this reform abolished the central notification system that had granted the Commission the exclusive power to exempt anticompetitive agreements and empowered the NCAs and national courts

Is a Blow to Liberal Europe', *Politico*, 22 July 2023, www.politico.eu/article/france-brussels-eu-fiona-scott-morton-economist-competition-emmanuel-macron/.

22 Nicholas Moussis, *Access to the European Union: Law, Economics, Policies*, 20th ed. (Cambridge: Intersentia, 2013), 394.

23 Eleanor M. Fox, 'Antitrust and Institutions: Design and Change', *Loyola University Chicago Law Journal* 41 (2010): 477.

of the Member States to fully apply the Treaty provisions that are now Articles 101 and 102 of the TFEU. For example, under Articles 5 and 22 of Regulation 1/2003, the NCAs, acting on their own initiative or based on a complaint, now have the power to conduct investigations, to adopt decisions, to prescribe penalties, and to grant exemptions; under Article 6 of Regulation 1/2003, national courts also have the power to apply Articles 101 and 102 when performing their judicial review functions. A Member State can have multiple NCAs sharing the enforcement power since Article 35 of Regulation 1/2003 requires the Member States to establish competition authorities or other authorities that fulfil the requirements but gives them the discretion to choose which institutions to be designated as NCAs.

The second major change was the transition from an *ex ante* enforcement approach to an *ex post* one. According to Articles 2 and 4 of Regulation 17, parties of an agreement, decision, or practice that could be caught by Article 85(1) of the Treaty must notify the Commission for an exemption. Until the Commission makes a decision of exemption or negative clearance, that agreement, decision, or practice should be presumed void. Consequently, the legality of an agreement or practice would be uncertain until the Commission explicitly granted an exemption or a negative clearance. This uncertainty was fixed by Regulation 1/2003, which, along with some BERs and the 'De Minimis Notice', established a review system in which an agreement or a concerted practice would be presumptively legal unless the Commission or the NCAs issued a decision declaring its incompatibility with Article 101(1) of the TFEU.

To be sure, though, the decentralization reform did not significantly alter the institutional structure. While the Commission's power was formally decentralized, it had in effect attained significant influence on the Member States' application of EU competition law. For instance, Article 11(6) of Regulation 1/2003 provides that the initiation of proceedings by the Commission under Articles 101 and 102 shall prevail over the NCAs' competence in applying those provisions; Article 15(3) of Regulation 1/2003 provides that the Commission may submit written or oral observations to a national court when the coherent application of Articles 101 and 102 is at stake. Admittedly, Regulation 1/2003 does provide a certain degree of institutional constraint on the Commission. For example, Article 14 of Regulation 1/2003 introduced the Advisory Committees, which consist of experts from the Member States and are to act as consultants and peer review panels for the Commission before the adoption of an enforcement decision. However, the opinions of these Advisory Committees are not binding upon the Commission. Currently, there are two Advisory Committees: the Advisory Committee on Restrictive Practices and Dominant Positions and the Advisory Committee on Concentrations.

In short, the adoption of Regulation 1/2003 has enabled the Commission to retain, if not strengthen, its central role in enforcing the Union law under Articles 101 and 102 of the TFEU. This came with the trade-off of delegating part of its enforcement power to Member States agencies and courts. The Commission's central role in the decentralized regime is reflected in the four types of enforcement power it wields: (1) the power to investigate (laid down in Articles 17–22 of Regulation 1/2003); (2) the power to make decisions (Articles 7–10); (3) the power to impose sanctions (Articles 23–24); and (4) the power to provide supervision and guidance (Articles 11–13 and 15–16). The Commission's central role implies that it would be able to draw support from a Union-wide enforcement network to pursue the mandates and responsibilities entrusted by the Union legislators. This could, on the one hand, further the market integration mandate of the Union, but on the other hand, it could also result in the potential marginalization of other social and industrial goals that should have been emphasized in the Member States.[24] Besides, it raises the concern of 'prosecutorial bias' of the Commission stemming from the accumulation of investigative, prosecutorial, and adjudicative powers.[25]

The CJEU as the judicial supervisor

Historical developments

In 1958, after the Treaty of Rome (the EEC Treaty) was enacted, two new Communities—the European Economic Community (the 'EEC') and the European Atomic Energy Community (the 'EAEC')—were established. The Member States of these two Communities signed the Convention on Certain Institutions Common to the European Communities, which mandated the establishment of a single Court of Justice for the two Communities. As a result, the Court of Justice of the European Communities was established.[26] It also replaced the Court of Justice of the European Coal and Steel Community (the 'ECSC'), which was established by the Treaty of Paris in 1951.[27]

Subsequently, based on the 1986 Single European Act and by a Council decision in 1988, the CFI of the European Communities was created and attached to the Court of Justice of the European Communities, with the aims to alleviate the increasingly overwhelming caseload and to foster more judicial expertise on economic factual issues.[28] The Treaty of Maastricht, enacted in 1993, confirmed the establishment of the CFI. Initially, the CFI had limited jurisdiction: it was only allowed to hear cases concerning disputes between the Communities and their employees, certain proceedings brought by undertakings against the Commission under the ECSC Treaty, and competition cases brought by undertakings under the EEC Treaty.[29] But in 1993 and 1994, a couple of Council Decisions expanded the

24 Stephen Wilks, 'Agency Escape: Decentralization or Dominance of the European Commission in the Modernization of Competition Policy?', *Governance* 18, no. 3 (2005): 440.

25 Donald Slater, Sebastien Thomas, and Denis Waelbroeck, 'Competition Law Proceedings before the European Commission and the Right to a Fair Trial: No Need for Reform?', *European Competition Journal* 5, no. 1 (2009): 129; *cf.* Wouter P. J. Wils, 'The Increased Level of EU Antitrust Fines, Judicial Review and the ECHR', *World Competition* 33, no. 1 (2010): 5–29.

26 Anthony Arnull, *The European Union and Its Court of Justice*, 2nd ed. (Oxford: Oxford University Press, 2006), 6–7.

27 Articles 33 and 38 of the Treaty establishing the European Coal and Steel Community, signed on 18 April 1951, effective on 23 July 1952, expired on 23 July 2002 (hereinafter, 'the Treaty of Paris (1951)').

28 Arnull, *The European Union and Its Court of Justice*, 25.

29 Arnull, *The European Union and Its Court of Justice*, 26.

CFI's jurisdiction to include all direct actions brought by both undertakings and natural persons.[30] Then in 2004, another Council Decision further expanded the CFI's jurisdiction to include direct actions brought by Community institutions and Member States.[31]

The Treaty of Nice (the EC Treaty) was signed in 2001 and became effective in 2003. Article 225a of the EC Treaty provided the possibility of creating subsidiary courts below the Court of Justice and the CFI to deal with special areas of law, resulting in the establishment of the EU Civil Service Tribunal in 2004. Most recently, the Treaty of Lisbon, which was signed in 2007 and became effective in 2009, changed the names of the Courts: the CFI has been renamed as the GC, and 'the Court of Justice of the European Union' (CJEU) now refers officially to the two levels of courts taken together. For future reference, this book refers to the higher and lower levels of the CJEU as 'the ECJ' and 'the CFI' or 'the GC', respectively.

Mission and competence

The CJEU is entrusted with the mission to safeguard the coherent interpretation of the Treaties. Article 19 of the TEU states that the CJEU 'shall ensure that in the interpretation and application of the Treaties the law is observed', and Article 17(1) of the TEU states that the Commission's application of Union law shall be overseen 'under the control of the CJEU'. To accomplish this mission, the CJEU is empowered with two sets of competence: hearing direct actions and making preliminary rulings.[32]

Vis-à-vis the first competence, the CJEU mainly hears two types of direct actions. First, infringement proceedings brought by the Commission or a Member State against another Member States that fail to comply with their Treaty obligations (as provided by Articles 258 and 259 of the TFEU) and infringement proceedings against a Union institution for failing to act (as provided by Article 265 of the TFEU). Second, annulment proceedings brought by the Member States, the Union institutions, or any natural or legal person regarding a measure adopted by a Union institution, as provided by Article 263 of the TFEU. In the realm of competition law, the measure-adopting Union institution is usually the Commission.

Vis-à-vis preliminary rulings, the CJEU holds the ultimate authority in interpreting EU law, including Treaty provisions and secondary acts. It also rules on the validity of secondary Union law in the light of primary law. A preliminary ruling procedure starts with a court or tribunal of the Member States submitting a question to the CJEU. The qualification of such a court or tribunal is elaborated in a series

30 Council Decision of 8 June 1993 Amending Council Decision 88/591/ECSC, EEC, Euratom Establishing a Court of First Instance of the European Communities [1993] OJ L 144, 21–2; Council Decision of 7 March 1994 Amending Decision 93/350/Euratom, ECSC, EEC Amending Decision 88/591/ECSC, EEC, Euratom Establishing a Court of First Instance of the European Communities [1994] OJ L 66, 29–9.

31 Council Decision of 26 April 2004 Amending Articles 51 and 54 of the Protocol on the Statute of the Court of Justice [2004] OJ L 132, 5–6.

32 Arnull, *The European Union and Its Court of Justice*, 33.

of case law.[33] According to Article 267 of the TFEU, it is mandatory for a national court of last instance to make a preliminary reference to the CJEU while optional for other courts and tribunals when they apply a Treaty provision or a secondary Union act.

Institutional hierarchy between the ECJ and the GC

With the establishment of the CFI, a hierarchy was also created between the CFI (later the GC) and the ECJ. As the CFI's jurisdiction expanded in the 1990s and 2000s, this hierarchy developed towards a two-tier judicial architecture. This was reflected in the change of expression in Article 220 of the EC Treaty, which removed the wording (in Article 168(a) of the EEC Treaty and, subsequently, Article 11 of the Single European Act) that the CFI was attached to the ECJ.

This two-tier setting is well shown in the CJEU's direct-action hearings: the ECJ only reviews issues on points of law not points of fact, as provided by Article 256(1) of the TFEU. This means the GC has final authority on factual issues brought to it while its rulings on points of law are subject to full scrutiny by the ECJ; any unjustified admission, rejection, or prejudice of evidence by the GC may constitute an error of law.[34] A GC judgment could be entirely or partially quashed by the ECJ if the parties chose to appeal and errors of law were found. But to be clear, not all direct actions are within the GC's jurisdiction. According to Article 256 of the TFEU and Article 51 of the CJEU Statute, the ECJ has exclusive jurisdiction over actions between the Union institutions and actions brought by a Member State against the European Parliament and/or the Council (with three exceptions). Except for these actions, the GC enjoys first-instance jurisdiction on all other actions, especially actions brought by individuals or a Member State against the Commission. In the realm of competition law, most of the direct actions fall in the GC's jurisdiction at first instance.

Meanwhile, preliminary ruling procedures do not reflect this two-tier setting because the ECJ has the *de facto* exclusive power to make preliminary rulings. It is technically possible for the GC to be empowered to make preliminary rulings under Article 256(3) of the TFEU, but no concrete measures have been adopted in this direction yet.

Composition and formations

Currently, the ECJ is composed of 27 judges (one from each Member State) and 11 Advocates General. Article 253 of the TFEU lays down the general qualifications and terms of office of these judges and Advocates General, while Article 255 of

33 Case C-24/92, *Corbiau v Administration des Contributions* [1993] ECR I 1277, para 15; Case C-54/96, *Dorsch Consult Ingenieurgesellschaft v Bundesbaugesellschaft Berlin* [1997] ECR I 4961, para 23.

34 C-413/06 P, *Bertelsmann and Sony Corporation of America v Impala* [2008] ECR I 4951, paras 61 and 102.

the TFEU stipulates the general selection process, including a seven-person panel selection. According to Article 9 of the Rules of Procedure of the Court of Justice, a President is elected among the 27 judges to represent the Court, to direct the work of the Court, and to ensure the proper functioning of the Court; according to Article 10, a Vice President is also elected to assist the President and to take the President's place when needed. Among the Advocates General, the Court designates a First Advocate General for each period of one year (Article 14). In each case proceeding, the President designates one judge as the Judge-Rapporteur, and the First Advocate General shall assign one Advocate General to that case (Articles 15–16).

As to the GC, the judges are selected according to the process laid down in Article 255 of the TFEU, and their qualifications and terms of office are laid down in Article 254 of the TFEU. Unlike the ECJ, the GC does not have any Advocate General position, although according to Article 49 of the CJEU Statute, in needed circumstances, a judge may be called upon to perform the functions of an Advocate General. Article 48 of the CJEU Statute stipulates that from 1 September 2016 onwards, there shall be 47 judges in the GC and two judges per Member State as of 1 September 2019.

Overall, the EU competition law regime can be characterized as centralized at the supranational level (see Figure 4.1). First, there is only public enforcement at

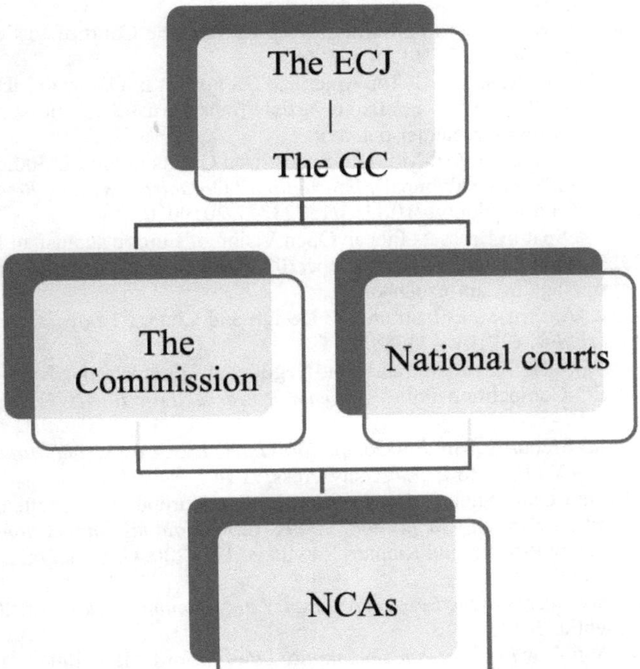

Figure 4.1 The centralized structure of the EU supranational competition law regime

the supranational level, and it is monopolized by the Commission. Beyond the supranational level, even though Regulation 1/2003 has to a large extent decentralized the public enforcement of EU competition law, the Commission still takes the centre stage in the Union-wide enforcement network by being entrusted with certain preferential enforcement powers over NCAs and national courts. The NCAs are subject to the coordination and leadership of the Commission on the one hand and the judicial supervision of domestic courts on the other. Second, the CJEU acts as the ultimate authority in interpreting Union competition law. It supervises the supranational public enforcement of the Commission through annulment procedures on the one hand while guiding Member State courts on adjudicating private enforcement cases through preliminary rulings on the other. There is a visible hierarchy at the supranational level not only between the CJEU and the Commission but also within the CJEU (i.e., between the ECJ and the GC). The EU regime poses an interesting contrast to the Chinese Anti-Monopoly Law regime, where public enforcement agencies are subject more to second-party control by administrative superiors than to third-party judicial control, and they compete with the courts in applying the AML. The Chinese regime is described in the next chapter.

Reference list

Arnull, Anthony. *The European Union and Its Court of Justice*. 2nd ed. Oxford: Oxford University Press, 2006.

Arnull, Anthony. 'Owning Up to Fallibility: Precedent and the Court of Justice'. *Common Market Law Review* 30, no. 2 (1993): 247–66.

Barber, Lionel. 'French Rejection of Top American Economist Is a Blow to Liberal Europe'. *Politico*, 22 July 2023. www.politico.eu/article/france-brussels-eu-fiona-scott-morton-economist-competition-emmanuel-macron/.

Butler, Graham. 'An Interim Post-Mortem: Specialised Courts in the EU Judicial Architecture after the Civil Service Tribunal'. *International Organizations Law Review* 17, no. 3 (2020): 586–632. https://doi.org/10.1163/15723747-2019010.

The Economist. 'A Spat in Brussels Pits an Open Vision of Europe against an Insular One'. 19 July 2023. www.economist.com/europe/2023/07/19/a-spat-in-brussels-pits-an-open-vision-of-europe-against-an-insular-one.

Fox, Eleanor M. 'Antitrust and Institutions: Design and Change'. *Loyola University Chicago Law Journal* 41 (2010): 473–88.

Hofmann, Herwig C. H. 'Negotiated and Non-Negotiated Administrative Rule-Making: The Example of EC Competition Policy'. *Common Market Law Review* 43, no. 1 (2006): 153–78.

Jones, Alison, and Brenda Sufrin. *EU Competition Law: Text, Cases, and Materials*. 5th ed. Oxford and New York: Oxford University Press, 2014.

Maher, Imelda, and Oana Stefan. 'Competition Law in Europe: The Challenge of a Network Constitution'. In *The Regulatory State: Constitutional Implications*, edited by Dawn Oliver, Tony Prosser, and Richard Rawlings, 178–200. Oxford: Oxford University Press, 2010.

Moussis, Nicholas. *Access to the European Union: Law, Economics, Policies*. 20th ed. Cambridge: Intersentia, 2013.

Senden, Linda. *Soft Law in European Community Law*. Oxford: Hart, 2004.

Slater, Donald, Sebastien Thomas, and Denis Waelbroeck. 'Competition Law Proceedings before the European Commission and the Right to a Fair Trial: No Need for Reform?'. *European Competition Journal* 5, no. 1 (2009): 97–143.

Stefan, Oana Andreea. 'European Competition Soft Law in European Courts: A Matter of Hard Principles?'. *European Law Journal* 14, no. 6 (2008): 753–72.
Wilks, Stephen. 'Agency Escape: Decentralization or Dominance of the European Commission in the Modernization of Competition Policy?'. *Governance* 18, no. 3 (2005): 431–52.
Wils, Wouter P. J. 'The Increased Level of EU Antitrust Fines, Judicial Review and the ECHR'. *World Competition* 33, no. 1 (2010): 5–29.

5 The federated Chinese Anti-Monopoly Law regime

Legal framework

The previous chapter describes the EU competition law regime at the supranational level, which features the Commission at the centre stage and the CJEU as the overarching supervisor. This chapter turns to its Chinese counterpart—the Anti-Monopoly Law enforcement regime.

Competition regulation before the Anti-Monopoly Law

The Anti-Monopoly Law (AML) was adopted on 30 August 2007 and entered into force on 1 August 2008. It was in the 1990s that the central government came to realize the need for a specialized law to foster and preserve market competition, as the nation continued transitioning from a centrally planned economy to a more market-oriented economy. However, lacking experience in that arena, the government opted for an incremental approach—adopting fragmented rules regarding the various aspects of competition regulation as a market-oriented economy developed.

Before the AML, there were several laws dealing with market competition, including the Anti-Unfair Competition Law (1993),[1] the Price Law (1997),[2] and the Provisional Regulation on Mergers with and Acquisition of Domestic Enterprises by Foreign Investors (2003). As the AML entered into force, it overlapped with both the Anti-Unfair Competition Law and the Price Law.[3] The 1993 Anti-Unfair

1 The Anti-Unfair Competition Law of the People's Republic of China (《中华人民共和国反不正当竞争法》), adopted by the Standing Committee of the National People's Congress on 2 September 1993, effective on 1 December 1993, www.lawinfochina.com/Display.aspx?lib=law&Cgid=6359 (accessed 1 May 2024) (hereinafter, 'the Anti-Unfair Competition Law'). The Law was revised in 2017 and then amended in 2019.

2 The Price Law of the People's Republic of China (《中华人民共和国价格法》), adopted by the Standing Committee of the National People's Congress on 29 December 1997, effective on 1 May 1998, http://en.pkulaw.cn/display.aspx?cgid=19158&lib=law (accessed 1 May 2024) (hereinafter, 'the Price Law').

3 Xingyu Yan, 'The Jurisdictional Delimitation in the Chinese Anti-Monopoly Law Public Enforcement Regime: The Inevitable Overstepping of Authority and the Implications', *Journal of Antitrust Enforcement* 6, no. 1 (2018): 126–7.

DOI: 10.4324/9781003479437-5

Competition Law overlapped with the AML in tackling the following types of infringements: abuse of dominant position by public undertakings, abuse of administrative power by governmental departments, undocumented loyalty rebates, pricing below costs in the aim of excluding competitors, bundling, and collusive tendering.[4] Meanwhile, the 1997 Price Law clashed with the AML regarding the practice of price-fixing agreements.[5] The overlaps in the Anti-Unfair Competition Law were dealt with in the Law's 2017 revision, but those in the Price Law remain, and the Price Law has been repeatedly applied to price-fixing agreements after the AML entered into force.[6] A possible justification for applying the Price Law is that the AML had not come into effect when these practices were carried out.[7]

Advent of the Anti-Monopoly Law

Legislative process

Adopting the AML was a protracted process, with the drafting of the law stretching from 1994 to 2007. One reason for this delay was the central government's fear that the domestic industries and enterprises might be too fragile to withstand incoming international competition.[8] Another reason was the challenge of formulating a sensible and effective competition law without undermining the government's control over strategically important industries and sectors.[9]

The AML legislative process was expedited in the early 2000s. In 2003, the newly restructured Ministry of Commerce (MOFCOM) was assigned to take over the drafting task. In 2004, it submitted the first draft to the State Council, which made several rounds of revision and presented a final draft to the Standing Committee of the National People's Congress in 2006.[10] The Standing Committee of the National People's Congress adopted the AML in 2007. According to the scholars who had advised the legislation, the main reason for the speedup was China's marketization: around the millennium, the marketization was reaching a point where widespread administrative monopolies, a legacy from the central planning era, had become a major roadblock; in addition, marketization itself was generating

4 See Articles 3(2), 6, 7, 8, 11, 12, and 15 of the 1993 Anti-Unfair Competition Law. For the distinction of anti-monopoly law and anti-unfair competition law in the Chinese context, see Xiaoye Wang, *The Evolution of China's Anti-Monopoly Law* (Cheltenham: Edward Elgar, 2014), 272–85.

5 See Article 14(1) of the 1997 Price Law.

6 Yichen Yang, 'Price-Related Cartels under the Chinese Anti-Monopoly Law Regime: The Need to Clarify Four Substantive and Procedural Issues', *World Competition* 39, no. 3 (2016): 484–5.

7 Thomas K. Cheng, 'The Meaning of Restriction of Competition Under the Monopolistic Agreements Provisions of the PRC Anti-Monopoly Law', *World Competition* 40, no. 2 (2017): 341.

8 Yong Huang, 'Pursuing the Second Best: The History, Momentum, and Remaining Issues of China's Anti-Monopoly Law', *Antitrust Law Journal* 75, no. 1 (2008): 118.

9 Bruce M. Owen, Su Sun, and Wentong Zheng, 'China's Competition Policy Reforms: The Anti-Monopoly Law and Beyond', *Antitrust Law Journal* 75, no. 1 (2008): 240.

10 Zhenguo Wu, 'Perspectives on the Chinese Anti-Monopoly Law', *Antitrust Law Journal* 75, no. 1 (2008): 77–8.

problematic private monopolies at the regional level.[11] Additionally, there was also an institutional factor: 2007 was the last year for the incumbent legislators to fulfil their promise to the people of establishing a 'fairly comprehensive legal system' for the socialist market economy before they had to hand over the legislative power to their successors.[12] Lastly, adopting the AML was part of the government's efforts to honour its promises made before joining the WTO in 2001: when applying for WTO membership, the Chinese representatives unequivocally assured the WTO that 'China was now formulating the law on Anti-Monopoly';[13] in the WTO accession agreement, the WTO also required China to adopt positive measures to 'allow prices for traded goods and services in every sector to be determined by market forces, and multi-tier pricing practices for such goods and services shall be eliminated'.[14]

Text of the Anti-Monopoly Law

Although the drafting of the AML was green-lighted, there were still disputes about what to put in the law. Some advised that the law should follow either the US or the EU model and focus on regulating private market power. But many others considered it imperative to also address the distortion of competition by public power, which they deemed a far more serious market problem in the context of China.[15] Eventually, after many rounds of consultation, negotiation, and compromise-making, the text of the 2007 AML was finalized as consisting of the following chapters: (1) 'General Principles', which lays down the objectives, scope of application, institutional setting, and relevant legal concepts of the AML; (2) 'Monopolistic Agreement'; (3) 'Abuse of Market Dominance'; (4) 'Concentration of Undertakings'; (5) 'Abuse of Administrative Power to Exclude or Restrict Competition'; (6) 'Investigation of Monopolistic Behaviour'; (7) 'Legal Liabilities'; and (8) 'By-law'.

The AML was revised in 2022 to better deal with the digital economy that has risen to prominence in the past 15 years. Notable changes are the significantly heightened penalties for AML infringements, clearer rules for assessing vertical agreements, additional references to abuse of dominance in digital platform markets, and procedural improvements in merger review. The overall structure remains the same.[16]

11 Angela Huyue Zhang, 'Bureaucratic Politics and China's Anti-Monopoly Law', *Cornell International Law Journal* 47, no. 3 (2014): 703.

12 Huang, 'Pursuing the Second Best', 119.

13 See the WTO, *Report of the Working Party on the Accession of China*, 1 October 2001, 12, http://docsonline.wto.org/imrd/directdoc.asp?DDFDocuments/t/WT/ACC/CHN49.doc (accessed 1 May 2024).

14 See the WTO, *Accession of the People's Republic of China*, 23 November 2001, 6, http://docsonline.wto.org/imrd/directdoc.asp?DDFDocuments/t/WT/L/432.doc (accessed 1 May 2024).

15 Wu, 'Perspectives on the Chinese Anti-Monopoly Law', 77, 93–4.

16 For an official English version of the 2007 AML, see the MOFCOM, *Anti-Monopoly Law of People's Republic of China*, 16 October 2019, http://mg.mofcom.gov.cn/article/policy/201909/20190902895917.shtml (accessed 1 May 2024). For the 2022 revised AML (in Chinese), see www.samr.gov.cn/zw/zfxxgk/fdzdgknr/fgs/art/2023/art_f0fae9eb3a684fc39e84d89eabfc2caa.html (accessed 1 May 2024).

Secondary to the AML text, the public enforcement agencies have adopted a series of implementation regulations. These regulations are introduced in the next section.

The bygone tripartite public enforcement regime

The 2007 AML text made only two references to the institutional design. First, Article 9 mandated the State Council to establish an Anti-Monopoly Commission responsible for coordinating the activities of the enforcement agencies. Second, Article 10 delegated the State Council to appoint the AML enforcement agencies before the AML came into force. This was consistent with the legislative custom in China: The legislature normally does not specify any enforcement agency that a forthcoming law needs; it delegates this task to the State Council instead. Then before that law enters into force, the State Council will issue one or more 'Three-Designation Orders', a kind of internal document that stipulates each enforcement agency's main responsibilities, internal organization structure, and staff composition.[17] This section critically describes how the AML enforcement power was split three ways and how those enforcement agencies have performed over the years. But first, it introduces the AMC, which was established to coordinate the original three AML enforcement agencies.

The Anti-Monopoly Commission

Article 9 of the 2007 AML requires the State Council to set up the Anti-Monopoly Commission (AMC) responsible for organizing, coordinating, and guiding anti-monopoly work. Its duties include the following: studying and drafting policies on competition, conducting investigations and assessments of market competition and publishing assessment reports, formulating and releasing anti-monopoly guidelines, coordinating the administrative enforcement of the AML, and other duties as prescribed by the State Council.

The AMC was established fairly quickly. In July 2008, on the eve of the AML's entering into force, the State Council issued a Notice concerning the staff composition and main responsibilities of the AMC.[18] According to the Notice, the board of the AMC shall consist of 19 Commissioners. A vice prime minister of the State Council, the minister of the MOFCOM, the director of the NDRC, the director of the SAIC, and the deputy secretary general of the State Council should each take a Commissioner position. The other 14 positions are taken by three deputy directors from the NDRC, the SAIC, and the MOFCOM, respectively, and 11 deputy directors from 11 other ministries. In 2009, though not formally announced, the

17 Yan, 'The Jurisdictional Delimitation in the Chinese Anti-Monopoly Law Public Enforcement Regime', 127.

18 The State Council, *Notice of the General Office of the State Council on the Main Functions and Members of the Anti-Monopoly Commission of the State Council* (《国务院办公厅关于国务院反垄断委员会主要职责和组成人员的通知国办发[2008]104 号》), 28 July 2008, www.lawinfochina.com/display.aspx?lib=law&id=7190&CGid (accessed 1 May 2024).

total number of ministries expanded to 16, with the accession of the People's Bank of China and the National Bureau of Statistics.[19] Additionally, an expert panel was formed in December 2011 to provide advisory opinions for policymaking. This expert panel consists of 21 lawyers, economists, and technology experts who work only part-time in the AMC. The part-time nature of these expert positions creates a rent-seeking opportunity and so a risk of regulatory capture, as exemplified by the bribery scandal of an ex-panellist.[20]

As a consultative and coordinating body, the AMC carries out its responsibilities only through inter-ministerial meetings within the State Council. It has no power to take administrative actions.[21] Some people suggested that the setting up of the AMC was the legislators' last-ditch effort to ensure a consistent and consolidated enforcement regime against the backdrop of fragmented pre-AML rules and the inevitability of having more than one enforcement agency.[22] During the tripartite era from 2008 to 2018, the MOFCOM handled the AMC's daily work. Then it was the newly established State Administration for Market Regulation (SAMR) that took over the work.

The AMC has kept a rather low profile. Its most notable work was the issuing of the Guidelines on the Definition of the Relevant Markets in 2009 and the Anti-Monopoly Guidelines for the Platform Economy in 2021.[23] Due to the lack of visibility, the AMC has largely escaped public scrutiny as to how well it has fulfilled its responsibilities for the past 16 years.

Three central ministries contending for the AML enforcer position

Before the AML was adopted, there were three central agencies involved in competition regulation: the MOFCOM, the National Development and Reform

19 See the list of signatures in the Notice concerning the adoption of the Guide of the Anti-Monopoly Committee of the State Council for the Definition of the Relevant Market (国务院反垄断委员会关于印发《关于相关市场界定的指南》的通知), 6 July 2009. For a current list of these ministries, see www.gov.cn/zhengce/content/2018-07/19/content_5307747.htm (in Chinese) (accessed 1 May 2024).

20 Tang Ming and Liu Nan, *Anti-Monopoly Expert Being Discharged Suddenly: What Is the Expert Panel in the Anti-Monopoly Commission?* (反垄断专家突遭解聘　反垄断委员会专家咨询组到底是个啥), 13 August 2014, http://finance.cnr.cn/gs/201408/t20140813_516216117.shtml (in Chinese) (accessed 1 May 2024).

21 See Article 6 of the Regulations on the Administration of the Establishment and Staffing of the Administrative Agencies of the State Council (《国务院行政机构设置和编制管理条例》), adopted by the State Council on 3 August 1997, effective on 3 August 1997, www.lawinfochina.com/display.aspx?lib=law&id=14544&CGid= (accessed 1 May 2024).

22 Qian Hao, 'The Multiple Hands: Institutional Dynamics of China's Competition Regime', in *China's Anti-Monopoly Law: The First Five Years*, ed. Adrian Emch and David Stallibrass (Alphen aan den Rijn: Wolters Kluwer International, 2013), 22.

23 Wei Huang et al., *Antitrust Guidelines for the Platform Economy in the Era of Enhanced Antitrust Scrutiny*, CPI Antitrust Chronicle March 2021, www.competitionpolicyinternational.com/wp-content/uploads/2021/03/10-Antitrust-Guidelines-for-the-Platform-Economy-in-the-Era-of-Enhanced-Antitrust-Scrutiny-By-Wei-Huang-Wendy-Zhou-Xiumin-Ruan-Xi-Zhang.pdf (accessed 1 May 2024).

Commission (NDRC), and the State Administration for Industry and Commerce (SAIC). All three agencies were motivated to become the enforcer of the AML because the power to safeguard market competition would only elevate their position in the central government as China develops further towards a market-oriented economy. Having the AML enforcement power in hand, these agencies would not only be able to enhance their pre-existing non-antitrust mandates[24] but they would also be able to aggressively pursue ends and strategies outside their defined mandates.[25] Leaders of these agencies were personally motivated as well since the internal structure of the State Council is characterized by technocracy and the technocratic officials' promotions depend heavily on their accumulation of administrative merits ('zhengji').[26] Thus, the three agencies entered into a hidden race for the AML enforcement agency position.

The MOFCOM

The MOFCOM staked a claim for the AML enforcement agency position based on its contribution to drafting the AML and its experience in handling mergers involving foreign investors.

When the State Council started the drafting of the AML in 1994, it assigned the work to two central agencies: the State Economic and Trade Commission and the SAIC. As the State Economic and Trade Commission was dissolved in the 2003 government restructuring, its drafting responsibility was reassigned to the MOFCOM, which was established in that restructuring to replace the Ministry of Foreign Trade and Economic Cooperation.[27] Rising to the occasion, the MOFCOM began presenting itself as a suitable candidate for the AML enforcement agency position. In the first AML draft that the MOFCOM submitted to the State Council in 2004, it proposed to appoint itself as the sole enforcement agency,[28] but that proposition was scratched out in later drafts because of strong objections from other agencies.[29]

The MOFCOM was created to govern domestic commerce and foreign trade, and to that end, it was given the authority to control mergers involving foreign investors. From there, it founded and gradually developed the merger review regime

24 Zhang, 'Bureaucratic Politics and China's Anti-Monopoly Law', 693–4.

25 Tom Ginsburg, 'Administrative Law and the Judicial Control of Agents in Authoritarian Regimes', in *Rule by Law: The Politics of Courts in Authoritarian Regimes*, ed. Tom Ginsburg and Tamir Moustafa (New York: Cambridge University Press, 2008), 59.

26 Victor C. Shih, *Factions and Finance in China: Elite Conflict and Inflation* (Cambridge: Cambridge University Press, 2007), 5, 54.

27 Shang Ming, *China's Developing Competition Policy and Legislation* (发展中的中国竞争政策与立法), Website of Department of Treaty and Law of the MOFCOM, 22 April 2005, http://tfs.mofcom.gov.cn/article/bc/200504/20050400081489.shtml (accessed 1 May 2024).

28 Yan, 'The Jurisdictional Delimitation in the Chinese Anti-Monopoly Law Public Enforcement Regime', 125.

29 Owen, Sun, and Zheng, 'China's Competition Policy Reforms', 261.

in China.[30] In 2003, the MOFCOM adopted, in collaboration with three other agencies, a merger and acquisition ('M&A') Regulation, in which the MOFCOM added four articles empowering itself as a co-authority on merger review along with the SAIC.[31] The MOFCOM reinforced its merger control authority in 2006 when it issued a notification guideline to implement the M&A Regulation.[32] In contrast, despite holding the title of a co-authority on merger review, the SAIC never adopted any secondary regulation to strengthen its authority. It was observed that in practice, the MOFCOM was far more active than the SAIC in terms of merger review.[33] This significantly boosted the MOFCOM's qualification as a merger control authority under the AML.

The MOFCOM also used its transnational channels to strengthen its merger review expertise and reputation. For instance, in 2004, the MOFCOM established a dialogue with the European Commission on competition policy, and since then, this dialogue has been held annually.[34] It also invited the American Bar Association several times to comment on the AML drafts.[35] Eventually, the MOFCOM secured the position as the exclusive merger review authority under the AML.

The SAIC

The SAIC also staked a claim in the AML enforcer position, based on its experience in enforcing the Anti-Unfair Competition Law since 1993. As mentioned earlier in the chapter, the 1993 Anti-Unfair Competition Law covered many types of monopolistic conduct that were later written in the AML. In 1994, the SAIC established a Fair Trade Bureau, under which an Anti-Monopoly Office was set up to deal with anti-monopoly cases exclusively. Soon, local Administrations for Industry and Commerce (AICs) followed the SAIC's internal structure and established their Fair Trade divisions. In 2002, the State Council upgraded the SAIC to

30 Hao, 'The Multiple Hands', 31–2.

31 Articles 19–22 of the Provisional Regulation on Mergers and Acquisitions of Domestic Undertakings by Foreign Investors (《外国投资者并购境内企业暂行规定》), adopted by the Ministry of Foreign Trade and Economic Cooperation, the State Administration of Taxation, the State Administration of Industry and Commerce, and the State Administration of Foreign Exchange on 13 March 2003, effective on 12 April 2003, http://tfs.mofcom.gov.cn/article/date/i/s/200509/20050900366385.shtml (in Chinese) (accessed 1 May 2024). This Regulation has been abolished.

32 Tingting Weinreich-Zhao, *Chinese Merger Control Law: An Assessment of Its Competition-Policy Orientation after the First Years of Application*, Munich Studies on Innovation and Competition (Berlin, Heidelberg: Springer-Verlag, 2015), www.springer.com/gp/book/9783662438671. 33.

33 Hao, 'The Multiple Hands', 31, 33.

34 News Office of the MOFCOM, *The MOFCOM Held Press Conference on the Anti-Monopoly Enforcement of 2011* (商务部召开"2011 年反垄断工作主要情况"专题新闻发布会), The MOFCOM Website, 27 December 2011, www.mofcom.gov.cn/article/ae/ztfbh/201112/20111207901483.shtml (in Chinese) (accessed 1 May 2024).

35 See the American Bar Association: Joint Submission of the American Bar Association's Sections of Antitrust Law and International Law and Practice on the Proposed Anti-Monopoly Law of the People's Republic of China, 15 July 2003, http://apps.americanbar.org/webupload/commupload/IC990000/newsletterpubs/abaprc2005fin.pdf (accessed 1 May 2024).

the ministerial level ('zhengbu ji'), making it the direct subordinate of the State Council in charge of market supervision and regulation.[36] Furthermore, with the adoption of the 2003 M&A Regulation, the SAIC held the title of co-controller of mergers of domestic undertakings by foreign investors alongside the MOFCOM.

The SAIC's participation in the early stage of the AML drafting process also supported its claim. In 1994, when the legislature added the AML to the agenda, it was the SAIC that was entrusted with the drafting task, along with the former State Economic and Trade Commission. Since then, the SAIC had been participating in the drafting process, until 2003, when the State Economic and Trade Commission was dissolved and the drafting task was mostly taken over by the MOFCOM.[37] When the MOFCOM proposed to name itself as the sole AML enforcer, it was the SAIC that united other ministries to block that proposition. To demonstrate its qualification as a suitable candidate, the SAIC released an investigation report about the anticompetitive practices of multinational companies in China and prescribed a few corrective measures.[38] Eventually, the SAIC secured an enforcement agency position.

The NDRC

The NDRC built its claim to be an AML enforcement agency around its long-standing authority on price control. Its predecessor was the State Planning Commission, which was established in 1952 and used to manage nearly all aspects of the nation's centrally planned macro-economy. The NDRC replaced the State Planning Commission in 2003, as the latter had become incompatible with China's embrace of market economy.[39] The NDRC has since then assumed the following main responsibilities: (1) formulating, implementing, and coordinating plans and strategies concerning macro-economy and social development; (2) reviewing and approving the central government's investments and key construction projects; (3) summarizing and analysing fiscal and financial situations; and (4) maintaining the balance and control over important commodities.[40]

Two features of the NDRC are remarkable. The first one is its omnipresent influence as a policymaker over a wide range of areas that concern macro-level policy formulation and strategic economic control. The second feature is its heavy-handed approach to regulation. The NDRC inherited many interventionist missions from its predecessor, and price control was one of them, as exemplified by its sole authority

36 Yan, 'The Jurisdictional Delimitation in the Chinese Anti-Monopoly Law Public Enforcement Regime', 126.
37 Owen, Sun, and Zheng, 'China's Competition Policy Reforms', 236.
38 Owen, Sun, and Zheng, 'China's Competition Policy Reforms', 260–1.
39 Peter Martin, 'The Humbling of the NDRC: China's National Development and Reform Commission Searches for a New Role Amid Restructuring', *China Brief* 14, no. 5 (2014): 15.
40 The NDRC, *Main Functions of the NDRC*, The NDRC Website, https://en.ndrc.gov.cn/aboutndrc/mainfunctions/ (in Chinese) (accessed 1 May 2024).

to enforce the 1997 Price Law.[41] Not surprisingly, this gave the NDRC a leading position in the race. After all, price control of certain industries remains strategically crucial in the blueprint of the 'socialist market economy', and in that regard, no other agency is more experienced or authoritative than the NDRC.[42]

Most importantly, the State Council had no intention to create any new agencies for the AML.[43] So it eventually decided to strike a compromise among the three contenders: on the eve of the AML's entering into effect, the State Council issued a Three-Designation Order for each of these three agencies, validating all three's claims for the AML enforcer position. Consequently, the AML enforcement power was split three ways, and the division of labour aligned with these agencies pre-existing mandates and experience: the MOFCOM was entrusted with the responsibility to review concentrations of undertakings,[44] the SAIC was responsible for regulating non-price-related anticompetitive agreements and abuse of dominant position,[45] and the NDRC was responsible for regulating price-related anticompetitive agreements and abuse of dominant position.[46] During the tripartite era from 2008 to 2018, these three agencies carried out enforcement activities in their respective jurisdictions. The following three subsections look at their enforcement records.

Enforcement record of the MOFCOM

Merger control had been one of the many responsibilities of the MOFCOM, and it was the Anti-Monopoly Bureau within the MOFCOM that handled the merger review work.[47] For carrying out its merger review responsibility under the AML, the MOFCOM reportedly had about a total of 35 staff members across seven divisions.[48]

41 Yan, 'The Jurisdictional Delimitation in the Chinese Anti-Monopoly Law Public Enforcement Regime', 126–7.

42 Zhang, 'Bureaucratic Politics and China's Anti-Monopoly Law', 696.

43 Huang, 'Pursuing the Second Best', 126.

44 The State Council, *The Notice of the General Office of the State Council on the Principal Responsibilities and Staffing of the Ministry of Commerce* (《国务院办公厅关于印发商务部主要职责内设机构和人员编制规定的通知(国办发[2008]77 号)》), Article 15 of Part I and Art 11 of Part III (15 July 2008).

45 The State Council, *The Notice of the General Office of the State Council on the Principal Responsibilities and Staffing of the State Administration for Industry and Commerce* (《国务院办公厅关于印发国家工商行政管理总局主要职责内设机构和人员编制规定的通知(国办发[2008]88 号)》), Article 6 of Part II and Art 3 of Part III (11 July 2008).

46 The State Council, *The Notice of the General Office of the State Council on the Principal Responsibilities and Staffing of the National Development and Reform Commission* (《国务院办公厅关于印发国家发展和改革委员会主要职责内设机构和人员编制规定的通知(国办发[2008]102 号)》), Article 3 of Part II and Art 23 of Part III (15 July 2008).

47 The MOFCOM, *Mission*, http://english.mofcom.gov.cn/column/mission.shtml (accessed 1 May 2024).

48 Yong Huang and Richean Zhiyan Li, 'An Overview of Chinese Competition Policy: Between Fragmentation and Consolidation', in *China's Anti-Monopoly Law: The First Five Years*, ed. Adrian Emch and David Stallibrass (Alphen aan den Rijn: Wolters Kluwer International, 2013), 9. The

In the first four years, the merger reviews by the MOFCOM were characterized by unusually lengthy procedures and obscure substantive analyses.[49] These problems were attributable to the MOFCOM's lack of experience and manpower at the time. Admittedly, these problems persisted more or less till the end of the tripartite era, but over the years, particularly from 2013 onward, the MOFCOM had made visible efforts to mitigate these problems.[50]

The MOFCOM began accepting merger notifications immediately after the AML came into effect. On 18 November 2008, it published the first conditional approval decision. Since then, the MOFCOM had unconditionally cleared most of the merger cases. By the time it handed over its merger control authority, the MOFCOM had produced two prohibition decisions and 36 conditional clearance decisions.[51]

Enforcement record of the SAIC

The SAIC had the primary responsibilities of maintaining market order and protecting the rights and legitimate interests of businesses and consumers. Because of the micro-management nature of these responsibilities, the SAIC frequently delegated its AML enforcement authority to local AICs. Also, it was observed that the SAIC used to have a *de facto* lower status than the NDRC and the MOFCOM, despite having the same administrative rank as them.[52]

Following the State Council's Three-Designation Order in 2008, the SAIC established an Anti-Monopoly and Anti-Unfair Competition Bureau to enforce the AML against non-price-related anticompetitive agreements, abuse of dominant position, and abuse of administrative power to restrain competition. Local AICs quickly followed suit and established their own Competition Enforcement Bureaus. There were eight divisions within the Anti-Monopoly and Anti-Unfair Competition Enforcement

---

Anti-Monopoly Bureau of the MOFCOM, *Internal Departments* (内设机构), The Anti-Monopoly Bureau Website, 13 March 2010, http://fldj.mofcom.gov.cn/article/gywm/200811/20081105868495.shtml (accessed 1 May 2024).

49 Zhang, 'Bureaucratic Politics and China's Anti-Monopoly Law', 689; Caroline Cauffman and Qian Hao, 'Comparison of the EU and Chinese System of Procedural Rights', in *Procedural Rights in Competition Law in the EU and China*, ed. Caroline Cauffman and Qian Hao (Berlin, Heidelberg: Springer Berlin Heidelberg, 2016), 237–8.

50 Fei Deng and Cunzhen Huang, 'A Five Year Review of Merger Enforcement in China', *The Antitrust Source* (blog), October 2013, www.clearygottlieb.com/-/media/organize-archive/cgsh/files/news-pdfs/a-five-year-review-of-merger-enforcement-in-china.pdf, 4; Fei Deng and Cunzhen Huang, 'A Ten-Year Review of Merger Enforcement in China', *The Antitrust Source* (blog), August 2018, www.clearygottlieb.com/-/media/files/a-tenyear-review-of-merger-enforcement-in-china-pdf, 5.

51 For the list of the cases, see Cauffman and Hao, note 49. For a statistical overview of these cases, see Shao Geng, *The Compilation and Statistics of the MOFCOM's Review Announcements and Penalty Decisions on Concentration between Undertakings* (商务部经营者集中反垄断审查公告、处罚决定(函)汇编及统计数据), Zhihu Website, https://zhuanlan.zhihu.com/p/20357507 (in Chinese) (accessed 1 May 2024).

52 Hao, 'The Multiple Hands', 30.

Bureau, and three of them were responsible for the AML enforcement. The actual officials handling anti-monopoly cases in the SAIC were no more than 20.[53]

The SAIC had been rather inactive from 2008 to 2013, possibly due to the limited staff power. It adopted two procedural regulations for the implementation of the AML in June 2009, and two substantive regulations on anticompetitive agreements and abuse of dominance, respectively, in December 2010. A highlight during this period was the launch of an investigation against Tetra Pak, which was the SAIC's first AML operation against a multinational company. This case was closed on 9 November 2016, with Tetra Pak being fined heavily for committing three abuse of dominance offenses.[54]

It was not until 2013 that the SAIC started publishing its enforcement cases on its website.[55] By the time the tripartite regime was ended, the SAIC had handled a total of 70 announcements of AML public enforcement cases. These announcements are summarized in Table 5.1.

Three points are notable regarding these enforcement announcements. First, a decision to terminate a case investigation usually followed a decision made previously

Table 5.1 AML enforcement announcements issued by the SAIC from 2013 to 2018

	2013	*2014*	*2015*	*2016*	*2017*	*2018*
Penalty decisions of anticompetitive agreement cases	12	3	4	4	3	2
Penalty decisions of abuse of dominance cases		4	3	9	4	1
Decisions to suspend a case investigation		1	5		1	2
Decisions to terminate a case investigation			1	1	5	3
Penalty decisions for being uncooperative during investigation			1			
In total (each year)	12	8	14	14	13	8

53 This number was estimated based on a statement made by the NDRC Director. See the NDRC, *The Minutes of Director Kunlin Xu Attending the Antitrust Enforcement Press Release Held by the State Council Information Office* (许昆林局长参加国务院新闻办公室反垄断执法工作情况新闻吹风会实录), The NDRC Website, http://jjs.ndrc.gov.cn/gzdt/201409/t20140915_625585.html (in Chinese) (accessed 1 May 2024). See also, Hao, 'The Multiple Hands', 31.

54 Xingyu Yan, 'Whither Antitrust Regulation of Loyalty Rebates in China: The Tetra Pak Decision and Lessons from the EU', *World Competition* 40, no. 4 (2017): 613–14.

55 All of the enforcement cases disclosed by the SAIC are currently available in Chinese at www.samr.gov.cn/fldys/tzgg/xzcf/index.html (accessed 1 May 2024). For a statistical overview of those decisions, see Shao Geng, *The Compilation and Statistics of the SAIC's Disclosed Anti-Monopoly Enforcement Case Decisions* (工商总局已公布反垄断执法案件处理决定汇编与数据统计), Zhihu Website, https://zhuanlan.zhihu.com/p/20373716?columnSlug=competitionlaw (in Chinese) (accessed 1 May 2024).

to suspend the investigation, but there are two exceptions: the termination of the *Ordos City Gas* case in 2017 (suspended in 2016 but no announcement published) and the termination of the *Jiangsu Hai'an Power Grid* case in 2016 (suspended in 2014 but no announcement published). By the end of the tripartite era, there had been one case being suspended of investigation: the *Ningxia Mobile* case (suspended in 2015). Second, as the announcement record shows, the SAIC had imposed penalties in 50 cases during the tripartite era: 29 of them were anticompetitive agreement cases, and the other 21 were abuse of dominance cases. Importantly, the date of a penalty decision being made did not always correspond to the date it was announced; there was often a delay in the announcement, which could be up to two or three years, as exemplified by some of the case decisions announced in 2013. Third, only two cases were personally handled by the SAIC (the *Tetra Pak* case in 2016 and the *Beijing Shengkai* case in 2015, which was terminated without penalty). The rest of the cases were all handled by provincial AICs under case-by-case delegations from the SAIC.[56] This exemplifies the SAIC's dependence on local AICs for enforcing the AML.

Enforcement record of the NDRC

In the 2008 Three-Designation Order, the Stated Council put the NDRC in charge of regulating 'price-related monopolistic conduct', which echoed its long-standing authority on price control.

From 2008 to 2013, the NDRC as an AML enforcer focused on adopting implementation regulations and building its capacity. In 2010, it adopted the Regulation on Anti-Price Monopoly, which clarified the scope of 'price-related monopolistic conduct' as including price-related monopolistic agreements and abuse of dominant position through price manipulation.[57] It also adopted the Regulation on the Administrative Enforcement Procedures of Anti-Price Monopoly, which laid down the procedural rules for its AML enforcement. In 2011, the NDRC renamed the Department of Price Supervision and Examination, which it established under the instruction of the Three-Designation Order, as the Bureau of Price Supervision and Anti-Monopoly. It expanded this Bureau's staff by adding three work units and 20 employees, all of who were to handle AML work exclusively.[58] During this period, the NDRC also established dialogues with the DG Comp of the European Commission, the Department of Justice and the Federal Trade Commission of the US, the Office of Fair Trading of the UK, and the Fair Trade Commission of South Korea.

From 2008 to 2013, there were only four enforcement cases announced on the NDRC's website. Two cases were handled in 2011, and both were about horizontal

56 Yan, 'The Jurisdictional Delimitation in the Chinese Anti-Monopoly Law Public Enforcement Regime', 137.

57 Articles 3 and 5–9 of the Regulation on Anti-Price Monopoly (《反价格垄断规定》), adopted by the NDRC on 29 December 2010, effective on 1 February 2011, www.gov.cn/flfg/2011-01/04/content_1777969.htm (in Chinese) (accessed 1 May 2024).

58 Sohu News, *The Anti-Monopoly "Hunter"* (反垄断"猎人") Business Sohu, 20 August 2014, http://business.sohu.com/s2014/jrzj328/ (in Chinese) (accessed 1 May 2024).

price-fixing agreements.[59] The other two were handled in 2013, one about horizontal price-fixing and the other about resale price maintenance.[60] All four cases resulted in financial penalties, but the NDRC never published the formal prohibition decisions. Another noteworthy case happened in November 2011, when the NDRC announced its AML investigation against China Telecom and China Unicom, two of the largest Chinese state-owned enterprises.[61] The NDRC declared sometime later that the two had violated the AML, but it never imposed any penalty. The case was eventually buried after Telecom and Unicom promised to rectify their monopolistic practices.[62] This case had ambivalent implications for the AML: on the one hand, going after powerful state-owned enterprises showed the NDRC's commitment to antitrust enforcement, but on the other hand, how the investigation fizzled out showed the political pressure and resistance that the enforcement is up against.[63]

The NDRC began publishing its enforcement decisions in 2014. It gave general authorizations to local DRCs to enforce the AML, whereas the SAIC delegated the enforcement power to local AICs on a case-by-case basis.[64] Compared to the SAIC, the NDRC performed worse in disclosing its enforcement decisions. Local DRCs also handled AML cases, but they were not systematically published by the NDRC. Several cases resulted in fines but no formal decisions were disclosed by the NDRC, such as the *Wuliangye* case handled by the DRC of Sichuan Province.[65] The case decisions that were published by the NDRC are listed in Table 5.2 according to the years they were made.[66]

59 The NDRC, *The Paper Association of Fuyang, Zhejiang, Severely Punished for Implementing Price Cartelization* (浙江省富阳市造纸行业协会组织实施价格垄断行为受到严厉处罚), www.gov.cn/gzdt/2011-01/04/content_1778091.htm (in Chinese) (accessed 1 May 2024); *Two Pharmaceutical Companies Severely Punished for Monopolizing Compound Reserpine* (两医药公司垄断复方利血平原料药受到严厉处罚), www.gov.cn/gzdt/2011-11/14/content_1992667.htm (in Chinese) (accessed 1 May 2024).

60 The NDRC, *Six Foreign Undertakings Punished for Implementing Price Monopoly of LCD Panels* (六家境外企业实施液晶面板价格垄断被依法查处), www.gov.cn/banshi/2013-01/04/content_2304387.htm (in Chinese) (accessed 1 May 2024); *Baby Formula Producers Fined ¥668.73 Million for Violating the Anti-Monopoly Law* (合生元等乳粉生产企业违反反垄断法限制竞争行为共被处罚6.6873亿元), www.ndrc.gov.cn/xwdt/xwfb/201308/t20130807_956179.html (in Chinese) (accessed 1 May 2024).

61 Ma Xiaofang and Guo Liqin, *The Unexpected Investigation against Telecom and Unicom: The AML Shaking Centrally-Owned Enterprises for the First Time* (电信联通意外遭调查《反垄断法》首撼央企), Yicai News, 10 November 2011, www.yicai.com/news/1187660.html (in Chinese) (accessed 1 May 2024).

62 China News Net, *The NDRC: China Telecom and Unicom Have Rectified Their Monopolistic Conduct* (发改委: 中国电信和联通已就反垄断案进行整改), Sina Finance, 19 February 2014, http://finance.sina.com.cn/chanjing/cyxw/20140219/111018264145.shtml (in Chinese) (accessed 1 May 2024).

63 Wang, *The Evolution of China's Anti-Monopoly Law*, 398–9.

64 Yan, 'The Jurisdictional Delimitation in the Chinese Anti-Monopoly Law Public Enforcement Regime', 137.

65 For a brief news report on this case, see the Sichuan DRC, *Wuliangye Being Fined ¥202 Million for Implementing Price-Monopoly* (五粮液公司实施价格垄断被处罚2.02亿元), Sina Finance, 22 February 2013, http://finance.sina.com.cn/chanjing/b/20130222/164314620476.shtml (in Chinese) (accessed 1 May 2024).

66 These NDRC cases are now archived by year on the SAMR's website: www.samr.gov.cn/fldys/tzgg/xzcf/ (in Chinese) (accessed 1 May 2024).

Table 5.2 AML enforcement decisions issued by the NDRC from 2008 to 2018

	2013	*2014*	*2015*	*2016*	*2017*	*2018*
Cases of horizontal anticompetitive agreements	1	1	1	2	1	0
Cases of vertical anticompetitive agreements	0	0	0	1	0	1
Cases of abuse of dominance	0	0	1	0	1	0

Consolidating the three agencies

The tripartite regime was in place for almost a decade. On 13 March 2018, the State Council proposed to the National People's Congress a government-restructuring plan, part of which was to merge the three AML enforcement agencies. More specifically, it proposed to rename the SAIC as 'the State Administration for Market Regulation' (SAMR) and to reallocate the AML responsibilities of the MOFCOM and the NDRC to the SAMR.[67] In addition to the AML responsibilities, the SAMR would also absorb the responsibilities of the State Administration for Quality Supervision and Inspection and Quarantine and the State Food and Drug Administration.[68] On 17 March 2018, the National People's Congress approved this restructuring plan. On 21 March 2018, the tripartite era was officially over and the SAMR was established to lead the new AML public enforcement regime.

The new public enforcement regime led by the SAMR

The SAMR and the State Anti-Monopoly Bureau

Following the Three-Designation Order issued by the State Council, the SAMR established an internal Anti-Monopoly Bureau to handle the AML public enforcement exclusively.[69] The Anti-Monopoly Bureau of the SARM had only about 40 official posts ('bianzhi'),[70] so it was unable to receive all the staff from the antitrust branches

67 Adrian Emch, 'China to Merge Antitrust Authorities', *Kluwer Competition Law Blog* (blog), 21 March 2018, https://competitionlawblog.kluwercompetitionlaw.com/2018/03/21/china-merge-antitrust-authorities/.

68 Xing Bingyin, *The Government Restructuring Plan: To Establish the State Administration for Market Regulation and No Longer Maintaining the SAIC* (机构改革方案：组建国家市场监督管理总局，不再保留工商总局), The Paper, 13 March 2018, www.thepaper.cn/newsDetail_forward_2026804 (in Chinese) (accessed 1 May 2024).

69 Wang Jun, *The Three-Designation Order for the SAMR Disclosed: Appointing 1 Director and 4 Vice-Directors* (国家市场监管总局三定方案出炉：设局长1名，副局长4名), The Paper, 13 August 2018, www.thepaper.cn/newsDetail_forward_2342433 (in Chinese) (accessed 1 May 2024).

70 On 'bianzhi', see Kjeld Erik Brødsgaard, 'Institutional Reform and the *Bianzhi* System in China', *The China Quarterly* 170 (June 2002): 361–86, https://doi.org/10.1017/S0009443902000232.

of the MOFCOM and the NDRC. In other words, the consolidation of AML enforcement agencies actually reduced the enforcement capacity at a time when the public was calling for more antitrust attention to tech giants in the digital economy.

Realizing this issue, the State Council decided in November 2021 to upgrade the Anti-Monopoly Bureau within the SAMR to the deputy-ministerial level and rename it as the State Anti-Monopoly Bureau. This new agency is still under the general management of the SAMR, but it gained more nominal independence and, more importantly, larger room for capacity building.[71] Currently, the State Anti-Monopoly Bureau consists of three divisions: Competition Policy Coordination Division, Anti-Monopoly Enforcement Division I, and Anti-Monopoly Enforcement Division II. Division I enforces the AML against anticompetitive agreements, abuses of dominance, and administrative monopolies, whereas Division II reviews mergers.

Enforcement record of the SAMR

The publication of cases has improved greatly since the SAMR consolidated the AML enforcement powers.[72] As of 31 December 2023, the enforcement decisions published by the SAMR (including the State Anti-Monopoly Bureau) are summarized in Tables 5.3, 5.4, and 5.5 according to the date they were published:

As Table 5.5 indicates, antitrust enforcement by the SAMR from 2018 to 2020 was relatively mild, comparable to the combined enforcement record of the SAIC and the NDRC before 2018. Particularly remarkable is 2021: first, this year saw a sudden peak in enforcement, particularly the number of penalty decisions against unapproved mergers. That number was down in 2022 to less than half that of 2021, then further down to zero in 2023, possibly because most of the unapproved mergers had been brought under the law and because the penalties had effectively deterred merging parties. Second, in 2021, the SAMR issued the first-ever AML penalty decision on abuse of dominance by a Big Tech platform, Alibaba. The case took the SAMR only five months from start to finish, and it resulted in the largest amount of fines in the AML enforcement history.[73] Six months later, the SAMR fined another domestic tech giant, Meituan, for committing the same type of dominance abuse.[74]

71 *China Appoints Chief of National Anti-monopoly Bureau*, Reuters, 16 November 2021, www.reuters.com/business/china-appoints-chief-national-anti-monopoly-bureau-2021-11-15/ (accessed 1 May 2024); Yicai, *Establishing the National Anti-Monopoly Bureau: From Three to One, then One to Three* (国家反垄断局挂牌，从三合一到一变三), Tencent, 19 November 2021, https://new.qq.com/rain/a/20211118A0D78A00 (accessed 1 May 2024).

72 All the published decisions can be found on the SAMR website: www.samr.gov.cn/fldys/tzgg/ (accessed 1 May 2024).

73 The case decision is published on the SAMR website. See www.samr.gov.cn/fldys/tzgg/xzcf/art/2023/art_65135bd83ef94f65a9bd50014a4c1218.html (in Chinese) (accessed 1 May 2024).

74 For the case decision, see www.samr.gov.cn/fldys/tzgg/xzcf/art/2023/art_1ee8b4651010426cadd7251c71e00089.html (in Chinese) (accessed 1 May 2024).

Table 5.3 Intervention by the SAMR against abuses of administrative power that restrict competition from 2018 to 2023

	2018	*2019*	*2020*	*2021*	*2022*	*2023*
Correction cases (no administrative penalties)	17	0	8	38	70	22

Table 5.4 Conditional clearance and prohibition decisions by the SAMR in reviewing concentrations of undertakings from 2018 to 2023

	2018	*2019*	*2020*	*2021*	*2022*	*2023*
Conditional clearance	3	5	4	4	5	4
Prohibition decisions	0	0	0	1	0	0
In total (each year)	3	5	4	5	5	4

Table 5.5 Enforcement by the SAMR against anticompetitive agreements, abuses of dominance, and other AML infringements from 2018 to 2023

	2018	*2019*	*2020*	*2021*	*2022*	*2023*
Penalty decisions of horizontal anticompetitive agreement cases	2	8	9	12	11	11
Penalty decisions of vertical anticompetitive agreement cases	0	1	0	1	4	1
Penalty decisions of abuse of dominance cases	0	4	7	11	9	8
Decisions to suspend a case investigation	0	2	0	0	0	0
Decisions to terminate a case investigation	1	2	2	0	0	0
Penalty decisions for being uncooperative during investigation	0	0	1	0	0	0
Penalty decisions for implementing concentrations without prior approval	1	16	13	94	45	0
In total (each year)	4	33	32	118	69	28

Compared to 2021 and 2022, the enforcement in 2023 returned to a relatively mild level that was seen in 2019 and 2020. This suggests that there had been a campaign-style antitrust crackdown circa 2021 and 2022. This crackdown came from the top leaders and was aimed at reining in homegrown Big Tech platforms.[75] Chinese tech giants, which include but are not limited to Alibaba and Tencent, are behind most of those penalized unapproved mergers. For years, they had enjoyed a laissez-faire regulatory environment—along with the negligible amount of fine for concentrating without approval and the practically non-existent AML enforcement in the tech sector, so these tech incumbents had the easy way to entrench their market power through horizontal, vertical, and conglomerate acquisitions.[76] But as the top policymakers decided to shift their stance on tech regulation, these tech firms were inevitably brought to reckoning.

Remarkably, however, the SAMR is not the only authority trying to regulate digital market competition. For example, the People's Bank of China has proposed measures to curb the duopoly in mobile payments,[77] the Cyberspace Administration of China has intervened against exploitative data collection practices by tech platforms,[78] and the Ministry of Industry and Information Technology has stepped in to dismantle the 'blockades' that Big Tech ecosystems have raised against each other.[79] Each of these instances suggests a likelihood of abuse of dominance practices being at play and so would warrant action from the SAMR. The consequential question is how the SAMR should interact with those sector-specific regulators if it were to take action. The AMC, which was established under the AML to coordinate antitrust enforcement within the State Council, may be of some help, but in the absence of formal mechanisms to resolve jurisdictional conflicts, an uneasy relationship will likely persist between the SAMR and other sector regulators, especially now that there has been a global trend of *ex post* antitrust enforcement shifting towards *ex ante* regulation vis-à-vis digital markets. To make the situation worse, there is a severe lack of judicial supervision of Chinese administrative agencies. This is discussed in the next section.

Judicial supervision of the AML public enforcement

Judicial supervision on concrete administrative actions

Legal basis

Article 65 of the 2022 amended AML provides the legal basis for administrative litigations against the enforcement decisions of the SAMR. An administrative

75 Jing Yang, Keith Zhai, and Quentin Webb, 'China's Corporate Crackdown Is Just Getting Started. Signs Point to More Tumult Ahead', *The Wall Street Journal*, 5 August 2021, www.wsj.com/articles/china-corporate-crackdown-tech-markets-investors-11628182971.

76 Tong Qian, Ruiyang Yuan, and Wei Han, 'In Depth: China Applies Closer Scrutiny to Sprawling Tech Acquisitions', 11 January 2021, www.caixinglobal.com/2021-01-11/in-depth-china-applies-closer-scrutiny-to-sprawling-tech-acquisitions-101648867.html.

77 Xingyu Yan, 'Towards a More Competitive Mobile Payment Industry: Standardization and Beyond', *Journal of Competition Law & Economics* 17, no. 2 (11 June 2021): 407.

78 *China: CAC Fines Didi RMB 8 Billion for PIPL, CSL, DSL Violations*, DataGuidance, 21 July 2022, www.dataguidance.com/news/china-cac-fines-didi-rmb-8-billion-pipl-csl-dsl (accessed 1 May 2024).

79 Edwin Chan and Yuan Gao, 'China Tech Watchdog Warns Internet Firms Against Blocking Rivals', *Bloomberg*, 13 September 2021, www.bloomberg.com/news/articles/2021-09-13/china-tech-watchdog-warns-internet-firms-against-blocking-rivals.

reconsideration procedure is prerequisite for a party seeking to challenge a merger review decision before a court, but it is optional for parties seeking to challenge an enforcement decision dealing with anticompetitive agreements or abuse of dominance.

Importantly, though, not all AML enforcement activities of the SAMR can be sued. According to Article 13(2) of the Administrative Litigation Law, which is the *lex generalis* to AML administrative litigations, only administrative actions with specific addressees are judicially reviewable.[80] This means only concrete decisions that impose penalties and coercive measures by the SAMR could be subject to judicial supervision.[81] Meanwhile, abstract administrative actions, such as the ruling-making activities by the enforcement agencies, are exempted from judicial supervision.

Case record

I define AML administrative suits as proceedings brought by an undertaking or relevant third parties before a court to seek review of the AML enforcement agency's decision to penalize that undertaking. On that basis, I found 11 AML administrative suits in the 'China Judgements Online'[82] database by 31 December 2023. The case count from 2014 to 2017 is consistent with the one made by practitioners.[83] I located them through a three-step search:

- first, I searched with the combination of the following entries: (i) case type: 'administrative case' (案件类型: 行政案件); (ii) document type: 'judgment' (文书类型: 判决书); and (iii) search throughout the document: 'anti-monopoly law' (全文检索: 反垄断法);
- second, in addition to the three-entry combination, I entered in the 'cause of action' (案由) box (i) 'administrative subject—administration for industry and commerce' (行政主体-工商行政管理), (ii) 'administrative subject—price administration' (行政主体-物价行政管理), and (iii) 'administrative conduct—administrative punishment' (行政行为-行政处罚) alternatively for three separate search attempts. The database returned 47 judgments in search attempt (i), 26 in search attempt (ii), and 21 in search attempt (iii);

80 Administrative Litigation Law of the People's Republic of China (《中华人民共和国行政诉讼法》), adopted by the Seventh National People's Congress on 4 April 1989, effective on 1 October 1990, last revised on 27 June 2017, www.registrationchina.com/articles/law/the-administrative-litigation-law-of-the-peoples-republic-of-china-2017/ (accessed 1 May 2024).

81 Jessica Su and Xiaoye Wang, 'China The Competition Law System and the Country's Norms', in *The Design of Competition Law Institutions: Global Norms, Local Choices*, ed. Eleanor M. Fox and Michael J. Trebilcock (Oxford: Oxford University Press, 2012), 205.

82 It is currently the only official online database of Chinese court rulings that is available to the public. See http://wenshu.court.gov.cn (中国裁判文书网) (in Chinese).

83 See Dentos Antitrust Team, *Administrative Litigation: Decade of AML Enforcement* (《反垄断法》实施十周年回顾: 不服处罚决定的行政诉讼案件综述), https://mp.weixin.qq.com/s/vEgYVtFAy84o8HlitSV4fQ (in Chinese) (accessed 1 May 2024).

- third, I hand-collected all the judgments displayed in the search results and analysed the content of each judgment to ascertain if they fitted the profile of AML administrative suits and whether they were judgments addressed to different plaintiffs but of the same case facts. I found 62 judgments that fit the profile, and they pertain to 11 separate cases, which are listed in Table 5.6. It should be noted this list of cases is possibly non-exhaustive, as some AML administrative litigation cases may not have been properly labelled when they were entered into the database and, therefore, could not be identified through the three-step search.

Practical absence of judicial supervision on AML public enforcers

As Table 5.6 indicates, the rate of AML public enforcement decisions being challenged is extremely low, and so far, the success rate of those challenges remains zero. Commentators had predicted early on that administrative litigations would be insignificant under the AML as long as businesses were fearful of retaliation from the enforcement agencies.[84] The scarcity of AML administrative suits confirms that prediction, and it may also be indicative of the level of confidence that businesses generally have in judicial supervision of AML public enforcement.

That being said, the 11 cases in Table 5.6 provide room for nuance. It seems that when the stakes are high enough, undertakings could be highly motivated to challenge an enforcement decision to the point that they are willing to exhaust whatever recourse possible. Exemplifying this point is the three parallel litigation strategies employed in the 2016 *Shandong Accounting Firms* case and the fact that in most of the cases, the plaintiffs chose to appeal right after the first instance judgments ruled against them. Here, a relevant question arises: When a sufficiently motivated plaintiff manages to bring an enforcement decision before a court, to what extent would this court be willing to engage in substantive scrutiny? The answer to this question lies in the unique role that administrative litigations play in the Chinese governance system: they are a third-party mechanism for the 'ruler' (principal) to monitor the agencies with delegated powers (agents), and so they are intended to constrain only low officials and not high ones.[85]

In other words, a court would likely refrain from or engage only perfunctorily in judicial scrutiny of an enforcement decision made by a central agency.[86] The cases listed in Table 5.6 confirm this. First, these litigated enforcement decisions all came from local agencies. Second, in the two cases where a central agency (the SAIC) was subsequently involved in the administrative litigation procedures (for upholding the original enforcement decisions at the end of two administrative reconsideration proceedings), the courts reviewed only the original decisions—instead of

84 Su and Wang, 'China The Competition Law System and the Country's Norms', 206.

85 Ginsburg, 'Administrative Law and the Judicial Control of Agents in Authoritarian Regimes', 68–9.

86 Angela Huyue Zhang, 'Taming the Chinese Leviathan: Is Antitrust Regulation a False Hope', *Stanford Journal of International Law* 51, no. 2 (2015): 211–12.

Table 5.6 AML administrative suits by 31 December 2023

Year of action filed	*Plaintiffs*	*Defendants*	*Handling courts*	*Conduct involved*	*Case outcomes*
2014	Two concrete manufacturers in Nanjing, Jiangsu Province[87]	The DRC of Jiangsu Province	Nanjing Intermediary Court	Horizontal price-fixing agreements	Dismissal of actions for exceeding the statutory limitations
2016	22 accounting firms in Shandong Province	The AIC of Shandong Province; the Government of Shandong Province; the SAIC[88]	(1) Lixia District Court of Jinan Municipality (first instance); Jinan Intermediary Court (appeal); (2) Xicheng District Court of Beijing Municipality (first instance); Beijing Second Intermediary Court (appeal); Beijing High Court (retrial)	Market-sharing agreements	Upholding wholly the initial enforcement decision
2016	A provider of auto-check services in Xi'an, Shaanxi Province	The DRC of Shaanxi Province	Railway Transport Court of Xi'an (first instance); Railway Transport Intermediary Court of Xi'an (appeal)	Horizontal price-fixing agreements	Upholding wholly the initial enforcement decision

(*Continued*)

87 The NDRC, *Two Concrete Manufactures in Jiangsu Province Lost Their Appeal against the Antitrust Penalty Decision* (江苏省两家混凝土企业不服反垄断处罚败诉), The NDRC Website, http://jjs.ndrc.gov.cn/gzdt/201412/t20141208_651321.html (in Chinese) (accessed 1 May 2024). See also, Yan, 'The Jurisdictional Delimitation in the Chinese Anti-Monopoly Law Public Enforcement Regime', 144.

88 These 22 accounting firms split into three teams with three different litigation strategies: Eight of them initiated an administrative litigation before the Lixia District Court immediately after receiving the sanction decision. Another eight of them filed for an administrative reconsideration before the Shandong People's Government and launched an administrative litigation after the reconsideration was decided against them. The remaining seven of them filed for an administrative reconsideration before the SAIC and launched an administrative litigation in Beijing after the SAIC decided against them.

Table 5.6 (Continued)

Year of action filed	*Plaintiffs*	*Defendants*	*Handling courts*	*Conduct involved*	*Case outcomes*
2017	A fodder producer in Haikou, Hainan Province	The DRC of Hainan Province	Haikou Intermediary Court (first instance); Hainan High Court (appeal)	Resale price maintenance	First instance judgment quashed the enforcement decision, but the appeal judgment reversed the first instance judgment.[89]
2017	A supplier of electronic payment cipher instruments in Shanghai	The AIC of Anhui Province; the SAIC[90]	Xicheng District Court of Beijing Municipality (first instance); Beijing Second Intermediary Court (appeal)	Horizontal agreements of market-sharing and price-fixing	Upholding wholly the initial enforcement decision
2018	13 driving schools in Guizhou Province	The DRC of Guizhou Province	Guiyang Intermediary Court (first instance); Guizhou High Court (appeal)	Horizontal price-fixing agreements	Upholding wholly the initial enforcement decision
2019	Two fireworks manufacturers in Guangxi Province	The AIC of Guangxi Province	Railway Transport Court of Nanning	Horizontal market-sharing agreements	Upholding wholly the initial enforcement decision

(Continued)

89 The Hainan High Court reasoned that for a resale price maintenance agreement to violate the AML, it is not necessary to meet the condition of having anticompetitive effects.

90 After being sanctioned by the Anhui AIC, the undertaking in question first applied for an administrative consideration before the SAIC. After the SAIC decided against it, the undertaking resorted to administrative litigation.

Table 5.6 (Continued)

Year of action filed	*Plaintiffs*	*Defendants*	*Handling courts*	*Conduct involved*	*Case outcomes*
2020	A concrete manufacturer in Maoming, Guangdong Province	The AMR of Guangdong Province	Guangzhou Intellectual Property Court (first instance); Supreme Court (appeal)	Horizontal price-fixing agreements	Upholding wholly the initial enforcement decision
2020	A brick supplier in Chongqing	The AMR of Chongqing	Yubei District Court of Chongqing Municipality (first instance); Chongqing First Intermediary Court (appeal)	Horizontal price-fixing and quota-restriction agreements	Upholding wholly the initial enforcement decision
2021	Six firefighting equipment suppliers	The AMR of Hainan Province	Intellectual Property Court of Hainan Free Trade Port	Horizontal price-fixing agreements	Upholding wholly the initial enforcement decision
2023	A concrete manufacturer in Chongqing	The AMR of Chongqing	Chongqing First Intermediary Court (first instance); Supreme People's Court (appeal)	Horizontal price-fixing and market-sharing agreements	Upholding wholly the initial enforcement decision

the SAIC's reconsideration decisions—before concurring with the SAIC's conclusions. The lack of judicial supervision on central AML agencies reflects the larger, gloomy landscape of administrative litigation in China: the courts lack institutional independence because the one-party polity would not allow it,[91] so they tend to shy away from reviewing administrative acts that carry certain political weight, despite being legislatively empowered to do that.[92]

Judicial supervision of local agencies does not seem in any way more present in the 11 cases. Admittedly, the situation is more intricate at the local judiciary level, in the sense that the local courts with the supervisory duty may be pressured by local governments to stay deferential on the one hand and be urged by higher courts to carry out their judicial review mandate on the other.[93] However, in the AML context where the decision-making power of local agencies always stems from the central agencies (either by delegations on an individual basis from the SAIC and the SAMR or a general authorization from the NDRC), the political stakes to exercise judicial review could simply be too high for local courts and for those higher courts too.[94] A higher court could turn out to be even more deferential than a subordinate court, as evidenced by the 2017 *Hainan Fodder* case.

The upshot is that there is virtually no judicial supervision placed on the AML public enforcement. First, it is extremely rare for an enforcement decision to be litigated, which could be attributed to the sanctioned undertakings' fear of retaliation from the enforcement agencies and their low confidence in judicial impartiality. Second, in the few instances where enforcement decisions were litigated, the handling courts showed a level of judicial deference so high that one may reasonably doubt if they had truly intended to conduct judicial scrutiny. The fact that no plaintiff has ever won an administrative suit entrenches this doubt. Businesses may have been in doubt already, which would feed back into their low confidence in judicial impartiality and increase their reluctance to litigate when being sanctioned under the AML.

Requirement to self-evaluate the competitive impact of abstract administrative actions

While external constraints from the judiciary are lacking, there is still—at least on paper—an internal source of constraints: the policy requirement of 'establishing a fair competition review system'.

On 1 June 2016, the State Council issued a policy document titled 'Opinion on Establishing a Fair Competition Review System during the Development of

91 Minxin Pei, *China's Crony Capitalism: The Dynamics of Regime Decay* (Cambridge, MA: Harvard University Press, 2016), 32, 217.

92 Haibo He, 'Litigations without a Ruling: The Predicament of Administrative Law in China', *Tsinghua China Law Review* 3 (2011): 265–6.

93 He, 'Litigations without a Ruling', 267.

94 Eric C. Ip and Kelvin Hiu Fai Kwok, 'Judicial Control of Local Protectionism in China: Antitrust Enforcement against Administrative Monopoly on the Supreme People's Court', *Journal of Competition Law & Economics* 13, no. 3 (2017): 560, 569.

Market-oriented Systems' (hereinafter, 'Opinion on Fair Competition Review').[95] This opinion is set out to safeguard market competition by delineating the boundaries of governmental intervention in markets. To that end, it requires government agencies at all levels to self-evaluate their abstract administrative measures that would affect market competition. It disapproves the adoption of administrative measures without a self-evaluation beforehand, as well as measures that would turn out in the self-evaluation to have a restrictive impact on competition. There are four sets of criteria for the self-evaluation: (1) the impact on market entry and exit, (2) the impact on the free movement of goods and other elements, (3) the impact on undertakings' operation costs, and (4) the impact on undertakings' operational behaviour. This self-evaluation requirement is meant to constrain administrative powers internally, but due to a lack of independent implementation mechanisms, it is unclear how much strength this policy truly has.[96] Besides, as the practice shows, this requirement is directed at government agencies whose abstract administrative measures are not antitrust in substance but may nevertheless affect market competition; AML enforcement agencies have not appeared to be at the receiving end of this requirement.[97]

The parallel track of private enforcement

Legal basis and enforcement records

Article 60 of the 2022 amended AML subjects undertakings infringing the AML to civil liabilities. It also empowers procuratorates at or above the municipal level to initiate civil public interest litigations against undertakings that have infringement the AML and harmed the public interest. Additionally, the Supreme People's Court issued a Judicial Interpretation in 2012 to clarify the issues relating to the AML's application in civil litigations. This Judicial Interpretation has been the primary legal basis for private AML enforcement to date.[98]

Right after the AML came into effect, civil litigations began to emerge. When issuing the AML Judicial Interpretation, the Supreme Court disclosed that by the end of 2011, there were 61 AML civil cases filed and 53 closed across the nation.[99] It

95 The State Council, *The Opinion on Establishing a Fair Competition Review System during the Development of Market-oriented Systems* (国务院关于在市场体系建设中建立公平竞争审查制度的意见 国发[2016]34号), 1 June 2016, www.gov.cn/zhengce/content/2016-06/14/content_5082066.htm (in Chinese) (accessed 1 May 2024).

96 Yong Huang and Baiding Wu, 'China's Fair Competition Review: Introduction, Imperfections and Solutions', *CPI Antitrust Chronicle*, 15 March 2017.

97 Implementation of this requirement is documented on the SAMR website. See www.samr.gov.cn/fldys/tzgg/gpjzsc/index.html (in Chinese) (accessed 1 May 2024).

98 Provisions of the Supreme People's Court on Several Issues concerning the Application of Law in the Trial of Civil Dispute Cases Arising from Monopolistic Conduct (最高人民法院《关于审理因垄断行为引发的民事纠纷案件应用法律若干问题的规定》), issued by the Supreme People's Court on 3 May 2012, revised on 23 December 2020 (hereinafter, 'the AML Judicial Interpretation').

99 Xinhua New Agency, *The Supreme Court Answers Journalists' Questions Regarding the Nation's First Judicial Interpretation for Anti-Monopoly Trials* (最高法就我国第一部反垄断审判

also disclosed that the majority of those cases were abuse of dominance cases and that the winning rate of the plaintiffs was very low. The Supreme Court attributed this low winning rate to the heavy burden of proof on the plaintiffs. There are no officially disclosed numbers, but according to a news report, the number of civil cases under the AML was rising each year, at least up until 2015. The numbers contained in this report are listed in Table 5.7. There was no mention of the numbers after 2015 in this news report.[100]

The parallel enforcement tracks and the ensuing institutional dynamics

Having a track of private enforcement parallel to public enforcement is common, although the significance of private enforcement differs across regimes. For example, the EU has seen a limited number of private enforcement cases over the years despite the boosting efforts at the Member State level. Meanwhile, the number of private antitrust actions in the US has been increasing to the point that the judiciary tends to discourage such actions.[101] The idiosyncrasy of the AML regime is that, against the backdrop of the dual-track setting, the public enforcement agencies are subject to almost no judicial supervision. Consequently, a unique set of institutional dynamics comes into being between the AML enforcement agencies and the courts.

On the one hand, since the judicial system is not up to the task of (third-party) supervising the SAMR and the tripartite enforcement agencies before it, hierarchical administrative (second-party) control by the State Council has to be put in place instead. Hierarchical control is one of the three mechanisms—besides obedience-internalization and judicial supervision—for a power-delegating principal to supervise a delegated agent, and one way to accomplish it is to demand the

Table 5.7 AML civil cases filed each year from 2008 to 2015

2008–2009	*2010*	*2011*	*2012*	*2013*	*2014*	*2015*
10	33	18	55	72	86	156

司法解释答记者问), The State Council Website, 8 May 2012, www.gov.cn/jrzg/2012-05/08/content_2132662.htm (in Chinese) (accessed 1 May 2024).

100 See Zhang Hongbing, *Ten Years after the Adoption of the AML: Hardening "Three Teeth" to Siege Administrative Monopolies* (反垄断法颁布十年: 磨硬"三颗牙齿"合围行政垄断), Jurisprudence Daily, 31 August 2017, www.chinacourt.org/article/detail/2017/08/id/2986162.shtml (in Chinese) (accessed 1 May 2024).

101 Loannis Lianos and Arianna Andreangeli, 'The European Union: The Competition Law System and the Union's Norms', in *The Design of Competition Law Institutions: Global Norms, Local Choices*, ed. Eleanor M. Fox and Michael J. Trebilcock (Oxford: Oxford University Press, 2012), 404; Daniel A. Crane, *The Institutional Structure of Antitrust Enforcement* (Oxford: Oxford University Press, 2011), 57–62.

promulgation of internal rules for exercising agency discretion.[102] The implication is that, from an institutional structure perspective, the discretion of the AML agencies in carrying out their enforcement responsibilities is significantly expanded because the State Council is internally structured on the basis of technocracy.[103] Provided that this hierarchical control does not lose its grip, two possible scenarios will emerge:

- on the upside, when the higher command defers to agency discretion, the SAMR—as the public enforcer of a young competition law regime in a developing country—will be facilitated to develop more technocracy and to shape the AML application to meet the regime-specific antitrust demands;[104]
- on the downside, when a deferential atmosphere shrinks, the SAMR's exercise of discretion will to a large extent be controlled by political influences that flow in via the administrative chain of command. Those political influences would be unaccountable due to the absence of a third-party (judicial) check. They would undermine to a further extent the agency's independence and thus perpetuate inadequate and opportunistic enforcement.[105]

Either way, the issue boils down to whether administrative control should (and if yes, to what extent) respect technocratic agency discretion. To be sure, the administrative superior has a wide range of institutional and policy factors to consider when deciding whether to respect an antitrust agency's discretion, but ultimately, the agency must have a decent track record to prove itself worthy of the respect. This leads us to Chapter 7, which reviews the AML agencies' performances in developing theories of harm in individual cases.

Meanwhile, when virtually relieved from the duty to supervise administrative agencies, the High Courts and the Intermediary Courts play only the role of adjudicator on private AML suits. In that event, they become 'competitors' of the public enforcement agencies when it comes to interpreting the law and clarifying legal issues. This is in addition to the competitive dynamics that are already palpable between the SAMR and other sector-specific central agencies in the area of Big Tech regulation. The institutional dynamics between the Supreme Court and the central AML enforcement agencies are more intricate: on the one hand, the Supreme Court also adjudicates private AML suits and, therefore, sits on the enforcement track parallel to AML agencies, but on the other hand, it frequently performs legislation-equivalent functions by adopting Judicial Interpretations, and disregarding these Interpretations could cause too much political risk for the AML agencies.

102 Ginsburg, 'Administrative Law and the Judicial Control of Agents in Authoritarian Regimes', 61–2.

103 Shih, *Factions and Finance in China*, 5, 54.

104 Yane Svetiev and Lei Wang, 'Competition Law Enforcement in China: Between Technocracy and Industrial Policy', *Law and Contemporary Problems* 79, no. 4 (2016): 191–4.

105 Yan, 'The Jurisdictional Delimitation in the Chinese Anti-Monopoly Law Public Enforcement Regime', 144.

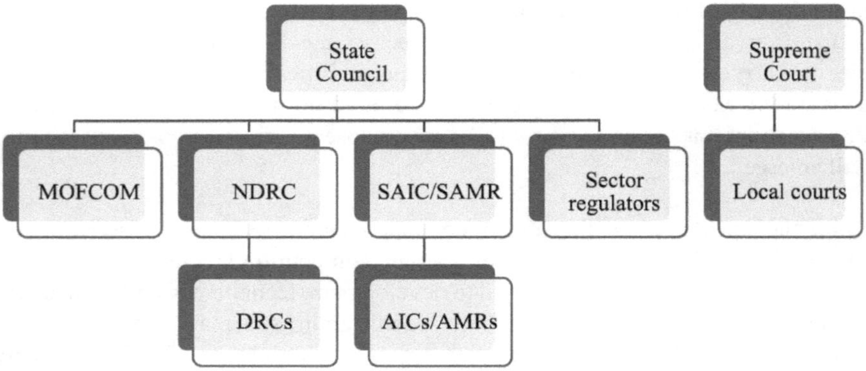

Figure 5.1 The federated structure of the Chinese AML enforcement regime

Overall, the AML enforcement regime can be characterized as federated (see Figure 5.1). There, the public enforcement agencies are subject more to second-party control by administrative superiors than to third-party judicial control, and they compete with the courts in applying the AML and with sector-specific regulatory agencies in regulating digital market competition. Considering that the AML text is highly generalized and that the second-party control by the State Council usually takes the form of campaign-style regulatory instructions,[106] an interesting question is how those competitive dynamics manifest in individual cases and affect decisional outcomes. Chapter 7 addresses this question by critically reviewing the theories of harm developed in a selection of cases. But before that, Chapter 6 shifts the focus back to the EU regime. It looks at the production of theories of harm in the EU regime and the underlying institutional dynamics based on the institutional descriptions in Chapter 4.

Reference list

Brødsgaard, Kjeld Erik. 'Institutional Reform and the *Bianzhi* System in China'. *The China Quarterly* 170 (June 2002): 361–86. https://doi.org/10.1017/S0009443902000232.

Cauffman, Caroline, and Qian Hao. 'Comparison of the EU and Chinese System of Procedural Rights'. In *Procedural Rights in Competition Law in the EU and China*, edited by Caroline Cauffman and Qian Hao, 223–71. Berlin, Heidelberg: Springer Berlin Heidelberg, 2016. https://doi.org/10.1007/978-3-662-48735-8_9.

Chan, Edwin, and Yuan Gao. 'China Tech Watchdog Warns Internet Firms Against Blocking Rivals'. *Bloomberg*, 13 September 2021. www.bloomberg.com/news/articles/2021-09-13/china-tech-watchdog-warns-internet-firms-against-blocking-rivals.

Cheng, Thomas K. 'The Meaning of Restriction of Competition Under the Monopolistic Agreements Provisions of the PRC Anti-Monopoly Law'. *World Competition* 40, no. 2 (2017): 323–54.

106 Angela Huyue Zhang, 'In China, Behave or Face a Campaign', *Bloomberg*, 7 January 2021, www.bloomberg.com/opinion/articles/2021-01-06/china-s-regulators-turn-to-communist-style-campaigns-to-keep-things-in-line.

Crane, Daniel A. *The Institutional Structure of Antitrust Enforcement*. Oxford: Oxford University Press, 2011. https://doi.org/10.1093/acprof:oso/9780195372656.001.0001.
Deng, Fei, and Cunzhen Huang. 'A Five Year Review of Merger Enforcement in China'. *The Antitrust Source* (blog), October 2013. www.clearygottlieb.com/-/media/organize-archive/cgsh/files/news-pdfs/a-five-year-review-of-merger-enforcement-in-china.pdf.
Deng, Fei, and Cunzhen Huang. 'A Ten-Year Review of Merger Enforcement in China'. *The Antitrust Source* (blog), August 2018. www.clearygottlieb.com/-/media/files/a-teny ear-review-of-merger-enforcement-in-china-pdf.pdf.
Emch, Adrian. 'China to Merge Antitrust Authorities'. *Kluwer Competition Law Blog* (blog), 21 March 2018. https://competitionlawblog.kluwercompetitionlaw.com/2018/03/21/china-merge-antitrust-authorities/.
Ginsburg, Tom. 'Administrative Law and the Judicial Control of Agents in Authoritarian Regimes'. In *Rule by Law: The Politics of Courts in Authoritarian Regimes*, edited by Tom Ginsburg and Tamir Moustafa, 58–72. New York: Cambridge University Press, 2008.
Hao, Qian. 'The Multiple Hands: Institutional Dynamics of China's Competition Regime'. In *China's Anti-Monopoly Law: The First Five Years*, edited by Adrian Emch and David Stallibrass, 15–34. Alphen aan den Rijn: Wolters Kluwer International, 2013.
He, Haibo. 'Litigations without a Ruling: The Predicament of Administrative Law in China'. *Tsinghua China Law Review* 3 (2011): 257–81.
Huang, Yong. 'Pursuing the Second Best: The History, Momentum, and Remaining Issues of China's Anti-Monopoly Law'. *Antitrust Law Journal* 75, no. 1 (2008): 117–31.
Huang, Yong, and Richean Zhiyan Li. 'An Overview of Chinese Competition Policy: Between Fragmentation and Consolidation'. In *China's Anti-Monopoly Law: The First Five Years*, edited by Adrian Emch and David Stallibrass, 3–11. Alphen aan den Rijn: Wolters Kluwer International, 2013.
Huang, Yong, and Baiding Wu. 'China's Fair Competition Review: Introduction, Imperfections and Solutions'. *CPI Antitrust Chronicle*, 15 March 2017. https://ssrn.com/abstract=3143289.
Ip, Eric C., and Kelvin Hiu Fai Kwok. 'Judicial Control of Local Protectionism in China: Antitrust Enforcement against Administrative Monopoly on the Supreme People's Court'. *Journal of Competition Law & Economics* 13, no. 3 (2017): 549–75. https://doi.org/10.1093/joclec/nhx018.
Lianos, Loannis, and Arianna Andreangeli. 'The European Union: The Competition Law System and the Union's Norms'. In *The Design of Competition Law Institutions: Global Norms, Local Choices*, edited by Eleanor M. Fox and Michael J. Trebilcock, 384–443. Oxford: Oxford University Press, 2012.
Martin, Peter. 'The Humbling of the NDRC: China's National Development and Reform Commission Searches for a New Role Amid Restructuring'. *China Brief* 14, no. 5 (2014): 14–18.
Owen, Bruce M., Su Sun, and Wentong Zheng. 'China's Competition Policy Reforms: The Anti-Monopoly Law and Beyond'. *Antitrust Law Journal* 75, no. 1 (2008): 231–65.
Pei, Minxin. *China's Crony Capitalism: The Dynamics of Regime Decay*. Cambridge, MA: Harvard University Press, 2016.
Qian, Tong, Ruiyang Yuan, and Wei Han. 'In Depth: China Applies Closer Scrutiny to Sprawling Tech Acquisitions', 11 January 2021. www.caixinglobal.com/2021-01-11/in-depth-china-applies-closer-scrutiny-to-sprawling-tech-acquisitions-101648867.html.
Shih, Victor C. *Factions and Finance in China: Elite Conflict and Inflation*. Cambridge: Cambridge University Press, 2007.
Su, Jessica, and Xiaoye Wang. 'China The Competition Law System and the Country's Norms'. In *The Design of Competition Law Institutions: Global Norms, Local Choices*, edited by Eleanor M. Fox and Michael J. Trebilcock, 194–231. Oxford: Oxford University Press, 2012.
Svetiev, Yane, and Lei Wang. 'Competition Law Enforcement in China: Between Technocracy and Industrial Policy'. *Law and Contemporary Problems* 79, no. 4 (2016): 187–222.

Wang, Xiaoye. *The Evolution of China's Anti-Monopoly Law*. Cheltenham: Edward Elgar, 2014.

Weinreich-Zhao, Tingting. *Chinese Merger Control Law: An Assessment of Its Competition-Policy Orientation after the First Years of Application*. Munich Studies on Innovation and Competition. Berlin, Heidelberg: Springer-Verlag, 2015. www.springer.com/gp/book/9783662438671.

Wu, Zhenguo. 'Perspectives on the Chinese Anti-Monopoly Law'. *Antitrust Law Journal* 75, no. 1 (2008): 73–116.

Yan, Xingyu. 'The Jurisdictional Delimitation in the Chinese Anti-Monopoly Law Public Enforcement Regime: The Inevitable Overstepping of Authority and the Implications'. *Journal of Antitrust Enforcement* 6, no. 1 (2018): 123–49. https://doi.org/10.1093/jaenfo/jnx018.

Yan, Xingyu. 'Towards a More Competitive Mobile Payment Industry: Standardization and Beyond'. *Journal of Competition Law & Economics* 17, no. 2 (11 June 2021): 405–36. https://doi.org/10.1093/joclec/nhaa029.

Yan, Xingyu. 'Whither Antitrust Regulation of Loyalty Rebates in China: The Tetra Pak Decision and Lessons from the EU'. *World Competition* 40, no. 4 (2017): 613–36.

Yang, Jing, Keith Zhai, and Quentin Webb. 'China's Corporate Crackdown Is Just Getting Started. Signs Point to More Tumult Ahead'. *The Wall Street Journal*, 5 August 2021. www.wsj.com/articles/china-corporate-crackdown-tech-markets-investors-11628182971.

Yang, Yichen. 'Price-Related Cartels under the Chinese Anti-Monopoly Law Regime: The Need to Clarify Four Substantive and Procedural Issues'. *World Competition* 39, no. 3 (2016): 479–512.

Zhang, Angela Huyue. 'Bureaucratic Politics and China's Anti-Monopoly Law'. *Cornell International Law Journal* 47, no. 3 (2014): 671–708.

Zhang, Angela Huyue. 'In China, Behave or Face a Campaign'. *Bloomberg*, 7 January 2021. www.bloomberg.com/opinion/articles/2021-01-06/china-s-regulators-turn-to-communist-style-campaigns-to-keep-things-in-line.

Zhang, Angela Huyue. 'Taming the Chinese Leviathan: Is Antitrust Regulation a False Hope'. *Stanford Journal of International Law* 51, no. 2 (2015): 195–228.

6 Development of theories of harm in the centralized EU regime

The market integration mandate

As mentioned in Chapter 3, the development of theories of harm under Article 102 TFEU has essentially two sources of input: economic theories and policy mandates. Chapter 3 has described the economic theories underpinning Article 102 as various schools of thought, so this chapter starts with describing the second source of input, the most important of which is market integration.

A key imperative of the EU

Market integration is an omnipresent imperative embedded in the EU legal framework.[1] This imperative was originally expressed as the establishment of a Common Market in Article 3 of the EEC Treaty. According to the Court of Justice of the European Communities (hereinafter, 'the ECJ'), it means 'the elimination of all obstacles to intra-Community trade in order to merge national markets into a single market bringing about conditions as close as possible to those of a genuine internal market'.[2] It entails two aspects of government action. The first one is negative integration, meaning that existing obstacles to Community integration should be removed. Negative integration was the primary task of the EC throughout the 1960s and the 1970s.[3] The highlight was the *Casis de Dijon* case,[4] in which the ECJ upheld the free movement of goods within the EC. The second aspect is positive integration, meaning the EU legislature (the Council and the European Parliament) should adopt affirmative policies to encourage trade between the Member States.[5] The need to proactively regulate the Common Market arose after the significant

1 Claus-Dieter Ehlermann, 'The Contribution of EC Competition Policy to the Single Market', *Common Market Law Review* 29, no. 2 (1992): 257; Norbert Reich, Annette Nordhausen Scholes, and Jeremy Scholes, *Understanding EU Internal Market Law*, 3rd ed. (Cambridge: Intersentia, 2015), 3–4.

2 Case 15/81 *Gaston Schul Douane Expediteur BV v Inspecteur der Invoerrechten en Accijnzen, Roosendaal* [1982] ECR 1409, para 33.

3 Reich, Nordhausen Scholes, and Scholes, *Understanding EU Internal Market Law*, 5–6.

4 Case 120/78 *Rewe-Zentral AG v Bundesmonopolverwaltung für Branntwein* [1979] ECR 649.

5 Barry E. Hawk, 'Antitrust in the EEC—The First Decade', *Fordham Law Review* 41, no. 2 (1972): 231.

DOI: 10.4324/9781003479437-6

progress in terms of negative integration in the 1970s, and it persisted from the mid-1980s to the mid-1990s.[6]

The integration mandate was accentuated in the Single European Act in 1987. The expression of 'internal market' replaced the old expression of 'Common Market'. The 1985 Commission White Paper proposed to establish an internal market by the end of 1992 and suggested various measures to achieve that goal.[7] On that basis, the Single European Act revised the EEC Treaty provisions and defined the internal market as 'an area without internal frontiers in which the free movement of goods, persons, services and capital is ensured in accordance with the provisions of this Treaty'.[8] To establish an internal market, a qualified majority voting system was introduced. It expanded the Council's legislative power for adopting 'measures for the approximation of the provisions laid down by law, regulation or administrative action in Member States which have as their object the establishment and functioning of the internal market'.[9] This definition of the internal market and the supranational power created under this mandate has since been kept in place, as provided by Article 26(2) and Article 114(1) of the TFEU.

Market integration and EU competition law

To understand the relationship between the market integration mandate and EU competition law, it is necessary to clarify three points. First, the EU has multiple layers of legal objectives, and the market integration mandate could be seen as an intermediary that links the fundamental values of the EU with the envisaged functions of the EU competition law regime. As referred to in the preamble and Article 3 of the TEU, fundamental values overarching the EU legal framework include, *inter alia*, peace, freedom, economic prosperity, and social progress. Market integration as a more specific mandate is written in Article 3(3) of the TEU, which identifies the establishment of an internal market as a means to achieve economic growth and other fundamental objectives enshrined in the founding Treaties.[10] One of the core methods to achieve the internal market is strict control of anticompetitive practices.[11] This method was stipulated in Article 3(f) of the EEC Treaty (now it is in Protocol 27 of the TFEU), which states that the internal market includes 'a system ensuring that competition is not distorted'.

6 T. Koopmans, 'The Role of Law in the Next Stage of European Integration', *International and Comparative Law Quarterly* 35, no. 4 (1986): 926–7; Rein Wesseling, *The Modernisation of EC Antitrust Law* (Oxford: Hart Publishing, 2000), 59–60.

7 Completing the Internal Market: White Paper from the Commission to the European Council (Milan, 28–29 June 1985), COM (85) 310.

8 Article 13 of the Single European Act, [29 June 1987] OJ L 169, 1–28.

9 Article 18 of the Single European Act.

10 Valentine Korah, 'From Legal Form Toward Economic Efficiency—Article 85(1) of the EEC Treaty in Contrast to U.S. Antitrust', *Antitrust Bulletin* 35 (1990): 1010; Reich, Nordhausen Scholes, and Scholes, *Understanding EU Internal Market Law*, 14.

11 Reich, Nordhausen Scholes, and Scholes, *Understanding EU Internal Market Law*, 11.

In that light, the mandate of market integration constitutes an independent aim of EU competition law; in other words, competition law serves as an indispensable instrument to accomplishing integration,[12] even though the validity of this 'means-end' relationship is subject to dispute.[13] The 'means-end' relationship between EU competition law and the market integration mandate is reflected in Articles 101 and 102 TFEU, which use *incompatibility with the internal market* as the benchmark of conduct illegality.

Second, as frequently stressed in the existing literature, market integration is neither the sole objective nor a fundamental objective of EU competition law. As Motta (2004) observed, 'It is probably safe to say that competition was not an end in itself, but was intended as a way to promote economic progress and the welfare of European citizens'.[14] Other prominent objectives include the protection of the competitive process, fairness, freedom of choice, non-discriminatory treatment of customers, efficiency, and welfare considerations.[15] But despite the multiplicity of objectives, the integration mandate has always been a key booster of EU competition law development, as exemplified by the swift installation of state aid policy and merger control policy in the late 1980s and 1990s.[16]

Third, the interpretation of market integration is not static. For example, the two Treaty provisions that are now Articles 101 and 102 TFEU are written in a highly generalized and flexible manner 'as to be capable of bearing very different practical meanings at different times and in different circumstances', therefore allowing the Commission and the CJEU to refine and advance the antitrust jurisprudence relating to the integration mandate.[17] The evolving understanding of the integration mandate in the application of these two Treaty provisions is described in the following subsections. A key takeaway is that as the integration mandate was articulated and enriched in the case law, it gradually became intertwined with other competition law objectives, making the EU antitrust jurisprudence strongly market structure-oriented.[18]

12 Reich, Nordhausen Scholes, and Scholes, *Understanding EU Internal Market Law*, 230; Ehlermann, 'The Contribution of EC Competition Policy to the Single Market', 258–9.

13 Roger van den Bergh, Peter D. Camesasca, and Andrea Giannaccari, *Comparative Competition Law and Economics* (Cheltenham: Edward Elgar Publishing, 2017), 113–14.

14 Massimo Motta, *Competition Policy: Theory and Practice* (Cambridge: Cambridge University Press, 2004), 14.

15 Renato Nazzini, *The Foundations of European Union Competition Law: The Objective and Principles of Article 102* (Oxford: Oxford University Press, 2011), 14–49; Niamh Dunne, 'Fairness and the Challenge of Making Markets Work Better', *The Modern Law Review* 84, no. 2 (March 2021): 237.

16 Michelle Cini and Lee McGowan, *Competition Policy in the European Union*, 2nd ed. (Palgrave Macmillan, 2009), 32–3.

17 Reich, Nordhausen Scholes, and Scholes, *Understanding EU Internal Market Law*, 224; Motta, *Competition Policy*, 14.

18 Sigfrido M. Ramírez Pérez and Sebastian van de Scheur, 'The Evolution of the Law on Articles 85 and 86 EEC [Articles 101 and 102 TFEU]', in *The Historical Foundations of EU Competition Law*, ed. Kiran Klaus Patel and Heike Schweitzer (Oxford: Oxford University Press, 2013), 43–4.

Starting with Article 101: market integration as a wider context for Article 102

The influence of the integration mandate was leveraged from Article 101 to Article 102. Article 85 of the EEC Treaty (a preceding version of Art 101 TFEU) was the first activated segment of EU competition law, and it had been enforced for 13 years by the time Article 86 of the EEC Treaty (a preceding version of Article 102 TFEU) was activated in the *Continental Can* case.[19] When Regulation 17/62 was adopted to break the ground for antitrust enforcement, trade barriers were pervasive, threatening the very existence of the EEC.[20] The need to break down those market barriers resonated with the antitrust rationale of prohibiting anticompetitive agreements, so naturally, Article 85 of the EEC Treaty was perceived as a powerful instrument for achieving negative integration of the internal market.[21] During the 13 years when Article 85 was applied and Article 86 of the EEC Treaty was not, there were two cases worth mentioning: *Société Technique Minière* and *Consten and Grundig v Commission.*

The Société Technique Minière *case*

This was a preliminary ruling case about the applicability of Article 85 to exclusive distribution agreements. Based on the wording of Article 85(1), the ECJ approached the overall effects-centric assessment from two dimensions of consideration: 'effects on trade between Member States' and 'effects on competition'.[22]

The 'effects on trade between Member States' consideration is first and foremost a jurisdictional threshold, which requires an effect on 'trade between Member States' for a practice to trigger the application of Article 85(1). But the ECJ gave it much more weight than that. On page 249 of this preliminary ruling judgment, the ECJ stated that this consideration also meant a concern for 'a possibility that the realization of a single market between Member States might be impeded'. With this statement, the ECJ effectively incorporated the market integration mandate in the first layer of consideration. In other words, the ECJ construed the first layer of consideration as a substantive—rather than just jurisdictional—examination of whether a suspected anticompetitive agreement could bring about 'a partitioning of the market in certain products between Member States and thus rendering more difficult the interpenetration of trade which the Treaty is intended to create'. This is a concern associated with but distinct from market competition restriction.

19 Lee McGowan, *The Antitrust Revolution in Europe: Exploring the European Commission's Cartel Policy* (Cheltenham: Edward Elgar, 2010), 123–4; Cini and McGowan, *Competition Policy in the European Union*, 21–2.

20 Korah, 'From Legal Form toward Economic Efficiency', 1011.

21 McGowan, *The Antitrust Revolution in Europe*, 31–2; Caroline Heide-Jorgensen, 'The Relationship between Article 101(1) TFEU and Article 101(3) TFEU', in *Aims and Values in Competition Law*, ed. Caroline Heide-Jorgensen et al. (Copenhagen: DJØF Publishing, 2013), 97–8.

22 Case 56/65 *Société Technique Minière (L.T.M.) v Maschinenbau Ulm GmbH (M.B.U.)* [1966] ECR 235, 248.

The Consten and Grundig v Commission *case*

This was also an exclusive distributorship case. In 1964, the Commission issued the *Grundig-Consten* decision, which prohibited the exclusive distribution agreement between producer Grundig and its French distributor, Consten, along with an assisting trademark licensing agreement. In its verification of the 'trade between Member States' requirement stipulated in Article 85(1), the Commission revolved around the market integration mandate. As it stated, the exclusive distribution agreement, along with the trademark licensing, prevented other undertakings in France from importing Grundig products; it also prevented Consten from reselling Grundig products to other Member States. The Commission deemed the price difference between the French and the German markets as clear proof of the Common Market being undermined, and in its opinion, the fact that cross-state trade was increasing could not justify the negative impact of the agreement on Community trade.[23]

In this case concerning exclusive distributorship, the Commission carried out the 'trade between Member States' examination stipulated in Article 85(1) in a rather superficial manner. When this case was appealed before the ECJ, part of the dispute was whether the Commission should be subject to a low standard of proof or it should be required to perform a more in-depth analysis when examining an agreement's impact on cross-Community trade. On this matter, the ECJ chose to subject the Commission to a low standard of proof because it viewed market integration as an objective of Article 85. As the ECJ stated:

> The Treaty, whose preamble and content aim at abolishing the barriers between States, and which in several provisions gives evidence of a stern attitude with regard to their reappearance, could not allow undertakings to reconstruct such barriers. Article 85 (1) is designed to pursue this aim, even in the case of agreements between undertakings placed at different levels in the economic process.[24]

Since the ECJ held the opinion that 'Articles 85 and 86 seek to achieve the same aim on different levels',[25] it was no surprise that the enforcement practice under the Treaty provision that is now Article 102 TFEU developed in accordance with the same integration mandate underpinning the practice under the Treaty provision that is now Article 101 TFEU.[26] Nevertheless, as the establishment of the Common Market progressed, the integration mandate was taken into account in the enforcement of Article 102 increasingly comprehensively. This is demonstrated in the case analyses in the next section.

23 64/566/CEE: Décision de la Commission, du 23 septembre 1964, relative à une procédure au titre de l'article 85 du traité (IV-A/00004–03344 'Grundig-Consten') [20 October 1964] OJ 161, 2548–9.

24 Joined Cases 56 and 58/64 *Établissements Consten S.à.R.L. and Grundig-Verkaufs-GmbH v Commission of the European Economic Community* [1966] ECR 299, 340.

25 Case 6/72 *Europemballage Corporation and Continental Can Company Inc. v Commission of the European Communities* [1973] ECR 215, para 25.

26 Ehlermann, 'The Contribution of EC Competition Policy to the Single Market', 261.

Theories of harm under Article 102 TFEU: an overview

The selection of cases

As described in Chapter 4 of this book, a prominent feature of the EU competition law enforcement regime is that the Commission assumes the central role for public enforcement under the judicial supervision of the CJEU. Against this institutional background, it is worth discussing whether and to what extent the institutional dynamics between the Commission and the CJEU, which are defined by their institutional responsibilities, have impacted the enforcement outcomes. This chapter contributes to that discussion but focuses on the theories of harm developed in the enforcement decisions.

To that end, this chapter selects a number of cases as study samples. These cases consist of two categories: public enforcement cases launched by the Commission and preliminary ruling cases brought by the Member State courts before the ECJ. First, the selection of Commission cases is based on one essential criterion: whether a case involves both the Commission and the CJEU and, therefore, provides a basis for identifying and comparing the legal reasoning of these two institutional actors. Consequently, only Commission decisions that were appealed—either once to the GC or further to the ECJ—are considered. Second, the selection of preliminary ruling cases is based on the criterion of whether a case could provide an opportunity for observing how the CJEU identifies and elaborates competitive harms when the Commission is not taking the case-handling initiative. Third, due to the limited length of this chapter, only landmark cases about seven types of abusive conduct are analysed. The selection of these landmark cases takes into account the existing literature that has identified important cases under Article 102 TFEU from various perspectives.[27]

These cases are grouped according to the types of abusive conduct they contain. The theories of harm in these cases are critically described, with a focus on their internal consistency of logic and the degree to which they make economic sense. But before we get into the various types of abusive conduct, it is necessary to introduce the activation of Article 102 and the establishment of dominance, which is prerequisite for assessing abuse.

The activation of Article 86 of the EEC Treaty

More than a decade of dormancy

In 1958, when the EEC Treaty was signed, a provision governing abuse of dominance, namely, Article 86, was incorporated, but the Commission kept this provision on the shelf for more than a decade. The reason was said to be the difficulty of formulating a clear doctrine due to the vaguely stipulated concepts in that

27 See for example, Anne C. Witt, *The More Economic Approach to EU Antitrust Law*, Hart Studies in Competition Law, vol. 14 (Oxford: Hart Publishing, 2016), xxx; Pablo Ibáñez Colomo, 'The Law on Abuses of Dominance and the System of Judicial Remedies', *Yearbook of European Law* 32, no. 1 (1 January 2013): 410.

provision, including the requirement of the Common Market dimension, the notion of dominance, and the abuse thereof.[28] Consequently, the Commission was reluctant to pursue cases for fear of its decisions being overturned by the ECJ due to a lack of well-defined reasoning.[29]

To be sure, there were some attempts to operationalize Article 86. First, in 1965, a group of experts were put together to develop the principles and frameworks for the application of Articles 85 and 86 to mergers.[30] A report by these experts was published in 1966, but lacking constructive results, it merely concluded that to apply the concept of abuse, 'a direct causal link was required between the enterprise's power and its results in the market' in addition to a violation of the Treaty objectives.[31] Second, motivated by the pervasive fear that Article 86 would remain a dead letter,[32] the ECJ also began encouraging the filing of Article 86 cases: in three cases that took place between 1968 and 1971, the ECJ implied that exercising intellectual property rights to raise price could constitute an abuse of dominance by stating that the price level of a product could be a decisive indicator of abuse of dominance when it was particularly high and unjustified in light of the case circumstances.[33] However, the ECJ's encouragement was limited to the scope of exclusionary abuses; it remained reluctant to tackle cases concerning exploitative abuses.[34]

Activating abuse of dominance regulation for merger control: the Continental Can *case*

Continental Can ended the dormancy of Article 86 in 1971. In this case, the Commission accused Continental's acquisition of a competitor of infringing Article 86 of the EEC Treaty because this acquisition eliminated the competition remaining in the market. The Commission stated that a dominant undertaking's acquiring a major share of a competing undertaking could constitute an abuse of dominance under Article 86 if the following conditions were met: (1) the acquisition was used to reinforce the dominant position, (2) the acquisition would result in the elimination of actual or potential competition at the current level, and (3) the markets concerned

28 Pérez and Scheur, 'The Evolution of the Law on Articles 85 and 86 EEC', 35; I. Samkalden and I. E. Druker, 'Legal Problems Relating to Article 86 of the Rome Treaty', *Common Market Law Review* 3, no. 2 (1966): 169.

29 David Gerber, *Law and Competition in Twentieth-Century Europe: Protecting Prometheus* (Oxford: Oxford University Press, 2001), 356.

30 Pérez and Scheur, 'The Evolution of the Law on Articles 85 and 86 EEC', 35.

31 Gerber, *Law and Competition in Twentieth-Century Europe*, 357.

32 Samkalden and Druker, 'Legal Problems Relating to Article 86 of the Rome Treaty', 162.

33 Case 40/70 *Sirena S.r.l. v Eda S.r.l. and others* [1971] ECR 69, para 17. The other two cases were: Case 24/67 *Parke, Davis & Co v Probel* [1968] ECR 55; Case 78/70 *Deutsche Grammophon GmbH v Metro-SB-Grossmärkte* [1971] ECR 487.

34 Peter Behrens, 'The Ordoliberal Concept of "Abuse" of a Dominant Position and Its Impact on Article 102 TFEU', *SSRN Scholarly Paper* (Rochester, NY: Social Science Research Network, 9 September 2015), 17.

were a substantial part of the Common Market.[35] By this reasoning, a concentration would most likely be caught under Article 86 if it were between a dominant undertaking and a competitor in the same market since such a concentration would entail a scale of competition restriction that normal concentrations would not entail.[36] The Commission identified two competitive harms arising from this acquisition: (1) the negative modification of market structure and (2) the restriction of actual or potential choices for users resulting from the reduction of competitors (pp 37–9 of the Commission decision).

The ECJ annulled the Commission decision but upheld in large part the Commission's harm analyses. From the outset, the ECJ adopted the stance that measures altering the market structure may very well constitute anticompetitive practices within the meaning of Article 86 if they were carried out by a dominant undertaking (para 21). The ECJ based this stance on a two-fold teleological interpretation of Article 86: first, it held that the aim of Article 86 was to help institute 'a system ensuring that competition in the Common Market is not distorted' as provided by Article 3(f) of the EEC Treaty; second, it underscored the parallelism of Articles 85 and 86 as two separate Treaty instruments designed to achieve the same aim, so one should never become the backdoor for escaping proscriptions in the event of a practice being caught by the other. Relying on this two-fold teleological analysis, the ECJ validated the Commission's reasoning relating to the harm to market structure (paras 24–5).

Not only did the ECJ validate the harm-to-market-structure reasoning, but it also put this reasoning at the centre of the abuse assessment, thereby introducing a highly structural conception of what was protected under Article 86. The ECJ held that consumers' freedom of choice could be damaged not only directly by certain practices but also indirectly by practices that undermined the competitive structure of the market. In this way, the ECJ downplayed the importance of the harm to consumer choice to abuse of dominance assessments (para 26). This contradicted the AG opinion, which argued extensively that precisely defined harm to consumers was crucial for applying Article 86 (specifically second paragraph (b)) to conduct that did not explicitly involve the exercise of market power.[37] Eventually, the ECJ made the ground-breaking ruling that 'the strengthening of the position of an undertaking may be an abuse and prohibited under Article 86 of the Treaty, regardless of the means and procedure by which it is achieved', if 'the degree of dominance reached substantially fetters competition' (paras 26–7).

35 72/21/CEE: Décision de la Commission, du 9 décembre 1971, relative à une procédure d'application de l'article 86 du traité CEE (IV/26 811—Continental Can Company) [8 January 1972] OJ L 7, 37 (hereinafter, 'Commission decision on *Continental Can*').

36 Case 6/72 *Europemballage Corporation and Continental Can Company Inc. v Commission of the European Communities* [1973] ECR 215, 229 (hereinafter, 'ECJ judgment on *Continental Can*').

37 Opinion of Mr Advocate General Roemer (delivered on 21 November 1972) in Case 6/72 *Europemballage Corporation and Continental Can Company Inc. v Commission of the European Communities* [1973] ECR 215, 254–6 (hereinafter, 'the AG opinion on *Continental Can*').

The ECJ judgment's precedential implication was that to be outlawed by Article 86, a practice by a dominant undertaking needed not to be objectionable as a manner of exercising market power; rather, it would only need to meet the requirement of altering the market structure to an extent that 'seriously endangers the consumer's freedom of action', and this would be the case when a merger eliminated practically all competition in the market (para 29). For the Commission, the ruling meant a rather high standard of proof vis-à-vis the illegality of a practice: the Commission 'had to state legally sufficient reasons or, at least, had to prove that competition was so essentially affected that the remaining competitors could no longer provide a sufficient counterweight' (para 29). Under this standard, the ECJ found that the Commission failed to present enough findings and analyses to support its conclusion and so decided to annul the Commission decision. The upshot is that the ECJ annulled the Commission decision not because it disagreed with the Commission's reasoning but because the Commission failed to meet a rather than standard of proof; in fact, the ECJ built upon the Commission and laid down a highly structural conception of what was prohibited under Article 86. After *Continental Can*, Article 86 officially became operational.

Finding dominance: a prerequisite for assessing abuse

This chapter is mainly concerned with how the Commission and the CJEU assess various types of abusive conduct under Article 102 TFEU. However, this does not mean finding dominant positions is in any way less important. In fact, in the 'abuse of dominance' paradigm, proving the dominant position of an undertaking is prerequisite for assessing the (un)lawfulness of a practice of that undertaking; moreover, under Article 102, finding dominance has profound implications for the subsequent abuse examination. This is exemplified by the concept of special responsibility of a dominant undertaking.

The special responsibility concept did not appear in the case law until *Michelin I*, an annulment case that the ECJ closed in 1983 concerning loyalty rebates. Notably, vis-à-vis the special responsibility concept, *Michelin I* does not stand alone; it should be read in conjunction with several cases adjudicated before and after it. The preceding cases had established a strong tradition of focusing on market structural elements for finding dominance. It was following this tradition that the ECJ in *Michelin I* introduced the special responsibility concept to underscore the importance of finding dominance for abuse assessments.

Before introducing the special responsibility concept, the ECJ set the stage by reiterating the aim of Article 86 and the definition of dominance as elaborated in the preceding case law. First, the ECJ confirmed that the (at least direct) objective of Article 86 was the preservation of a competitive structure since it identified Article 3(f) of the EEC Treaty as the 'general aim' of Article 86 and clarified this general aim as 'the institution of a system ensuring that competition in the common market is not distorted'.[38] The choice of the word 'institution' implied that the

38 Case 322/81 *NV Nederlandsche Banden Industrie Michelin v Commission of the European Communities* [1983] ECR 3461, para 29 (hereinafter, 'ECJ judgment on *Michelin I*').

level of Community market competition was still suboptimal at that time, so there was a need to foster competition by, for example, breaking down trade barriers. In this way, the ECJ linked the aim of Article 86 with the market integration mandate. Second, following the case law of *Hoffmann-La Roche* and *United Brands*, the ECJ defined *dominance* as 'a position of economic strength' and stated that Article 86 'prohibits any abuse of a position of economic strength' enjoyed by a dominant undertaking.[39] This could be interpreted as the ECJ construing *abuse* as the exercise of market power held by a dominant undertaking, therefore clarifying the unclear link between abuse and dominance in the *Hoffmann-La Roche* judgment and disagreeing with AG Reischl's argument in *Hoffmann-La Roche* that for assessing abuse, 'the criterion is not the exercise of market power but that there is abuse where an undertaking in a dominant position influences the structure of competition by its acts'.[40]

The ECJ introduced the concept of special responsibility when trying to dismiss Michelin's contention that it was being punished by law for having superior performances. As the ECJ stated:

> A finding that an undertaking has a dominant position is not in itself a recrimination but simply means that, irrespective of the reasons for which it has such a dominant position, the undertaking concerned has a special responsibility not to allow its conduct to impair genuine undistorted competition on the common market.[41]

The special responsibility concept can be understood as the legal implication of finding a dominant position. Judging by the ECJ's wording, this concept is built upon the emphasis on the structural preservation of competition, although it is not entirely clear as to what legal implications this concept entails. For example, questions arise as to (1) whether this concept means a dominant undertaking is prohibited from carrying out certain conduct that would be acceptable when carried out by non-dominant undertakings; (2) if so, the exact kinds of conduct that are prohibited. The *Michelin I* judgment provided no precise answers to these questions, which were already looming in some cases before *Michelin I* and persisted in some cases after *Michelin I*. One may even argue that to this day, no satisfactory answers have been provided yet.[42] This is shown in the remainder of this chapter,

39 ECJ judgment on *Michelin I*, para 30; Case 85/76 *Hoffmann-La Roche & Co. AG v Commission of the European Communities* [1979] ECR 461, para 38; Case 27/76 *United Brands Company and United Brands Continentaal BV v Commission of the European Communities* [1978] ECR 207, para 65.

40 Opinion of Mr Advocate General Reischl (delivered on September 19, 1978) in Case 85/76 *Hoffmann-La Roche & Co. AG v Commission of the European Communities* [1979] ECR 461, 583. The *Hoffmann-La Roche* judgment is analysed later in this chapter.

41 ECJ judgment on *Michelin I*, para 57.

42 Xingyu Yan and Hans Vedder, 'Minimum Efficient Scale, Competition on the Merits, and the Special Responsibility of a Dominant Undertaking', *Journal of Competition Law & Economics* 19, no. 1 (13 March 2023): 124, 134–5.

which looks at how the Commission and the CJEU assess various types of abusive conduct with a view towards their different contributions to the development of theories of harm.

Restriction of resale

There are two leading cases pertaining to this type of abuse: *Suiker Unie* and *United Brands*. In these cases, the Commission and the ECJ shared a highly common understanding of protecting market integration through applying Article 86.

The Commission: a superficial theory of harm focusing on market integration

To prosecute resale restrictions under Article 86, the Commission in *Suiker Unie* came up with a rather superficial theory of harm that focused heavily on market integration. It identified the competitive harm to be the *impediment to market integration* and stated that this harm (1) was reflected in the accused undertakings' aim of limiting their dealers' 'principal sources of supply' and (2) had the possibility of impairing the Common Market by restricting cross–Member State sugar sales.[43] No further analysis was provided.

In *United Brands*, the Commission showed a consistent concern for market integration, with a marginal improvement in the reasoning. It alleged two harms caused by the resale restriction practice in question. The first one was *competition restriction at the distribution level*. As stated by the Commission, the prohibition of resale prevented the distributors and ripeners of UBC (the accused dominant firm) from 'entering into competition at the resale level with UBC and the other importer/distributors'. The second harm was *undermining the Common Market*, in the sense that the practice in question 'amounts to a prohibition on exports and thus maintains an effective market segregation'.[44] But the Commission did not further substantiate these allegations.

The ECJ: heightened market integration concern and limited competitive harm analyses

Both cases were brought before the ECJ, which largely endorsed the Commission's abuse assessments and enriched the competitive harm analyses, albeit to a limited extent. In the *Suiker Unie* judgment, the ECJ relied on the second paragraph (b) of Article 86 and articulated the harm caused by resale restrictions to be

43 73/109/EEC: Commission Decision of 2 January 1973 Relating to Proceedings under Articles 85 and 86 of the EEC Treaty (IV/26 918—European Sugar Industry) [26 May 1973] OJ L 140, 38–9 (hereinafter, 'Commission decision on *Suiker Unie*').

44 76/353/EEC: Commission Decision of 17 December 1975 Relating to a Procedure under Article 86 of the EEC Treaty (IV/26699—Chiquita), [9 April 1976] OJ L 95, 13–14 (hereinafter, 'Commission decision on *United Brands*').

the *limitation of production*. It translated this harm to a negative impact on trade between Member States.[45] Without any further elaboration, this opinion seemed more like a reiteration of the market integration mandate than a bona fide explanation as to why the identified limitation of production was anticompetitive. To be sure, later in the judgment, the ECJ did seem to suggest that resale restrictions could also result in the harm of *output-foreclosing* the dominant firm's competitors (para 486), but the ECJ did not delve into this; instead, it went back to a literal reading of Article 86. This was unfortunate because the output-foreclosure harm analysis would not have been very demanding considering the Commission had already found dominance of the accused undertakings.[46] Overall, because of the limited competitive harm analyses, it is difficult to ascertain what other competitive harms the ECJ had in mind besides the policy-driven concern for market integration.

The competitive harm analyses were even more scarce in the *United Brands* judgment. The ECJ spelled out two harms resulting from the resale restriction imposed by the dominant firm UBC: the *limitation of markets to the prejudice of consumers*, which was a direct reading of Article 86(b), and the *impediment to the Common Market* through partitioning national markets.[47] It expanded on neither. At certain points, the ECJ seemingly implied an additional competitive harm: the restriction of freedom of the distributors to trade (paras 157, 160) but it did not further explain how this restriction of freedom could translate to a restriction of competition, leaving one wonder whether this perceived restriction of freedom had foreclosed UBC's competitors' output or it had inhibited UBC's distributors from engaging in competition at the distribution level. In that light, it is safe to say the ECJ's concern rested primarily on market integration.

Exploitative pricing

Abuses of dominance can be broadly grouped into two categories: exclusionary abuses directed towards competitors and exploitative abuses directed towards customers and end consumers. There are far fewer exploitative abuse cases than exclusionary abuse cases because according to the teachings of neoclassical economics, exploitative abuses would be unlikely if competition was well preserved in the first place.[48] This section spotlights four leading cases concerning exploitative pricing under Article 102 TFEU: *General Motors, United Brands, DSD*, and *SABAM*. The first three are annulment cases, and the last one is a preliminary ruling case.

45 Joined Cases 40 to 48, 50, 54 to 56, 111, 113, and 114/73 *Coöperatieve Vereniging "Suiker Unie" UA and others v Commission of the European Communities* [1975] ECR 1663, para 401 (hereinafter, 'ECJ judgment on *Suiker Unie*').

46 For example, as the Commission stated, 'For lack of other large sources of supply, the two dealers had to give into these pressures from the RT'. See Commission decision on *Suiker Unie*, 38.

47 Case 27/76 *United Brands Company and United Brands Continentaal BV v Commission of the European Communities* [1978] ECR 207, para 159 (hereinafter, 'ECJ judgment on *United Brands*').

48 Richard A. Posner, *Antitrust Law*, 2nd ed. (Chicago: University of Chicago Press, 2001), 248.

The Commission: from market integration to competition foreclosure

The Commission's approach to excessive pricing in the early years was fairly rudimentary. In *General Motors*, it considered the pricing scheme in question to be an abuse under the second paragraph (c) of Article 86 because of 'the extraordinary disparity between actual costs incurred and prices actually charged'; in the Commission's opinion, this extraordinary price disparity caused the harm of *secondary-line competition distortion* in the sense that the customers being charged such high prices were unfairly disadvantaged vis-à-vis their competitors.[49] Interestingly, when trying to demonstrate the excessiveness of the prices, the Commission looked only at the intentions of the accused undertaking, instead of engaging in an objective price-cost comparison (paras 10–11 of the Commission decision). It was also interesting that the Commission framed the abusive conduct in question as excessive pricing, but it alleged the harm of secondary-line competition distortion rather than monopoly rent extraction, which was more commonly associated with excessive pricing conduct. There was not much elaboration on how the alleged harm would come about, but with the special attention paid to 'parallel imports', it seemed that the Commission's underlying concern was actually *market integration* (para 13). This concern also underpinned the Commission's analysis on the excessive pricing conduct in *United Brands*, in which it only made a vague reference to 'unfair prices to certain of its distributors/ripeners';[50] it made no attempt to prove the excessiveness of the prices or assessing the welfare loss resulting therefrom.

In *DSD*, the Commission had progressed from the narrow focus on market integration to the more theoretically grounded concern for welfare loss and competition foreclosure when assessing excessive pricing. In this case, the Commission considered the fees that the accused firm charged to its customers excessive because they were based not on the firm's service rendered but on the licensing of a trademark for which the accused firm bore minimal costs and had no justifiable grounds for charging fees.[51] The Commission considered this excessive pricing conduct to have caused two competitive harms: (1) monopolistic exploitation under the second paragraph (a) of Article 82 of the EC Treaty; and (2) output-foreclosure of competition, in the sense that the fees made it financially unappealing for the accused firm's customers to buy from the firm's competitors, and it expanded on the two harms with three groups of case analyses (paras 111–15, 117–35).

49 75/75/EEC: Commission Decision of 19 December 1974 relating to a proceeding under Article 86 of the EEC Treaty (IV/28.851—General Motors Continental), [3 February 1975] OJ L 29, para 8 (hereinafter, 'Commission decision on *General Motors*').

50 Commission decision on *United Brands*, 15.

51 2001/463/EC: Commission Decision of 20 April 2001 Relating to a Proceeding Pursuant to Article 82 of the EC Treaty (Case COMP D3/34493—DSD), [21 June 2001] OJ L 166, paras 100, 111–12 (hereinafter, 'Commission decision on *DSD*').

The ECJ: accentuating the concern for competition foreclosure and monopolistic exploitation

The ECJ annulled the Commission's finding of excessive pricing in *General Motors* because it found excessive pricing was justified in the temporary circumstances and was corrected soon after the undertaking had adjusted to the new situation. It nevertheless upheld the Commission's reasoning that excessive pricing by a dominant firm would generally lead to the harm of parallel-import inhibition.[52] Without further elaboration on how the harm could transpire and how it related to monopoly rent extraction, it seemed that the ECJ was also emphasizing the protection of market integration through Article 86.

This emphasis on market integration quickly shifted towards monopolistic exploitation in *United Brands*, where the ECJ stated the need to 'ascertain whether the dominant undertaking has made use of the opportunities arising out of its dominant position in such a way as to reap trading benefits which it would not have reaped if there had been normal and sufficiently effective competition' when assessing excessive pricing (para 249). Unfortunately, though, the ECJ did not provide a concrete enough analysis on this point. This statement suggested *a causal link* between the insufficiency of competition in the dominated market and the benefits that could be reaped, but later, it seemed to have set aside this causal link and just presumed that if a price was unreasonably high compared to the product value, that price should be deemed abusive without the need to ascertain whether it was a result of insufficient market competition (paras 250–1). In the *DSD* case, both the Court of First Instance (CFI) and, subsequently, the ECJ upheld the Commission decision, and they paid extra attention to the harm of competition foreclosure.[53]

More recently in *SABAM*, the ECJ drew from the principle of proportionality and elaborated on how to approach allegedly excessive prices by apparently monopolistic firms like a copyright management company. It held that the excessiveness of a price was to be measured against 'the economic value of the service' in question and suggested that this economic value could be assessed through various methods ranging from calculating the cost actually incurred to comparing the price in question with the price charged before or the prices charged by competitors.[54] Irrespective of the methods used, the key point was to take into account all circumstances and strike a proportionate balance between the potentially legitimate exploitation of monopolistic status and the legitimate interests of the customers. Along the line, the ECJ reasoned that SABAM's royalty-charging scheme based on

52 Case 26/75 *General Motors Continental NV v Commission of the European Communities* [1975] ECR 1367, paras 12, 21–2 (hereinafter, 'ECJ judgment on *General Motors*').

53 Case T-151/01 *Der Grüne Punkt—Duales System Deutschland GmbH v Commission of the European Communities* [2007] ECR II 1607, paras 139, 163–4 (hereinafter, 'CFI judgment on *DSD*'); Case C-385/07 P *Der Grüne Punkt—Duales System Deutschland GmbH v Commission of the European Communities* [2009] ECR I 6155, para 143 (hereinafter, 'ECJ judgment on *DSD*').

54 Case C-372/19 *Belgische Vereniging van Auteurs, Componisten en Uitgevers CVBA (SABAM) v Weareone.World BVBA and Wecandance NV*, ECLI:EU:C:2020:959, paras 28, 31–2 (hereinafter, 'ECJ ruling on *SABAM*').

the licensees' gross receipts from ticket sales was not abusive because the resulting high prices served the legitimate aim of safeguarding the rights of the creators and they were reflective of the significant value that the musical works brought to the public (paras 30, 37–41). Nevertheless, the ECJ suspected SABAM's scheme that calculated the number of musical works actually performed to be exploitatively abusive because there were viable alternative methods that could calculate more precisely (meaning lower and more transparent prices for the customers) without undermining the music creators' rights and interests (paras 52–9).

Predatory pricing

Predatory pricing is a typical exclusionary abuse of dominance. The abusiveness flows from temporarily selling below cost to push out competitors and entrench dominance. This section spotlights two leading cases concerning predatory pricing: *AKZO* and *Post Danmark I*. The former is an annulment case, and the latter is a preliminary ruling case.

The Commission in AKZO*: an underdeveloped theory of harm centring on anticompetitive intent*

The Commission considered the aggressive price-cutting in question to have caused the harm of competition foreclosure, and its conception of the harm hinged heavily on the market structure. Referring back to *Continental Can*, it stated that 'the strengthening of a dominant position held in a particular product market may constitute an abuse of that dominant position irrespective of the precise means adopted'.[55] The preservation of a competitive market structure entailed the view that a practice by a dominant firm did not have to be directly linked to its market power to constitute an abuse; this was because the presence of a dominant position was already a sign of weakened market competition, so any further weakening by the dominant firm would be unacceptable. This also meant that a practice did not have to take place in the dominated market to constitute an abuse, so the fact that AKZO's aggressive price-cutting happened in a market other than the dominated one could not prevent the Commission from finding an abuse (para 85 of the Commission decision).

The Commission tried to establish the general applicability of Article 86 to exclusionary practices. It referred to *Hoffmann-La Roche* to clarify that a dominant position could manifest not only as the ability to exploit but also the ability to exclude (paras 67, 74)[56] and described such exclusionary practices as 'unfair commercial practices on the part of a dominant undertaking intended to eliminate,

55 85/609/EEC: Commission Decision of 14 December 1985 relating to a proceeding under Article 86 of the EEC Treaty (IV/30.698—ECS/AKZO), [31 December 1985] OJ L 374, para 62 (hereinafter, 'Commission decision on *AKZO*').

56 The Commission was arguably wrong when it perceived *Hoffmann-La Roche* as a case 'where the infringement of Article 86 involved primarily the exploitation of customers' since the competitive

discipline or deter smaller competitors' (para 74). Theoretically, there was little doubt that Article 86 should generally apply to exclusionary practices. But by using vague prefixes such as 'unfair', 'intended', and 'smaller competitors', the Commission failed to convincingly ground this general applicability, as these prefixes did not help explain how the foreclosure harm would transpire; instead, they implied the consideration on non-foreclosure-related harms. Those harms were not clarified but could be fitted into the market structure-oriented conception of the foreclosure harm, thereby shaping the Commission's theory of harm for predatory pricing.

AKZO argued that the assessment of its price-cutting practices under Article 86 should revolve around verifying whether the price offered was below the average variable cost ('AVC'). But the Commission rejected this argument for two reasons. First, in the Commission's opinion, AKZO's formulation of the AVC was wrong because it treated costs of labour, repair, and maintenance as fixed costs. Second, the Commission found that there was certain strategic conduct accompanying the aggressive price-cutting, which enabled AKZO to effectively exclude competitors without having to price below average variable cost. Hence, the Commission refused to limit the examination to a price-cost comparison (paras 75–8). Based on the structural conception of competition foreclosure harm, the Commission was concerned that such strategic aspects could result in the exclusion of 'smaller but possibly more efficient firms' to the detriment of long-term market efficiency (para 77). However, with the reference to 'smaller but possibly more efficient firms', the Commission failed to address AKZO's argument that less efficient competitors should not be protected from exclusion under Article 86, leaving the question open as to when, if at all, less efficient firms should be protected.

When trying to assess those strategic aspects, the Commission introduced the element of anticompetitive intent. As it stated, 'There can thus be an anticompetitive object in price cutting whether or not the aggressor sets its prices above or below its own costs', and 'The pursuance by a dominant firm of a strategy of eliminating competitors or potential competitors by unfair means differing from normal competition would in principle fall under Article 86 whatever the detailed mode of implementation' (paras 79–80). It suggested looking into company internal documents and the specific case circumstances to identify such an anticompetitive intention. Following this route, the Commission concluded, without engaging in a price-cost verification, that AKZO had indeed abused its dominance through aggressive price-cutting.

This intention-based theory of harm raised a few issues. First, it is questionable whether the assessment of aggressive price-cutting should only include a finding of exclusionary intent and not a discussion on anticompetitive effects. The Commission did not engage in a balanced pro- and anticompetitive effects analysis, despite acknowledging the importance of such an assessment (para 80). Second, by

harms enunciated in that judgment included more than just the exploitation of customers. Nonetheless, this mistake does not invalidate the point raised by the Commission here.

refraining from engaging in an effects-based analysis, the Commission appeared overly dismissive when addressing AKZO's argument that less efficient competitors should not be protected under Article 86. The Commission seemed to hold the view that the need to preserve a competitive market structure should prevail over the need to respect a dominant undertaking's activities for advancing its own business interests even when those activities were not intended to restrict competition. Admittedly, not being intended to restrict competition does not preclude a practice from being found illegal, but at the same time, being intended to restrict competition does not necessarily result in competition-restrictive outcomes either because some competitors might be less efficient and so deserve to be excluded. That is why a balanced competitive-effects assessment is so important. In that light, the Commission's reasoning was flawed: instead of seeking a verification in the case circumstances, it simply presumed that those competitors were equally efficient, and therefore, their exclusion should not happen. Consequently, it failed to convincingly explain why and when the preservation of competition should prevail over the respect for an undertaking's legitimate business activity. Third, the Commission made references to some intuitively sensible but ultimately vague concepts. For example, it acknowledged that a dominant undertaking was entitled 'to compete on the merits', but it did not explain how to distinguish, under Article 86, competitive behaviour by virtue and competitive behaviour by abusing dominance nor did it distinguish performance superiority and advantages resulting from being an incumbent. Consequently, this seemingly sensible endorsement of competition on the merits brought no concrete implication to the application of Article 86.

The ECJ in AKZO*: a presumptive theory of the foreclosure harm and the intent-based AKZO formula*

In the appeal, the ECJ agreed with the Commission that competition foreclosure was the core harm of the case. It articulated its understanding of this foreclosure harm as the following:

> Article 86 prohibits a dominant undertaking from eliminating a competitor and thereby strengthening its position by using methods other than those which come within the scope of competition on the basis of quality.[57]

In other words, the ECJ suggested that there were two different kinds of pricing practices: one was the result of competition, and the other one was the result of situations where competition was missing or distorted. The ECJ thought the former to be permissible and the latter condemnable because it was the exploitation of a dominant firm's market power. By this reasoning, when assessing a pricing scheme,

57 Case 62/86 *AKZO Chemie BV v Commission of the European Communities* [1991] ECR I 3359, para 70 (hereinafter, 'ECJ judgment on *AKZO*').

one is advised to look beyond the structure and design of the scheme as such and assess how it related to and interacted with the market competition situation.

Similar to what the Commission did, the ECJ sidestepped the issue of whether the targeted competitors deserved to be excluded for having inferior performances. It only gave an ambiguous presumption that those excluded competitors 'are perhaps as efficient as the dominant undertaking' (para 72 of the ECJ judgment), without prescribing any concrete solutions on how to ascertain that presumption. Consequently, there was a potential error of protecting (less efficient) competitors instead of competition. A possible explanation for this unsoundly presumptive stance was the concern for market integration: it wanted this stance to serve as an expedient to rectify the practices of certain undertakings and an intermediary step to foster competition in the stage of establishing a Common Market.

The ECJ highlighted the element of intent in assessing predatory pricing. It agreed with the Commission that a price-cost comparison was not necessary for finding a price-cutting practice abusive, but such a comparison was nevertheless an important aspect of a balanced anticompetitive assessment (para 65). The underlying logic was that when the exclusionary intention of a dominant undertaking was not obvious, it could be useful to engage in a price-cost comparison, under the premise that below-cost pricing would definitely signify an intention to exclude. In that light, questions arise as to (1) whether such an intention would necessarily result in anticompetitive outcomes (even if other 'strategic aspects' of the price-cutting practice were taken into account) and (2) in what aspects an intention to exclude would qualitatively differ from a benign intention to compete on the merits. Regarding the first question, the ECJ's answer was that such an intention would presumptively entail anticompetitive outcomes because a dominant undertaking would have no interest in pricing below average variable costs except for eliminating competitors (para 71). The ECJ did not provide an answer to the second question in this case. But this question was discussed more thoroughly later in *France Télécom*, in which the GC used 'anticompetitive objective' as a proxy for 'anticompetitive effect'. As it stated, 'If it is shown that the objective pursued by the conduct of an undertaking in a dominant position is to restrict competition, that conduct will also be liable to have such an effect'. Then the GC referred to *AKZO* to explain how that proxy works: First, in a situation where the prices in question were found below AVC, 'the only interest which the undertaking may have in applying such prices is that of eliminating competitors', and therefore, a predatory intention could be presumed.[58] This line of reasoning was also consistent with the preceding *Tetra Pak* case, in which the ECJ upheld the CFI's ruling that no further proof of exclusionary intention was needed if the price in question was below AVC; it also held that there was no need to examine the possibility of recoupment.[59]

58 Case T-340/03 *France Télécom SA v Commission of the European Communities* [2007] ECR II 107, para 195, 197 (hereinafter, 'GC judgment on *France Télécom*').

59 Case C-333/94 P *Tetra Pak International SA v Commission of the European Communities* [1996] ECR I 5951, paras 41–2, 44.

Second, in a situation where the prices were above AVC but below average total costs ('ATC'), the Commission would be required to prove an anticompetitive objective ('a strategy of "pre-emption"'). In this case, the GC found an anticompetitive objective by looking into France Télécom's internal documents and the case circumstances.[60] The ECJ upheld the GC's reasoning in the appeal.

Eventually, in the *AKZO* case, the ECJ relied on the presumption of anticompetitive effects and the analytical focus on intent to construct a two-part AKZO formula for assessing predatory pricing: first, pricing below AVC by a dominant undertaking is *per se* abusive because it is an unequivocal indication of an intention to exclude; second, pricing below ATC but above AVC by dominant undertaking will be abusive if the pricing practice is 'part of a plan for eliminating a competitor' (para 72). According to paragraphs 143–6 of the judgment, there seems to be an implicit sub-presumption in this second part of the AKZO test: if there is no finding that a 'below ATC but above AVC' price is a response to competition, that price will be presumed as driven by an exclusionary intention.

The ECJ in **Post Danmark** *I: an 'all circumstances' approach to assessing competition foreclosure*

As a preliminary ruling case, *Post Danmark I* was also about predatory pricing, although its circumstances were somewhat different from *AKZO*: the pricing scheme in question was found below ATC but above its average incremental costs ('AIC'), which comprises AVC of the particular business in question and common variable costs of that business shared with other businesses. The referring court asked the ECJ how, if at all, a below-ATC-but-above-AIC pricing scheme by a dominant undertaking could be found abusive without finding an exclusionary intention.[61]

The ECJ identified the harm in this case to be competition restriction, which would further cause the harm to consumer welfare. The ECJ's conception of the competition restriction harm included primary- and secondary-line injuries to competition within the meaning of Art 82(c) of the EC Treaty (paras 20, 26). To elaborate on this harm, the ECJ referred to the concept of 'competition on the merits'. Based on *Michelin I, Compagnie maritime belge transports*, and *TeliaSonera*, it distilled the point that domination or monopolization 'on its own merits' was not condemnable *per se* because it could just be the result and manifestation of a healthy competitive process. Accordingly, it ruled that Article 82 of the EC Treaty protected competition rather than less efficient competitors since their being excluded was the expected result of competition on the merits (paras 21–2).

Based on the concept of competition on the merits and the *AKZO* case, the ECJ construed a scenario where a pricing practice would be prohibited under Article 82. This scenario contains two aspects of consideration: the *methods* and the *effects*

60 GC judgment on *France Télécom*, paras 202, 206–9, 210–14.

61 Case C-209/10 *Post Danmark A/S v Konkurrencerådet*, ECLI:EU:C:2012:172, paras 9, 18 (hereinafter, 'ECJ ruling on *Post Danmark I*').

of a pricing practice. The first one entails that to trigger the prohibition of Article 82, the methods employed should be non-merits-based. The second one entails that there should be exclusionary effects on as-efficient competitors. These two aspects of consideration essentially boil down to the same thing: a qualified level of anticompetitive effects that trigger the finding of abuse.[62] To carry out these two aspects of consideration, the ECJ suggested considering 'all the circumstances', which had been repeatedly stressed in the case law. The consideration of such circumstances includes, *inter alia*, the ATC, the AVC, and the exclusionary purpose as contained in the AKZO formula (paras 24–8).

The AKZO formula was inapplicable in this case because there was no evidence of an exclusionary intention and the cost benchmarks were different: AIC incorporates AVC of the particular business in question and common variable costs of that business shared with other businesses, and average fixed cost is included in ATC but not AIC (paras 29–35). So in light of case circumstances, the ECJ established a new formula for assessing predatory pricing, which was based on the as-efficient-competitor rationale and adhered to the all-circumstances assessment approach. According to this formula, when a price is below ATC but above the AIC pertaining to the particular business activity in question, it will be found abusive only if it can drive out equally efficient competitors. As an alternative to the AKZO formula, the Post-Danmark formula does not rely on a finding of exclusionary purposes. Instead, it focuses on finding effects in all the relevant circumstances, making the examination scope extend far beyond a price-cost comparison of the suspected undertaking itself (paras 38–9).

Infringement of regulatory rules

A dominant undertaking's infringement of non-antitrust regulatory rules may also constitute an abuse under Article 102 TFEU. This section examines two such cases: *AstraZeneca* and *Meta*. The former is an annulment case concerning the misuse of the patent process, while the latter is a preliminary ruling case concerning the infringement of the General Data Protection Regulation (GDPR).

The Commission in AstraZeneca*: finding potential anticompetitive effects through finding exclusionary purposes*

The Commission accused *AstraZeneca* of abusing its dominant position in the relevant markets by (1) making misleading representations to national patent authorities to obtain Supplementary Protection Certificates ('SPCs') that without the misleading representations, it would have obtained for a shorter period of validity or would not have obtained at all and (2) implementing a strategy that included the

62 Yan and Vedder, 'Minimum Efficient Scale, Competition on the Merits, and the Special Responsibility of a Dominant Undertaking', 137.

selective deregistration of market authorizations and the switching from capsules to tablet of the medical product in question.[63]

The Commission considered the first abuse to have caused the harm of competition restriction. In its opinion, since SPCs were exclusive rights that already had the inevitable effect of competition restriction, obtaining these rights by way of deception would exceed the tolerable level of competition restriction and so should be prohibited (paras 626, 767 of the Commission decision). The Commission's theory of harm was two-fold: First, it examined the deceptiveness of the SPC-obtaining conduct. It found that AstraZeneca had been continuously and deliberately making misleading representations and consequently had successfully implemented an overall exclusionary strategy. It held that the SPCs would not have been granted in the absence of the misleading representations and therefore AstraZeneca's acquisition of such SPCs was outside the scope of intellectual property rights ('IPRs') protection. Second, the Commission explained how this deceptive conduct had generated anticompetitive effects. Adopting the 'potential effects' criterion, it directed the finding of anticompetitive effects towards finding an anticompetitive objective, which it had successfully shown (paras 758–65).

The harm of the second abuse was also the restriction of competition. The Commission understood the harm as comprising two aspects: the prevention or delay of generic products from emerging and the limitation on parallel-traded products. On that basis, it identified the exclusionary purpose behind the conduct in question in three steps: (1) whether those two aspects of harm were the main purposes of AstraZeneca, (2) whether the conduct in question was planned and implemented to achieve those purposes, and (3) whether those two purposes were underpinned by the longer-term goal of restricting competition in a 'post-patent' scenario. After demonstrating the exclusionary purposes, the Commission moved on to analysing the anticompetitive effects. In that regard, it once again adopted the 'potential effects' criterion and considered AstraZeneca's confidence in implementing that conduct was enough proof that the potential anticompetitive effects had transpired (paras 789, 848).

The GC and the ECJ in **AstraZeneca***: distinguishing competition on the merits through an evaluation of intent*

In the appeals, both the GC and the ECJ upheld the Commission's theory of harm, and they refined it by digging into the issue of what is and is not 'competition on the merits'. The GC equated abuse with non-merits-based methods of competition, which was prohibited under Article 82 of the EC Treaty,[64] and it understood competition on the merits as 'competition on the basis of quality' that was referred

63 Commission Decision of 15 June 2005 relating to a proceeding under Article 82 of the EC Treaty and Article 54 of the EEA Agreement (Case COMP/A. 37.507/F3—AstraZeneca), paras 144, 255, 788 (hereinafter, 'Commission decision on *AstraZeneca*').

64 Case T-321/05 *AstraZeneca AB and AstraZeneca plc v European Commission* [2010] ECR II 2805, para 354 (hereinafter, 'GC judgment on *AstraZeneca*').

to in paragraph 70 of the ECJ's *AKZO* judgment. The ECJ endorsed this line of reasoning.[65] Moreover, the GC invoked the 'special responsibility of a dominant undertaking' rationale and construed the 'competition on the merits' concept as a derivative of that rationale (para 671 of the GC judgment). The ECJ also endorsed this (paras 98, 134, 149 of the ECJ judgment).

When it came to assessing whether a practice fell outside the scope of competition on the merits, the GC held in paragraph 359 that intent could be relevant but unnecessary due to the objective conception of abuse. The ECJ went further: it clarified that when assessing whether dishonest conduct such as the first abuse in question was outside the scope of 'competition on the merits', a contextualized approach should be taken, instead of declaring all fallible practices in regulatory proceedings condemnable under Article 82. In that sense, the ECJ seemed to suggest a consideration of the principle of proportionality for balancing competition preservation and respecting an undertaking's right to defend its legitimate business interests. This proportionality principle was also reflected in its examination of the second conduct in question, where the ECJ indicated the need for such a balance for delineating merits-based competitive behaviour from non-merits-based behaviour (paras 99, 129 of the ECJ judgment).

Regarding the first conduct in question, the GC held that such conduct was outside the scope of competition on the merits because it served the sole aim of restricting competition through misusing the patent process (para 608 of the GC judgment). The ECJ agreed, and to demonstrate that this conduct was not merits-based, it emphasized the deliberateness of AstraZeneca's supply of misleading information to the patent offices and its tactical concealment of the correct information as evidenced by various findings of fact (paras 76–9, 81–93 of the ECJ judgment). The second conduct in question was examined in a similar manner. By highlighting the exclusionary purpose of the deregistration, which was deemed to be unjustifiable from every angle, the ECJ agreed with the GC that the second conduct did not fall within the scope of competition on the merits either. The fact that AstraZeneca had the right to deregister did not preclude the possibility of infringing Article 82 (paras 130–2 of the ECJ judgment).

The ECJ in **Meta**: *finding exploitative abuse by establishing an infringement of the GDPR*

Meta was a preliminary ruling case. The referring court asked how, if at all, the German competition authority should assess the compliance of the conduct of an undertaking with the GDPR when trying to examine the legality of that conduct under Article 102 TFEU. The German competition authority argued that Meta (formerly Facebook) had abused its dominance by imposing unfair terms regarding user data collection and combination, causing the harms of exploiting end users

65 Case C-457/10 P *AstraZeneca AB and AstraZeneca plc v European Commission*, ECLI:EU:C:2012:770, para 75 (hereinafter, 'ECJ judgment on *AstraZeneca*').

on the one hand and input-foreclosing rivals vis-à-vis user data accumulation on the other. Instead of directly engaging in an 'exploitative & exclusionary' abuse analysis under Article 102, the German competition authority chose to prove the abusiveness of the conduct by way of a violation of the GDPR,[66] thereby making the case largely about a GDPR matter regarding the justifiable grounds for collecting and combining personal data.

Because of how this case was framed, the ECJ's preliminary ruling revolved more around the application of the GDPR than that of Article 102. Nonetheless, this is an important addition to the competition case law. First, it confirmed that a competition authority could make GDPR-compliance assessments when trying to apply Article 102, as long as it fulfilled the duty of cooperation with data protection authorities. Competition authorities should be allowed to make such assessments because they are required by a long line of Article 102 case law to consider all the case circumstances when trying to find an abuse of dominance.[67] Along this line, one could reason that such compliance assessments are not necessarily limited to data protection law; competition authorities could also make assessments in other sector-regulatory areas such as consumer protection, patent protection, and financial regulation.

Second, by clarifying what constituted unjustified personal data processing under Article 6(1) of the GDPR with a view towards abuse assessment under Article 102, the ECJ effectively provided a rather straightforward approach to assessing the potential unfairness—and so the exploitative abusiveness—of a dominant firm's data-processing practices (paras 97–126, 140–54). But to be sure, proving the practice's violation of the GDPR would only be part of the abuse-of-dominance assessment under Article 102; ideally, a competition authority would still need to articulate how the GDPR-incompatibility of the practice in question has contributed to or resulted from the restriction of competition. In that regard, the ECJ advised the examination of whether users had real choice when trading with the dominant firm—e.g., whether users could still buy a service without consenting to personal data processing and whether they could give separate consent to the processing of data relating to different services (paras 150–1).

Refusal to deal

Refusal to deal is a prominent type of abuse under Article 102 TFEU with a long string of precedents establishing a rather coherent theory of harm. The cases featured in this section include the following: (1) *Commercial Solvents*, (2) *United Brands*, (3) *BP*, (4) *CBEM-Telemarketing*, (5) *BPB Magill*, (6) *Bronner*, (7) *IMS Health*, (8) *Microsoft*, and (9) *Sot Lélos*. Among them, *CBEM-Telemarketing,*

66 Xingyu Yan and Huaiwen He, 'Fine-Tuning the *Ex Ante* Approach to Regulating Data Combination Practices', *Journal of Competition Law & Economics* 18, no. 4 (26 December 2022): 896.

67 Case C-252/21 *Meta Platforms Inc and Others v Bundeskartellamt*, ECLI:EU:C:2023:537, paras 47–8, 62–3 (hereinafter, 'ECJ ruling on *Meta*').

Bronner, IMS Health, and *Sot Lélos* are preliminary ruling cases. The rest are annulment cases.

The Commission in Commercial Solvents, United Brands, BP, *and* Magill: *primitive theories of harm*

The Commission showed a consistent concern for competitive market structures in these four cases, but the theories of harm therein were underdeveloped. In *Commercial Solvents*, it briefly identified two competitive harms caused by the refusal to supply: negatively affecting the market structure in the downstream market by eliminating a major competitor and limiting the production of the upstream raw material market within the meaning of Article 86(b) of the EEC Treaty.[68] There were no more analyses beyond that.

In *United Brands*, the Commission alleged the harm of output-foreclosure of competition. In its opinion, the refusal to supply at issue 'would discourage it and other distributors/ripeners from selling competing brands', thereby preventing UBC's competitors from having access to principal distributors. The Commission only provided a brief and theoretical account of how the harm had transpired. Seemingly, the Commission had a second competitive harm in mind: the restriction of customers' freedom of choice. As it stated in paragraphs 16–7 of the decision, 'A buyer must be allowed the freedom to decide what are his business interests, to choose the products he will sell, even if they are in competition with each other; in effect to determine his own sales policy'.[69] But no further analyses were provided.

The theory of harm was even more obscure in *BP*, a case in which the accused undertaking refused to supply petroleum to a customer after the oil crisis broke out in 1973. The Commission considered the conduct to have caused the harm of secondary-line competition distortion and prosecuted it under Article 86(c) of the EEC Treaty. To explain how this harm had transpired, the Commission did not look into the market where the refused customer operated; instead, it relied heavily on the presupposition that a dominant undertaking had the obligation to treat every customer non-discriminatorily and equitably.[70] On that basis, the Commission found the refusal in question abusive because it was disproportionate compared to the reduction of supply to other customers. This presupposition was questionable: it emphasized the value of maintaining the normal 'extent, regularity and continuity of commercial relationships' (p 10 of the Commission decision), but it offered no clarification on how that value related to competition protection. Specifically, it

68 72/457/CEE: Décision de la Commission, du 14 décembre 1972, relative à une procédure d'application de l'article 86 du traité instituant la Communauté économique européenne (IV/26.911—ZOJA/CSC—ICI), [31 December 1972] OJ L 299, 54 (hereinafter, 'Commission decision on *Commercial Solvents*').

69 Commission decision on *United Brands*, paras 16–17.

70 77/327/EEC: Commission Decision of 19 April 1977 relating to a proceeding under Article 86 of the EEC Treaty (IV/28.841—ABG/Oil companies operating in the Netherlands) [9 May 1977] OJ L 117, 9 (hereinafter, 'Commission decision on *BP*').

failed to clarify how obliging a dominant firm to maintain normal commercial relationships would necessarily increase competition when the dominant firm could also be entitled to and contributing to competition on the merits.

The theory of harm in *Magill* was more sensible but had limited substantiation. *Magill* concerned the refusal of three broadcasting organizations to grant copyright license to a TV-guide magazine publisher that wanted to use that license to publish TV scheduling information every week. The Commission found the three broadcasting companies to be *de facto* monopolies vis-à-vis the production of their weekly listings because 'it is not possible for third parties to produce reliable listings themselves'.[71] On that basis, it considered the refusal to license by these companies to be a disproportionately competition-restrictive way to exercise copyrights and to have caused two competitive harms: the limitation of production within the meaning of Article 86(c) and competition foreclosure in the market where the refused undertaking operated. The Commission's reasoning regarding the first harm was not so much a theory as it was a literal citation of Article 86(c). The Commission found the refusals to grant license, in conjunction with the threat to sue any unlicensed publication, to have prevented the emergence of a new product, namely, a comprehensive TV guide, for which there was a substantial potential demand. Regarding the second harm, the Commission alleged, with little analysis, that the refusals reserved the derivative market of weekly TV guides for the broadcasting companies themselves while eliminating potential competition from a more comprehensive TV guide (para 23 of the Commission decision).

The Commission in Microsoft*: two standard harm allegations and a theory adhering to the case law*

Microsoft took place after the ECJ had made a string of impactful preliminary rulings. In this case, the Commission accused Microsoft of abusing its dominant position in the market for PC operating systems by refusing to share interoperability protocol specifications with Sun, a firm that sought to provide work group server functions interoperable with the Windows domain architecture (particularly with the Windows client PC operating system). Like what it did in *Magill*, the Commission alleged two harms caused by Microsoft's refusal to interoperate: (1) limiting technical development to the prejudice of consumers, as stipulated in Article 82(b) of the EC Treaty, and (2) undermining the competitive structure to the detriment of consumer welfare.[72]

The Commission highlighted the case law including *Commercial Solvents, Télémarkting, Magill, Tiercé Ladbroke, Bronner*, and *Volvo*, which instructed that only

71 89/205/EEC: Commission Decision of 21 December 1988 relating to a proceeding under Article 86 of the EEC Treaty (IV/31.851—Magill TV Guide/ITP, BBC and RTE) [21 March 1989] OJ L 78, para 22 (hereinafter, 'Commission decision on *BPB Magill*').

72 Commission Decision of 24 March 2004 relating to a proceeding under Article 82 of the EC Treaty (Case COMP/C-3/37.792 Microsoft), paras 693–4, 704 (hereinafter, 'Commission decision on *Microsoft*').

in 'specific circumstances' would a refusal to license intellectual property rights by a dominant firm constitute an abuse (paras 547–59 of the decision). On that basis, it constructed a theory of harm consisting of the following aspects. First, it examined the indispensability of the withheld protocol information (specifically, 'a full specification of the protocols underlying the Windows domain architecture'). It found this information to be indispensable for Sun to compete in the work group server operating system market, and there were no real substitutes for the withheld information (paras 566–7, 586, 666–91). Second, the Commission assessed the refusal's competition restriction effects. It found Microsoft's refusal to be part of a broader strategy of 'not disclosing interoperability information to work group server operating system vendors' so as to promote the attractiveness of Microsoft's own work group server operating system in terms of its interoperability with the prevailing Microsoft client PC operating system (paras 575–7, 588, 638). Adopting the 'potential effects' criterion, the Commission listed evidence to show that Microsoft's increase in market shares was the result of successfully executing that broader strategy and took that as an indication of competitors being marginalized (paras 591–665). In the Commission's opinion, the very fact that customers perceived Microsoft's work group server operating system as the preferred option over other operating systems was already a sign of consumer harm, as those customers' choices were unduly influenced (para 706). Third, the Commission briefly explained how the refusal in question had limited technical development. According to the Commission, had the interoperability information been granted, there would have been products bringing additional value to the Windows work group networks and ultimately to consumer welfare (paras 696, 700).

The ECJ in **Commercial Solvents, United Brands, BP,** *and* **CBEM-Telemarketing***: a presumptive approach to protecting competitive market structures and market integration*

The ECJ's theory of harm in *Commercial Solvents* revolved closely around the concern for market structure. First, relying on Article3(f) of the EEC Treaty, it reasoned that the refusal to supply a customer by a dominant undertaking would infringe Article 86 if it risked eliminating 'all competition on the part of this customer', and to amount to that risk, it would suffice if the refusal was based on 'the object of reserving such raw material for manufacturing its own derivatives', namely, an exclusionary intention.[73] Second, the ECJ seemed to suggest that if the aforementioned two conditions were met, it would no longer be necessary to engage in a case-specific examination as to whether the refused customer was able to find alternative supplies on the grounds that 'that question is not relevant to the consideration of the conduct of the applicants' (para 26). Third, the ECJ interpreted

73 Joined Cases 6 and 7/73 *Istituto Chemioterapico Italiano S.p.A. and Commercial Solvents Corporation v Commission of the European Communities* [1974] ECR 223, para 25 (hereinafter, 'ECJ judgment on *Commercial Solvents*').

the 'effects on trade between Member States' requirement in Article 86 as much more than just a jurisdictional threshold: it stated that this requirement was aimed at preserving 'the effective competitive structure as envisaged by Article 3(f) of the Treaty', therefore linking this requirement to—and consequently reinforcing—the protection of a competitive market structure, which entailed that conduct by a dominant undertaking should be prohibited if it impaired the market structure by eliminating a competitor (paras 32–3). Fourth, the ECJ showed caution in identifying the discrimination of customers as a harm resulting from refusals to supply, as it disregarded the AG's suggestion of approaching the refusal in question from paragraph (c) of Article 86. In the AG's opinion, a refusal could be justifiable if it involved exclusive ownership and was for product integration but would be unjustifiable if it was targeted at (and, therefore, discriminating) a particular customer.[74]

Meanwhile, *United Brands* embodied the ECJ's concern for market integration in relation to refusals to deal. First, the ECJ identified two harms resulting from the refusal in question: *limiting markets to the prejudice of consumers* and *discriminating customers*, within the meaning of paragraphs (b) and (c) of Article 86, respectively. It did not provide much substantiation as to how these harms had transpired but simply presumed the abusiveness of a dominant undertaking's refusal to supply 'a long standing customer who abides by regular commercial practice' and whose purchasing orders 'are in no way out of the ordinary'.[75] By stating that such behaviour 'cannot be countenanced if its actual purpose is to strengthen this dominant position and abuse it', the ECJ seemed to have based the illegality primarily on anticompetitive intent; but its examination of the case circumstances suggested that there was no clear line between purposes of strengthening dominance and purposes of protecting legitimate commercial interests (paras 189–92). Second, the ECJ also alleged the restriction of freedom of trade as a supplementary harm, as it stated that the refusal 'amounts therefore to a serious interference with the independence of small and medium sized firms' (para 193). But it did not substantiate this allegation nor did it explain how this allegation related to competition protection since there was no discussion on any kind of competition surrounding the refused distributor. In that light, what underlay this supplementary harm allegation was most likely the concern for market integration.

The ECJ annulled the Commission's decision in *BP*. It held that all private undertakings were entitled to pursue their self-interests and so should not be expected to assume the governmental responsibility of allocating resources of production in times of emergency. In other words, an undertaking should not be expected to act in all fairness and equitability if that would hamper its freedom to pursue its legitimate business interests.[76] On this basis, the ECJ found no abuse.

74 Opinion of Mr Advocate General Warner (delivered on 22 January 1974) in Joined Cases 6 and 7/73 *Istituto Chemioterapico Italiano S.p.A. and Commercial Solvents Corporation v Commission of the European Communities* [1974] ECR 223, 268–70.

75 ECJ judgment on *United Brands*, paras 182–3.

76 Case 77/77 *Benzine en Petroleum Handelsmaatschappij BV and others v Commission of the European Communities* [1978] ECR 1513, para 34.

In the preliminary ruling case of *CBEM-Telemarketing*, the ECJ was asked whether an undertaking with a statutory monopoly position had infringed Article 86 by reserving for its subsidiary—to the exclusion of any other undertaking—an ancillary activity that could be carried out by an independent undertaking. The ECJ answered affirmatively. Referring back to *Commercial Solvents*, it identified the harm arising from this scenario to be the undermining of a competitive market structure, and it held that the total exclusion of a particular undertaking in the ancillary market would suffice to prove that harm, without needing to further examine the remaining level of competition in that market.[77]

Overall, from *Commercial Solvents* to *CBEM-Telemarketing*, the ECJ had constructed a presumptive theory of competitive harm on refusal to deal, and it was highly likely that the ECJ had the concern for market integration to back up this presumptive stance. One explanation for this presumptive stance is the ECJ's institutional role: as the judicial supervisor of the EEC, it was not institutionally motivated to show interest in building an economically elaborate theory of harm as long as the Treaty provisions and case law permitted it to reach a straightforward conclusion. Admittedly, this would entail a risk of making false positive errors, but there were no supervisors on top of the ECJ to neutralize that risk. So until the ECJ itself became aware of such errors being made, there would be no real motivation for it to change this disinterested-in-economics attitude. Besides, even when the ECJ decided to reduce such false positive errors by embracing more economics, it could still be held back by the consideration of case justiciability and judicial costs.

The CFI in Magill *and* Microsoft*: endorsing and polishing the Commission's reasoning*

In *Magill*, the CFI upheld the Commission decision and it enriched the Commission's theory of harm by elaborating on the balancing of IPRs protection and competition protection. First, it drew from a series of precedents to declare that the protection of IPRs should prevail over the application of Article 86 only if an IPR's competition-restrictive effects 'are inherent in the protection of the actual substance of the intellectual property right'.[78] On that basis, the CFI held that the exercise of an IPR would fall outside the protected scope if 'that right is exercised in such ways and circumstances as in fact to pursue an aim manifestly contrary to the objectives of Article 86' because in that case, 'the copyright is no longer exercised in a manner which corresponds to its essential function', which was 'to protect the moral rights in the work and ensure a reward for the creative effort' (para 71 of the CFI judgment). Subsequently, the CFI found that the refusal to license in question had gone beyond what was necessary to fulfil the 'essential function' and was

77 Case 311/84 *Centre belge d'études de marché—Télémarketing (CBEM) v SA Compagnie luxembourgeoise de télédiffusion (CLT) and Information publicité Benelux (IPB)* [1985] ECR 3261, para 27.

78 Case T-69/89 *Radio Telefis Eireann v Commission of the European Communities* [1991] ECR II 485, para 69 (hereinafter, 'CFI judgment on *BPB Magill*').

therefore arbitrary and unjustified. It also declared that the refusal was not related to the 'actual substance' of the copyright, although it did not clarify the relationship between 'essential function' and 'actual substance' (paras 71, 74).

The *Microsoft* case was only reviewed by the CFI, which ruled in complete favour of the Commission. The CFI expanded on the refusal-to-deal analytical framework that had been established by the case law and applied by the Commission. First, it confirmed the Commission's finding that the withheld interoperability information was indispensable for Sun and held that the refusal had caused the harm of competition foreclosure because Microsoft's competitors would not be able to stay viable in the downstream market without the withheld information. It also dismissed Microsoft's concern that the interoperability information would be used for cloning Microsoft products.[79] Second, regarding the balancing of IPRs protection and competition protection, the CFI relied on the Commission's reasoning and the existing case law to distil three cumulative conditions for finding a refusal to grant IPRs abusive: (1) the withheld information was indispensable to the refused party, (2) the refusal had resulted in competition restriction, and (3) the refusal had prevented a new product from emerging (paras 316–34 of the judgment). The CFI carried out the rest of the assessment in accordance with these three conditions. It deferred to the Commission's finding of indispensability on the grounds that the Commission enjoyed a margin of discretion vis-à-vis complex economic assessments, and it found competition restriction by adopting the 'potential effects' criterion. Regarding the third condition, the CFI observed that the competitors' products offered functions that were non-operability-related but were nonetheless valued greatly by consumers, and had the competitors been granted the interoperability information, they would have provided products with differentiated and advanced features. In that light, the 'prevention of a new product' requirement was met (paras 652, 654–5).

The ECJ in **Magill, Bronner, IMS Health,** *and* **Sot Lélos***: developing the indispensability test*

In *Magill*, the ECJ agreed with the Commission and the CFI that the refusal had caused two harms, namely, the limitation of production within the meaning of Article 86(b) and the foreclosure of competition in the derivative market. However, the ECJ sidestepped the issue of balancing IPRs protection and competition protection, which was featured extensively in the accompanying AG opinion. The ECJ's theory of harm was simple: although a refusal to license by a dominant undertaking did not constitute an abuse *per se*, in specific circumstances, that conduct could nevertheless constitute an abuse of dominance.[80] The ECJ explained such specific

79 Case T-201/04 *Microsoft Corp. v Commission of the European Communities* [2007] ECR II 3601, paras 229, 240–4 (hereinafter, 'CFI judgment on *Microsoft*').

80 Joined Cases C-241/91 P and C-242/91 P *Radio Telefis Eireann (RTE) and Independent Television Publications Ltd (ITP) v Commission of the European Communities* [1995] ECR I 743, paras 46–50 (hereinafter, 'ECJ judgment on *BPB Magill*').

circumstances as comprising the following elements: (1) a lack of actual or potential substitutes for the product that was prevented from emerging by the refusal, a product for which 'there was a specific, constant and regular potential demand on the part of consumers'; (2) a lack of justification for the refusal; and (3) the refusal had resulted in the exclusion of all competition in the said product market by denying access to the raw material indispensable to operate in that market (paras 52, 55–6 of the judgment).

Bronner was a preliminary ruling case concerning the refusal of a dominant firm to provide a competitor access to its national distribution system. Referring to *Commercial Solvents* and *CBEM-Telemarketing*, the ECJ emphasized the element of 'eliminating all competition on the part of the refused undertaking' when assessing the abusiveness of a refusal to supply. It also referred to *Magill* to underscore that only in 'exceptional circumstances' would an exercise of IPRs by a dominant undertaking constitute an abuse. The ECJ formulated the following criteria for assessing the abusiveness of a refusal to deal: (1) the likeliness of excluding all competition on the part of the refused undertaking in the market it intended to enter, (2) the refusal not being able to be objectively justified, and (3) the product in question being indispensable for the refused undertaking (having no actual or potential substitute).[81]

IMS Health was a preliminary ruling case concerning refusal to license. In this case, the ECJ first clarified on how to apply the indispensability criterion formulated in *Bronner*. It underscored two aspects of consideration: (1) 'whether there are products or services which constitute alternative solutions' and (2) 'whether there are technical, legal or economic obstacles capable of making it impossible or at least unreasonably difficult' to create the alternative products or services.[82] Second, the ECJ clarified on how to apply the excluding-all-competition criterion formulated in *Bronner* (for finding abusive refusals to deal in general) to refusals to license, which could be found abusive only in 'exceptional circumstances' (paras 34–7). It elaborated this criterion into two cumulative conditions: (1) The refusal had prevented the emergence of a new product. This entails that for a refusal to license to constitute an abuse, the refused undertaking must intend to develop a new product by using the withheld license instead of simply trying to duplicate the already existing product (paras 38, 48–9). (2) The refusal had excluded all competition in a secondary market. This entails the identification of two separate markets, although these markets do not need to be stringently defined; it would suffice if they could be identified potentially or hypothetically, for example, as two stages of production (paras 42, 44–5).

Sot Lélos was a preliminary ruling case in which a dominant pharmaceutical producer in Greece refused to supply some domestic distributors (Sot Lélos and others) that intended to engage in parallel exports to other Member States where

81 Case C-7/97 *Oscar Bronner GmbH & Co. KG v Mediaprint Zeitungs- und Zeitschriftenverlag GmbH & Co. KG, Mediaprint Zeitungsvertriebsgesellschaft mbH & Co. KG and Mediaprint Anzeigengesellschaft mbH & Co. KG* [1998] ECR I 7791, paras 38–41 (hereinafter, 'ECJ ruling on *Bronner*').

82 Case C-418/01 *IMS Health GmbH & Co. OHG v NDC Health GmbH & Co. KG* [2004] ECR I 5039, para 28 (hereinafter, 'ECJ ruling on *IMS Health*').

the prices of certain medical products were higher because of the different degrees of state intervention.[83] In answering how to approach this conduct under Article 82 of the EC Treaty, the ECJ first identified the harm of undermining a competitive market structure in close association with a concern for market integration: in its opinion, a refusal to supply an existing customer with the aim of restricting parallel trade should be considered as presumptively abusive. The reason was that parallel trade in and by itself would promote competition and benefit consumers (paras 37, 52–7). Second, the ECJ identified some potential justifications for rebutting this abuse presumption. The first one was an undertaking's right to defend its legitimate commercial interests, as long as the steps taken to defend such interests were reasonable and the underlying purpose was not to strengthen and abuse the dominant position (paras 49–50). The second possible justification was the presence of state intervention. The ECJ held that on the one hand, the mere presence of state intervention could not preclude the applicability of Article 82 to a limitation-on-parallel-trade case (paras 58–66), but on the other hand, a refusal to deal that threatened parallel trade could not be deemed as *per se* abusive anymore if the parallel trade was born out of the very existence of state intervention rather than natural competition. Consequently, the ECJ suggested a balanced approach to assessing the refusal in question, focusing on whether the refused orders from the customers were out of the ordinary (paras 67–70, 77).

Margin squeeze

Margin squeeze is a type of potentially abusive conduct that sits somewhere between predatory pricing and refusal to deal. It involves a situation where a vertically integrated undertaking abuses its dominant position in an upstream market by charging relatively high for products supplied to its rivals in a downstream market, therefore giving itself a cost advantage to those rivals downstream. This section highlights two cases: *Deutsche Telekom* and *TeliaSonera*. The former is an annulment procedure case, while the latter is a preliminary ruling case.

The Commission in **Deutsche Telekom***: proposing the margin squeeze test*

In *Deutsche Telekom*, the Commission accused DT of abusing its dominant position in the upstream wholesale market for local access to fixed telecommunications networks by overly charging its competitors in the downstream retail market for the wholesale access service. The Commission alleged the harm of competition foreclosure downstream, as DT's margin squeeze scheme had raised rivals' costs and would force them out even if they were as efficient as DT in the retail market.[84]

83 Joined Cases C-468/06 to C-478/06 *Sot. Lélos kai Sia EE and Others v GlaxoSmithKline AEVE Farmakeftikon Proïonton, Formerly Glaxowellcome AEVE* [2008] ECR I 7139, paras 9–11 and 23 (hereinafter, 'ECJ ruling on *Sot Lélos*').

84 2003/707/EC: Commission Decision of 21 May 2003 Relating to a Proceeding under Article 82 of the EC Treaty (Case COMP/C-1/37.451, 37.578, 37.579—Deutsche Telekom AG), [14 October 2003] OJ L 263, paras 108, 141 (hereinafter, 'Commission decision on *Deutsche Telekom*').

The Commission proposed a test for assessing the abusiveness of margin squeeze. First, it advanced two key considerations for establishing the abusiveness: (1) whether the gap between DT's wholesale charges to downstream competitors and DT's direct retail charges to end users was 'negative, or insufficient to cover the product-specific costs to the dominant operator of providing its own retail services on the downstream market', and (2) whether there was a downstream market in which the upstream dominant undertaking competed with other firms in providing the same service (paras 105–9 of the Commission decision). The background to these considerations was that the downstream competitors bore two distinguishable sets of costs: the wholesale charges by DT (as input costs) and the specific downstream (retail) costs. The principle underlying these considerations was that the wholesale charges by the upstream dominant operator 'must enable competitors to compete with that operator effectively, and at least to replicate the established operator's customer pattern' (paras 114, 127).

Second, based on these two considerations, the Commission focused on analysing the retail prices and wholesale charges of the dominant operator. It envisaged two scenarios where a margin squeeze scheme could be found abusive. First, when the average retail prices were below the level of the wholesale charges, there would definitely be an abuse. Second, when the average retail prices were above the level of the wholesale charges, there would be an abuse if 'the product-specific costs of providing the product or service in question to end-users' was higher than 'the extent of the positive spread between the retail charges and the wholesale charges' because a firm as efficient as the dominant firm would not be able to profitably operate in the retail market (paras 111, 138–9). Eventually, the Commission found DT's margin squeeze scheme abusive. It considered that, under the objective conception of abuse established in the case law, the existence of a margin squeeze scheme was enough proof of an abuse; no demonstration of anticompetitive effects was necessary.

The CFI and the ECJ in **Deutsche Telekom***: clarifying the application of the margin squeeze test*

The *Deutsche Telekom* case was appealed first to the CFI, and then to the ECJ. Both courts upheld the Commission decision and further clarified the margin squeeze test proposed by the Commission.

First, the CFI and the ECJ clarified that margin squeeze was a type of abuse distinct from predatory pricing. Specifically, the abusiveness of a margin squeeze scheme stemmed from the 'unfairness of the spread' between the wholesale charges and the retail charges rather than the predatory nature of the retail prices or the excessiveness of the wholesale charges as such.[85] Along the line, the ECJ dismissed DT's argument that by the Commission's margin squeeze test, it was caught in a

85 Case T-271/03 *Deutsche Telekom AG v Commission of the European Communities* [2008] ECR II 477, para 167 (hereinafter, 'CFI judgment on *Deutsche Telekom*'); Case C-280/08 P *Deutsche*

dilemma where it would either have to keep the existing retail price level that led to a finding of abuse, or it would have to increase the retail prices to the detriment to its end users' welfare. The ECJ considered this dilemma to be fallacious because the abusiveness stemmed from the unfairness of the spread, so DT could always remedy the situation by lowering its wholesale charges instead of raising retail prices (paras 175–82 of the ECJ judgment).

Second, the CFI and the ECJ found no problem in the Commission's focus on DT's own price-cost structure on two grounds. The first ground was the established case law (e.g., *AKZO*) to focus on the dominant undertaking's own price-and-cost structure when assessing the abusiveness of its pricing practices. The second ground was legal certainty in the sense that straying away from this focus would make an undertaking unable to self-assess the legality of its practices since they were not supposed to know other undertakings' price-and-cost structures (paras 188–9, 192 of the CFI judgment). The ECJ further added that the focus on the firm's own price-cost structure was inherently aligned with the as-efficient-competitor rationale, which was essential in ascertaining the alleged competition foreclosure harm (paras 198–200 of the ECJ judgment).

Third, the CFI and the ECJ corrected the Commission's logic that proving anticompetitive effects was unnecessary for finding an abusive margin squeeze. They stressed that under the objective conception of abuse, the Commission was required to show anticompetitive effects before finding an abuse of dominance. Nevertheless, such anticompetitive effects were measured by the 'potential effects' criterion pursuant to the structural conception of the foreclosure harm, so the Commission had already shown such effects with its application of the margin squeeze test.[86]

The ECJ in **TeliaSonera***: further clarifying the application of the margin squeeze test*

Based on existing case law, the ECJ reiterated that competition foreclosure was the harm relevant to margin squeeze and that the theory of harm should be consistent with the objective conception of abuse and the entailed 'all circumstances' analytical framework.[87] Along the line, the ECJ confirmed the *Deutsche Telekom* ruling that the abusiveness of margin squeeze stemmed from the unfairness of the spread rather than the excessiveness of wholesale prices or the predatory nature of retail prices as such. The ECJ also stressed that the demonstration of potential effects of excluding as-efficient competitors was required, but because such effects were inherent in the unfairness of the spread, no further proof was necessary (paras 30–4).

Telekom AG v European Commission [2010] ECR I 9555, paras 168–9, 183 (hereinafter, 'ECJ judgment on *Deutsche Telekom*').

86 CFI judgment on *Deutsche Telekom*, 233–7; ECJ judgment on *Deutsche Telekom*, paras 252–4.

87 Case C-52/09 *Konkurrensverket v TeliaSonera Sverige AB* [2011] ECR I 527, paras 24, 27–8 (hereinafter, 'ECJ ruling on *TeliaSonera*').

Subsequently, the ECJ discussed the relevance of several factors to the abuse assessment. First, it considered competitors' price-cost structures to be generally irrelevant due to the as-efficient-competitor rationale and the consideration of legal certainty. Nonetheless, it held that in particular circumstances where the price-and-cost structure of the dominant undertaking was not precisely measurable, competitors' price-cost structures might be relevant (paras 38–46). Second, the ECJ clarified that when there was a positive spread between the wholesale charge and the retail price, the indispensability of the wholesale product to downstream competitors would be a relevant but not necessary factor for assessing margin squeeze under the 'all circumstances' analytical framework (paras 69–77). Third, the ECJ understood margin squeeze as a separate type of abuse from refusal to supply, so the conditions for finding an abusive refusal to supply did not necessarily apply to margin squeeze cases (paras 55–6). Seemingly, the ECJ made this clarification because it perceived the conditions for finding abusive refusals to supply as too demanding and wanted to ensure that implicit refusals to supply in the form of margin squeeze would still be brought under regulation even if they failed to meet the standard refusal-to-supply conditions. However, as suggested by scholars, this concern was overblown because the approaches to assessing margin squeeze and refusal to deal are highly similar in the fine details.[88] After all, margin squeeze and refusal to deal are both about causing the harm of competition foreclosure in a downstream market, irrespective of whether they are conceptualized as independent from each other.

Loyalty rebates

Loyalty rebates are another prominent type of abuse under EU competition law featuring a long line of case precedents. This section analyses the following: (1) *Suiker Unie*, (2) *Hoffmann-La Roche*, (3) *Michelin I*, (4) *Michelin II*, (5) *Post Danmark II*, and (6) *Intel*. Only *Post Danmark II* is a preliminary ruling case, with the rest all being annulment procedure cases.

The Commission in **Suiker Unie** *and* **Hoffmann-La Roche***: limited harm analyses*

In *Suiker Unie*, the Commission considered the granting of fidelity rebates an abuse of dominance for causing two harms: discrimination of customers and impediment to market integration. The harm analysis was brief. First, the Commission held that the rebates constituted 'an unjustifiable discrimination against buyers' who also bought from the dominant firm's competitors. Second, it found the rebates in question to have the potential effect of enabling the dominant firm to control the customers' purchases from foreign producers. Overall, the Commission suggested

88 Niamh Dunne, 'Dispensing with Indispensability', *Journal of Competition Law & Economics* 16, no. 1 (30 April 2020): 95.

that the rebates should be *per se* illegal because they could serve the *aims* of limiting opportunities for imports and strengthening the dominant position.[89]

In *Hoffmann-La Roche*, the Commission alleged three harms caused by the rebate schemes in question: hampering the freedom of choice of the purchasers, output-foreclosure of competition (resulting from the hampering of freedom), and discrimination of the purchasers. The Commission reasoned that the first two harms had happened because (1) the rebate schemes showed an element of exclusivity that 'by its very nature removes all freedom of choice from purchasers'; (2) the rebate schemes had the desired *object* of inducing—either by express obligation or by providing financial incentives—the customers to buy all or a large proportion of their requirements from the dominant firm, therefore interfering with the competition; and (3) this desired object was presumably realized in light of the facts. It provided no analysis of the third harm, simply stating that the rebates infringed Article 86(c) by offering different prices to different customers.[90]

The ECJ in Suiker Unie *and* Hoffmann-La Roche*: a structural and form-based theory of harm to loyalty rebates*

The ECJ in *Suiker Unie* was mainly concerned with the harm to market integration. First, it introduced the notion of 'dissuasive effect' and indicated that, through the grant of a financial advantage, such rebates were designed and likely to prevent 'customers obtaining their supplies from competing producers'.[91] Second, the ECJ referred to second paragraph (c) of Article 86, seemingly to indicate that part of the harm was discrimination, although it refrained from explaining whether and how the discrimination had caused any competitive disadvantages. Third, it referred to second paragraph (b) of Article 86, suggesting that the rebates in question limited markets to the detriment of the Common Market (paras 523–4, 526 of the judgment).

In *Hoffmann-La Roche*, the ECJ rearranged the Commission's harm allegations into two more competition-focused ones: (1) output-foreclosure of competition resulting from the limitation on customers' freedom of choice and (2) distortion of downstream market competition resulting from the discriminatorily granted rebates. The ECJ's understanding of 'competition' was heavily market structure-based, as shown in its objective conception of abuse in paragraph 91 of the judgment. The ECJ categorized the rebates in question into three kinds and approached them separately. For the first kind, which imposed a specific obligation to obtain exclusively from Roche, it adopted a *per se* rule of illegality on the grounds that such rebates simultaneously caused four harms: limitation of freedom of choice, output-foreclosure of competition, discrimination under Article 86(c),

89 Commission decision on *Suiker Unie*, 39–40.

90 76/642/EEC: Commission Decision of 9 June 1976 relating to a proceeding under Article 86 of the Treaty establishing the European Economic Community (IV/29.020—Vitamins), [16 August 1976] OJ L 223, paras 22–4 (hereinafter, 'Commission decision on *Hoffmann-La Roche*').

91 ECJ judgment on *Suiker Unie*, para 518.

and strengthening the dominance through a distorted form of competition.[92] For the second kind, which incentivized customers to obtain all or a fixed percentage of their requirements from Roche, the ECJ only considered the potentially anticompetitive mechanism of these rebates, i.e., the fact that they were aimed at attaining the maximum portion (as opposed to quantity) of a customer's requirements. There was no examination of the actual or potential effects.[93] The structural and form-based harm analysis was also shown in the examination of the third kind of rebates, where the ECJ discussed only the anticompetitive incentive and the potentially anticompetitive mechanisms of the contracts and refrained from ascertaining whether and to what extent these incentives and mechanisms had been realized. In fact, the ECJ seems to have deliberately disregarded factors that might mitigate the anticompetitive effects of the practices in question, and the reason was the view that competition had already been weakened by the presence of dominance. A closer look at the ECJ's examination of the 'Union effect' dimension (paras 111–20, 125) would reveal that this view stemmed largely from the concern for market integration.

The Commission in **Michelin I** *and* **Michelin II***: a presumptive of the competition foreclosure harm*

Like in *Hoffmann-La Roche*, the Commission in *Michelin I* alleged three harms caused by the rebates in question: output-foreclosure of competition, restriction of customer choice, and discrimination of customers. The Commission's analysis of the foreclosure harm was largely presumptive, as it showed no evidence of competitors being foreclosed and only analysed how the rebate scheme in question had functioned in a loyalty-inducing manner. A closer look would reveal that this presumptive foreclosure-harm analysis was largely driven by the concern for market integration.[94] The Commission's analysis of the discrimination harm was also presumptive, as it only looked at how the rebates were discriminatory in form and refrained from assessing whether the discriminatory treatment had indeed put certain customers at a competitive disadvantage (paras 41–2).

In *Michelin II*, the Commission alleged three harms caused by the so-called 'quantity rebates' of Michelin: (1) unfairness in the sense that the rebates caused uneven relationships between the dominant firm Micheline and its dealers; (2) competition foreclosure, along with the restriction of customers' freedom of choice because the rebates in question were 'loyalty-inducing'; and (3) impediment to market integration, along with the harm of discrimination because the rebates were

92 Case 85/76 *Hoffmann-La Roche & Co. AG v Commission of the European Communities* [1979] ECR 461, paras 89–90 (hereinafter, 'ECJ judgment on *Hoffmann-La Roche*').

93 ECJ judgment on *Hoffmann-La Roche*, para 100.

94 81/969/EEC: Commission Decision of 7 October 1981 Relating to a Proceeding under Article 86 of the EEC Treaty (IV.29.491—Bandengroothandel Frieschebrug BV/NV Nederlandsche Banden-Industrie Michelin) [9 December 1981] OJ L 353, paras 37–51 (hereinafter, 'Commission decision on *Michelin I*').

'market-partitioning'.[95] First, the Commission stated that the harm of unfairness was reflected in the operational burdens and bargain disadvantages that the rebates had brought onto Michelin's customers (paras 219–24, 250–3, 263–6). Second, regarding the harm of competition foreclosure, the Commission introduced the concept of 'loyalty-inducing effects' to describe the design and workings of the rebates in question and, on that basis, presumed the transpiring of the foreclosure harm (paras 227–30, 239, 254–8, 267–9). Third, regarding the harm of impeding market integration, the Commission basically just claimed that the rebates in question limited both imports and exports of the French dealers, thereby isolating the French market (paras 242–6). Overall, although the Commission placed the competition foreclosure harm at the centre of its concerns, its theory of that harm was largely presumptive, as it looked mostly at how the rebates, by their purpose and design, had affected Michelin and its customers, instead of analysing how the rebates had actually affected Michelin and its competitors.

The ECJ in **Michelin I** *and the CFI in* **Michelin II***: a presumptive 'all circumstances' analytical framework on loyalty rebates*

The ECJ in *Michelin I* characterized the rebates in question as 'loyalty rebates', which were distinguished from 'quantity rebates' and 'rebates attached with exclusivity obligations'. The ECJ agreed with the Commission about the three harms at stake (limitation of choice, competition foreclosure, and discrimination), and it instructed an 'all circumstances' framework for assessing loyalty rebates:

> [I]t is therefore necessary to consider all the circumstances, particularly the criteria and rules for the grant of the discount, and to investigate whether, in providing an advantage not based on any economic service justifying it, the discount tends to remove or restrict the buyer's freedom to choose his sources of supply, to bar competitors from access to the market, to apply dissimilar conditions to equivalent transactions with other trading parties or to strengthen the dominant position by distorting competition.[96]

To show the first two harms (choice limitation and competition foreclosure) had happened, the ECJ examined the aim, structure, and functioning mechanisms of the rebate scheme in question, as well as the broader circumstances in which the scheme was implemented. It eventually concluded that the rebate scheme had limited 'the dealers' choice of supplier', made 'access to the market more difficult for competitors', and was not 'based on any countervailing advantage which may be economically justified' (paras 76–85). Notably, despite establishing the 'all

95 2002/405/EC: Commission Decision of 20 June 2001 Relating to a Proceeding Pursuant to Article 82 of the EC Treaty (COMP/E-2/36.041/PO—Michelin) [31 May 2002] OJ L 143, paras 218, 226, 240 (hereinafter, 'Commission decision on *Michelin II*').

96 Case 322/81 *NV Nederlandsche Banden Industrie Michelin v Commission of the European Communities* [1983] ECR 3461, para 71–3 (hereinafter, 'ECJ judgment on *Michelin I*').

circumstances' analytical framework, the ECJ's analyses were largely theoretical. This could be attributed to the structural focus it stated in paragraph 70: 'Article 86 covers practices which are likely to affect the structure of a market'. Regarding the third harm (discrimination of customers), the ECJ annulled the Commission's finding of infringement under Article 86(c) because the Commission had failed to prove 'such differences in treatment between different dealers are due to the application of unequal criteria' (para 90).

In *Michelin II*, the CFI fully endorsed the Commission decision. It also confirmed competition foreclosure as the core harm, although it worded the harm in a more market structure-based way as the rigidifying of the dominant position. This allowed the CFI to build a rather presumptive theory of harm without engaging in intensive fact-finding and anticompetitive effects examination.[97] As it reasoned, a rebate scheme would be loyalty-inducing when it had (1) significant variation of discount rates, (2) long reference periods, and (3) a calculation based on total turnover; in turn, this loyalty-inducing scheme would inherently produce competition foreclosure effects when carried out by a dominant firm and should therefore be prohibited (paras 57, 65, 95).

The CFI's presumption was strong. Throughout the judgment, the CFI repeatedly held that a rebate scheme would infringe Article 82 of the EC Treaty if it could not be justified on economic or objective grounds. It was dismissive towards arguments presented by Michelin, claiming that those arguments could not justify the subjectivity of the rebate scheme in question (paras 65, 98, 137, 140, 149, 160). The CFI referred to the 'special responsibility' concept to support this presumptive stance. Specifically, it translated the 'special responsibility' concept to a purpose-based standard for finding abuse: as it stated, 'such behaviour cannot be allowed if its purpose is to strengthen that dominant position and thereby abuse it' (paras 55, 98–100, 217). The CFI also referred to a series of precedents to ground the reasoning that 'establishing the anti-competitive object and the anti-competitive effect are one and the same thing' and suggested that the line between legal and illegal conduct under Article 82 boiled down to whether the purpose of the conduct was to strengthen and abuse the dominant position (paras 239–43).

A potential problem with this presumptive stance is its susceptibility to expansive application and false-positive errors. Admittedly, there are also potential false-negative errors, which would require the CFI to be stringent towards suspected anticompetitive practices. But ultimately, in balancing the two sides, the CFI would need to decide whether the Commission should be encouraged to make judgment calls or the Commission should be tightly controlled in exercising its discretion at least until antitrust theories reach a more solid consensus. It seems the CFI has opted for the former, demonstrating a clearly deferential attitude towards the Commission's reasoning.

97 Case T-203/01 *Manufacture française des pneumatiques Michelin v Commission of the European Communities* [2003] ECR II 4071, paras 209–10, 224 (hereinafter, 'CFI judgment on *Michelin II*').

The ECJ in **Post Danmark II***: a market structure-oriented conception of the foreclosure harm and the unnecessity of the AEC test*

In this preliminary ruling case, the ECJ reiterated that rebates as an abuse generated mainly the harm of competition foreclosure, which was construed as the undermining of a competitive market structure in the case law.[98] Observing that the rebates in question did not contain exclusive-dealing requirements, the ECJ held that instead of applying a *per* se rule, it was necessary to consider all circumstances, particularly, (1) the rebate scheme's structure and (2) the market characteristics. First, the ECJ highlighted two features of the rebate scheme's structure: retroactiveness and standardization. It considered that by being retroactive with a long reference period, the rebate scheme had a disproportionate suction effect on customers, incentivizing them to obtain all or a substantial proportion of their supplies from Post Danmark; meanwhile, being standardized (i.e., non-discriminatory) did not preclude the possibility of a rebate scheme being abusive (paras 22–5, 32–8). Additionally, it considered the wide customer coverage of the rebates, holding this as a relevant factor for determining the quantitative level of exclusionary effects (paras 43–6). Second, concerning the market circumstances, the ECJ highlighted that a very large market share (95%) made Post Danmark an unavoidable trading partner, along with the fact that the market was characterized by high barriers, economies of scale, and Post Danmark's statutory monopoly.

In this 'all circumstances' analytical framework for assessing non-exclusivity rebates, the ECJ considered the as-efficient-competitor test ('AEC test') to be a potentially useful but ultimately unnecessary element. This is because the ECJ viewed the AEC test, which entailed price-cost comparisons, as closely associated with predatory pricing conduct, which caused competitive harms in a different manner from rebate conduct (paras 55–9, 62). This view is debatable, as the application of the AEC test in past predatory pricing cases does not necessarily preclude its usefulness in emerging rebate cases. The ECJ also stated that the AEC had limited use because when a market was dominated, the emergence of an as-efficient competitor would be practically impossible (paras 59–60). This is also questionable, as the ECJ failed to see that the AEC test and, more broadly, the AEC rationale could be adjusted to accommodate the protection of potentially as-efficient competitors.[99]

The ECJ also clarified the likelihood and appreciability of anticompetitive effects. Regarding likelihood, it held that the (potential) effects required for finding abuse should not be purely hypothetical, but it needed not to be concrete either. Regarding appreciability, it stated that there was no need for establishing a threshold of effects for finding abuse because under the structural conception of the foreclosure harm and the concept of 'special responsibility', the finding of dominance was already serving as a threshold of effects (paras 64–6, 70–2).

98 Case C-23/14 *Post Danmark A/S v Konkurrencerådet*, ECLI:EU:C:2015:651, para 13 (hereinafter, 'ECJ ruling on *Post Danmark II*').

99 Yan and Vedder, 'Minimum Efficient Scale, Competition on the Merits, and the Special Responsibility of a Dominant Undertaking', 142–4.

The Commission in Intel*: a presumptive v an as-efficient-competitor approach to assessing the foreclosure harm*

The Commission fined Intel in 2009 for abusing its dominant position in the worldwide market for x86 CPUs for all computers to exclude the only remaining competitor (AMD) in that market through two practices: (1) rebates conditional on original equipment manufacturers ('OEMs') purchasing all or almost all of their x86 CPUs from Intel and (2) 'naked restrictions', meaning payments conditioned on three OEMs postponing or cancelling the launch of AMD CPU-based products and limiting the distribution channels of those products.[100] The core harm that the Commission had in mind was unquestionably the output-foreclosure of competition, which was underpinned by concerns for consumer choice and innovation. Additionally, the Commission also alleged the harm of restricting customers' freedom of choice (paras 924, 1001, 1616).

The Commission adopted a formalistic approach to assessing the foreclosure harm caused by the first practice. It found that the rebates were *de facto* conditional upon the customers purchasing all or most of their x86 CPU requirements from Intel. On that basis, the Commission characterized those rebates as 'fidelity discounts' defined in the case law and stated that such rebates should be *per se* abusive (paras 920, 924–5, 1001). Regarding the second practice, the Commission found that there was a customer demand for AMD products and that Intel's conditional payments to the OEMs were directly responsible for such a demand being unsatisfied. In that light, the Commission stated that customer choice was limited and competition on the merits was inhibited. It stated that those payments constituted 'recourse to methods different from those governing normal competition' and so were abusive (paras 1679–81).

Interestingly, although insisting that the rebate schemes were presumptively abusive, the Commission carried out an extensive AEC test to show that the rebates would still be found abusive with a non-presumptive approach. This as-efficient-competitor analysis eventually became the main point of contention in subsequent appeals to the GC and the ECJ.

The GC in Intel*: a failed attempt to champion the presumptive approach to exclusivity rebates*

The GC heard the case and issued the first-instance judgment in 2014. It upheld the Commission decision. Intel further appealed to the ECJ, which decided in 2017 to refer the case back to the GC for a retrial. The GC issued the retrial judgment in 2022, this time ruling in favour of Intel. The Commission decided to appeal, and now the case is pending a judgment from the ECJ.

100 Commission Decision of 13 May 2009 relating to a proceeding under Article 82 of the EC Treaty and Article 54 of the EEA Agreement (COMP/C-3/37.990—Intel), paras 835–6, 912, 924–5, 1000, 1641–2 (hereinafter, 'Commission decision on *Intel*').

The referred-back 2014 judgment

The GC ruled in favour of the Commission in 2014, but it replaced the Commission's AEC-test-adjacent reasoning with an illegality-presuming theory of harm. First, the GC drew from the case law and distinguished three categories of rebates, assigning to them vastly different analytical routes: (1) *quantity rebates*, which were linked solely to the volume of purchases so should generally be considered benign; (2) *exclusivity rebates*, which were 'conditional on the customer's obtaining all or most of its requirements' from the dominant undertaking and should be considered *per se* abusive because they were by their very nature capable of restricting competition; and (3) *rebates of a third category*, which were 'not directly linked to a condition of exclusive or quasi-exclusive supply' but their granting mechanism may have a fidelity-building effect, so they should be subject to the 'all circumstances' analytical framework.[101] The GC considered the rebates granted by Intel to be exclusivity rebates.

Second, the GC elaborated its reasoning behind the *per se* rule of illegality on exclusivity rebates. To begin with, it highlighted the distinction of contestable and non-contestable shares of demand resulting from the finding of Intel's dominant position and suggested that the 'exclusivity' property of the rebates would create a financial incentive and a threat (to stop supplying the non-contestable share of demand) for the customers to stop trading with the competitors, thereby helping Intel leverage its market power from the non-contestable share of market to the contestable share and foreclose the output of its competitors (paras 91–3). Subsequently, the GC accentuated the special responsibility of a dominant undertaking and the structural conception of the competition foreclosure harm: a dominant position would already be a deterioration of the competitive market structure, so any additional interference by the dominant undertaking with the market structure—such as the granting of inherently anticompetitive exclusivity rebates—would constitute an abuse (paras 88–90, 111, 139).

With this *per se* illegality stance, the GC dismissed the need to consider elements not directly related to the exclusivity of the rebates. For example, it held that there was no need to consider 'the level of the rebates' because even a rebate of a minimum amount would still be capable of foreclosing competition nor the consideration of the extent of foreclosure was necessary because it was not for the dominant undertaking to dictate what degree of competition should exist (paras 108–9, 117, 124). Most importantly, the GC dismissed the need to consider the 'all circumstances' of the case—i.e., the need to prove any actual or potential foreclosure effect—when assessing exclusivity rebates. The GC reasoned that (1) the element of exclusivity made the rebates essentially different from the other categories of abusive pricing practices and (2) according to established case law on rebates,

101 Case T-286/09 *Intel Corp. v European Commission*, ECLI:EU:T:2014:547, paras 75–85 (hereinafter, 'the referred-back GC judgment on *Intel*').

the 'all circumstances' analytical framework was never extended to exclusivity rebates (paras 97–9, 103–4).

Much as the GC's *per se* rule of illegality aligned with the special responsibility of a dominant undertaking and the structural conception of the competition foreclosure harm, it did not fit well with another key concept established in the case law: competition on the merits, which cautions against the protection of less efficient competitors. Consequently, a question arises as to whether the structural conception of the foreclosure harm should be qualified with an 'as-efficient-competitor' threshold, according to which an exclusivity rebate scheme would be abusive only if it had foreclosed as-efficient competitors instead of just any competitors. Intel had incorporated this question into its defence. The Commission addressed this question in a fallback scenario where it excused itself from the legal obligation to perform that test. But the GC denied the applicability of the AEC test to exclusivity rebates altogether, for the same reason it dismissed the need to consider 'all circumstances': the exclusivity element had inherently resulted in the competition foreclosure harm, which the GC conceptualized highly rigidly as occurring 'not only where access to the market is made impossible for competitors' but also where the access 'has been made more difficult' (paras 143–50). In that light, the GC failed to address the aforementioned question, let alone examine the Commission's answer to that question.

The 2022 retrial judgment

The ECJ reviewed the case and referred it back to the GC for a retrial in 2017, precisely because of the aforementioned failure of the GC. In its opinion, the AEC test, despite being declared unnecessary by the Commission, had *de facto* 'played an important role in the Commission's assessment', so it must be substantively reviewed by the GC.[102]

The GC was, therefore, forced to reform its rigid conception of the competition foreclosure harm, so as to equip itself to comprehensively assess the economic evidence at hand and scrutinize whether the Commission had convincingly proven the rebates' anticompetitive effects. After all, the element of exclusivity, coupled with the finding of dominance, might have been a workable proxy for proving anticompetitive effects in the past, but now that more theoretically sound and practically feasible approaches to assessing anticompetitive effects had become available, the GC should, by all means, adapt to fulfil its judicial supervising responsibilities.[103] Eventually, the GC found the Commission had failed to sufficiently prove the foreclosure effects of the rebates.[104]

102 Case C-413/14 P *Intel Corp. v European Commission*, ECLI:EU:C:2017:632, paras 143–6, 149.
103 Yan and Vedder, 'Minimum Efficient Scale, Competition on the Merits, and the Special Responsibility of a Dominant Undertaking', 137.
104 Case T-286/09 RENV *Intel Corp. v European Commission*, ECLI:EU:T:2022:19, paras 167–482.

In a sense, we could say that the initiative taken by the Commission to apply the AEC test in *Intel* had backfired not only on itself but also on the GC: the Commission eventually found itself being held legally accountable for applying that test even though it had intentionally exempted itself from accountability when applying the test; subsequently, because the Commission had taken the initiative to apply the AEC test, the GC could no longer stay in the comfort zone of existing case law and find anticompetitive effects by reiterating the highly structural conception of the foreclosure harm. In retrospect, it may be tempting to conclude that had the Commission not taken the initiative, the case might have gone a different way, but we have to see the larger picture against which the Commission's initiative-taking was somewhat inevitable: economic theories have been evolving and increasingly embedded into antitrust decision-making, so the Commission ought to be worried that going forward, the presumptive and formalistic theories of harm that had worked in past might not work so well for it anymore in passing judicial reviews and gaining public support.

Interim conclusions

A division of labour between the Commission and the CJEU

The allegation of harms

In all the annulment cases, the Commission consistently took the lead in alleging the harms at issue. Only on rare occasions did the Commission refrain from explicitly alleging the harms. Such was the case in *United Brands* (concerning excessive pricing). There, because the Commission did not identify the harm, the ECJ alleged the harm of monopoly exploitation in appeal. In most cases, the CJEU deferred to the Commission's allegations of harm, although it sometimes rephrased and regrouped the harms alleged by the Commission. Only in rare cases did the ECJ disapprove of the Commission's allegations of harm. An example is *Commercial Solvents*, where the ECJ implicitly dismissed discrimination as a competitive harm caused by refusal to deal. In some cases, the Commission's decisions were annulled in subsequent appeals, but its allegations of harm were unchallenged. One example is *General Motors*, where the ECJ annulled the Commission's decision regarding abusive excessive pricing on factual grounds and did not question its theory of harm to parallel imports.

The elaboration of theories

While the Commission took the lead in alleging harms, the CJEU played a main role in elaborating and developing the theories of the alleged harms. This can be described from two aspects.

First, by comparing the annulment and preliminary ruling cases, we can see the preliminary ruling cases showed a high level of consistency in elaborating the competitive harms. For example, the four preliminary ruling cases concerning refusal to deal (*CBEM-Telemarketing, Bronner, IMS Health*, and *Sot Lélos*) contributed greatly to establishing the legal standard for assessing this type of abuse. In *CBEM-Telemarketing*, the ECJ accentuated the presumptively construed harm of competition foreclosure; it began to elaborate the theory of harm in *Bronner* by introducing the benchmark of 'exceptional circumstances' and formulating the three criteria for assessing refusals to supply. The ECJ took one step further in *IMS Health*, where two sub-criteria for determining indispensability were formulated and the two other Bronner criteria were regrouped into three cumulative conditions in the context of IPRs protection. After clearing the obstacles in applying those conditions, the ECJ in *Sot Lélos* moved on to expanding on the criterion of no objective justification.

Second, by comparing the harm analyses of the Commission and the CJEU in annulment cases, we can see that the CJEU has the upper hand when cooperating with the Commission to produce theories of harm in individual cases; there was no routinized deference to the Commission. This is discussed in the following subsections about the different types of harms.

The harm to market integration

The harm to market integration is the most identifiable, simply by looking for the references to the Common Market and the concerns for cross–Member State trade in individual cases. This harm was expressly alleged in several cases: *Continental Can, Suiker Unie, General Motors, United Brands*, and *Michelin II*. All of these cases were from the 1970s except *Michelin II*. In these cases, it was always the Commission that initially alleged the harm. The CJEU processed the harm allegations in three alternative ways. The first one is upholding the Commission's allegation by referring to the Treaty provision that is now Art 102 TFEU or providing more elaborate reasoning. *Suiker Unie* (restriction of resale) was a case of the former option, whereas *Suiker Unie* (loyalty rebates) and *General Motors* were examples of the latter. *United Brands* (restriction of resale and refusal to supply) was an example of both. The second way is upholding the Commission's allegation and adding new harm allegations. Such was the case in *United Brands* (discriminatory pricing), which is left out of this chapter. The third way is accepting the Commission's allegation but shifting the focus from the harm to market integration to the harm of structural competition restriction. Such was the case in *Continental Can.*

The harm of structural competition foreclosure

Competition foreclosure is another repeatedly alleged harm. It is also the most consistently developed harm conception. This is easily understandable: most abuse of dominance cases pertain to exclusionary abuses, which inevitably raise foreclosure concerns. So the more interesting issue is not whether this harm is alleged but how it is construed. As shown throughout this chapter, the competition foreclosure harm has been construed in a highly market structure-oriented fashion from the start. The structural conception of the harm has made it easy to accommodate the concern for market integration, leading to the eventuality that the harm to integration and the harm of competition foreclosure become extremely blurry.

Underlying the structural conception of the foreclosure harm is a special institutional dynamic: the CJEU took the centre stage by assuming its upper-hand role in elaborating this harm, whereas the Commission took a back seat with its role in alleging this harm. This can be explained from three aspects. First, some of the cases alleging the foreclosure harm are preliminary ruling proceedings in which the Commission played no direct part. Second, in the early enforcement cases, the Commission tended to merely imply the harm of competition foreclosure without explaining its understanding of this harm. For example, the Commission in *Continental Can* stashed its concern for competition foreclosure underneath the allegation of user-choice restriction, and it was the ECJ that highlighted the foreclosure harm from a structural view. In *Commercial Solvents*, the Commission expressed the concern for the maintenance of effective conditions of competition in the Common Market, which suggested both the integration harm and the foreclosure harm, and it was the ECJ that accentuated the foreclosure harm. In *Hoffmann-La Roche*, the Commission's clarification of the foreclosure harm was simply the observation that the loyalty rebates induced exclusivity; it was left to the ECJ to clarify the foreclosure harm in light of primary- and secondary-line injuries. Third, the Commission began elaborating its understanding of the foreclosure harm in *Michelin I*, but that elaboration was just a refined reiteration of the ECJ's structural conception of the foreclosure harm in *Hoffmann-La Roche*. The same is true in *AKZO, Magill, Michelin II, Microsoft, DSD, Deutsche Telekom, AstraZeneca*, and *Intel*, in which the Commission deferentially referred to previous case law and briefly reiterated the structural conception of foreclosure harm.

Supplementary harms

Some of the cases analysed in this chapter referred to the enumerated abuse examples in the Treaty provision that is now Article 102 TFEU, second paragraph (a) to (d). But these examples are worded in such an open-ended way that the harms they can accommodate are neither exhaustive nor mutually exclusive. As a result, directly referring to these examples serves somewhat as a leeway for the Commission and the CJEU to find abuse without unequivocally identifying and substantiating the competitive harms at hand. It is, therefore, likely that when Article 102(a), (b), and (c) were referred to in the following cases, other types of harm were alleged.

Article 102(a)

One case referred to Art 102(a): *DSD*. There, the Commission alleged the harm of monopoly exploitation in the form of imposing unfair prices and trading conditions. The CFI and the ECJ fully supported this harm allegation in the subsequent appeals.

Article 102(b)

Many allegations were made by referring to Article 102(b), which addresses the limitation of 'production, markets or technical development to the prejudice of consumers'. Cases making such references include the following: *Continental Can, Commercial Solvents, Suiker Unie* (restriction of resale and loyalty rebates), *United Brands* (refusal to supply), *Magill*, and *Microsoft* (refusal to supply). It is not entirely clear what harms underpin Article 102(b), thus giving the CJEU the upper hand in the cooperative process (with the Commission) for developing theories of harm. After all, the CJEU holds the ultimate authority in interpreting a Treaty provision.

First, in some cases, the reference to Article 102(b) was a way to elaborate on the harm of structural competition foreclosure and the supplementary harm of restriction on freedom of choice. For example, in *Continental Can*, the Commission brought up the restriction on freedom of choice with the underlying concern for competition restriction; in the appeal judgment (para 26), the ECJ linked the restriction of freedom to the indirect undermining of competitive market structure through Article 86(b). In *Commercial Solvents*, the Commission alleged product limitation by implicitly quoting Article 86(b); in appeal (para 25), the ECJ adjusted the Commission allegation towards structural competition foreclosure.

Second, in some other cases, the reference to Article 102(b) was associated with the harm to integration. For example, in *Suiker Unie*, while the Commission clearly considered the protection of integration but provided little reasoning, the ECJ cited Article 86(b) to back up the concern for the Common Market (paras 398, 526). In *United Brands* (refusal to supply), after the Commission brought up the concern for freedom of choice with a mere statement, the ECJ used Article 86(b) to build that concern towards market integration (para 183).

Third, there were also the cases of *Magill* and *Microsoft* (refusal to supply). In *Magill*, the Commission quoted Article 86(b) for the literal interpretation of 'product limitation' as an additional source of harm of the refusal to license in question; in *Microsoft*, the Commission invoked Article 86(b) to support its concern for consumer welfare. These two references were fully endorsed by the ECJ and CFI, respectively.

Article 102(c)

References were also frequently made to Article 102(c) to allege the harm of customer discrimination, possibly underpinned by the harm of downstream competition distortion. The following cases made such references: *Commercial Solvents, Suiker Unie* (loyalty rebates), *United Brands* (refusal to supply), *BP, Hoffmann-La Roche, Michelin I,* and *Michelin II.* A close look at the theories of harm in these cases would suggest once again a set of institutional dynamics where the CJEU had the upper hand: the Commission showed a habit of superficially referring to Article 102(c) to support its allegation of discrimination as a type of harm, but the CJEU tended to be cautious about validating this.

The CJEU's caution was first demonstrated in *Commercial Solvents*. There, although the Commission did not allege the harm of discrimination, the AG proposed the harm of discrimination by referring to Article 86(c); nonetheless, that proposition was set aside by the ECJ. In *Suiker Unie*, the Commission began to allege the harm of discrimination without any analysis; the ECJ placed that harm under Article 86(c) but only as a supplementary concern (para 523).

In subsequent cases including *BP, Hoffmann-La Roche, Michelin I*, and *Michelin II*, the Commission continued invoking Article 86(c) and perceived discrimination as harmful at face value, while sidestepping how the discrimination had resulted in competition distortion in secondary-line markets.

The CJEU was consistently cautious. In *BP*, the ECJ annulled the Commission decision on the grounds that there was no abuse found. In *Hoffmann-La Roche*, the ECJ recognized discrimination as harmful under Article 86 but downplayed it as a concern supplementary to competition foreclosure (para 80). In that sense, the ECJ picked up the issue of 'secondary-line competition distortion' when the Commission had sidestepped it. Along the line, the ECJ annulled the Commission's finding of discrimination under Article 86(c) in *Michelin I* (para 90). In *Michelin II*, the CFI excluded the examination on discrimination altogether; instead, it advanced 'unfairness' as a supplementary concern to the concern for market integration (paras 141, 147).

Reference list

Behrens, Peter. 'The Ordoliberal Concept of "Abuse" of a Dominant Position and Its Impact on Article 102 TFEU'. *SSRN Scholarly Paper*. Rochester, NY: Social Science Research Network, 9 September 2015. https://papers.ssrn.com/abstract=2658045.

Bergh, Roger van den, Peter D. Camesasca, and Andrea Giannaccari. *Comparative Competition Law and Economics*. Cheltenham: Edward Elgar Publishing, 2017.

Cini, Michelle, and Lee McGowan. *Competition Policy in the European Union*. 2nd ed. Palgrave Macmillan, 2009.

Dunne, Niamh. 'Dispensing with Indispensability'. *Journal of Competition Law & Economics* 16, no. 1 (30 April 2020): 74–115. https://doi.org/10.1093/joclec/nhaa004.

Dunne, Niamh. 'Fairness and the Challenge of Making Markets Work Better'. *The Modern Law Review* 84, no. 2 (March 2021): 230–64. https://doi.org/10.1111/1468-2230.12579.

Ehlermann, Claus-Dieter. 'The Contribution of EC Competition Policy to the Single Market'. *Common Market Law Review* 29, no. 2 (1992): 257–82.

Gerber, David. *Law and Competition in Twentieth-Century Europe: Protecting Prometheus*. Oxford: Oxford University Press, 2001.

Hawk, Barry E. 'Antitrust in the EEC—The First Decade'. *Fordham Law Review* 41, no. 2 (1972): 229–92.

Heide-Jorgensen, Caroline. 'The Relationship between Article 101(1) TFEU and Article 101(3) TFEU'. In *Aims and Values in Competition Law*, edited by Caroline Heide-Jorgensen, Christian Bergqvist, Ulla Neergaard, and Sune Troels Poulsen, 91–114. Copenhagen: DJØF Publishing, 2013.

Ibáñez Colomo, Pablo. 'The Law on Abuses of Dominance and the System of Judicial Remedies'. *Yearbook of European Law* 32, no. 1 (1 January 2013): 389–431.

Koopmans, T. 'The Role of Law in the Next Stage of European Integration'. *International and Comparative Law Quarterly* 35, no. 4 (1986): 925–31.

Korah, Valentine. 'From Legal Form toward Economic Efficiency—Article 85(1) of the EEC Treaty in Contrast to U.S. Antitrust'. *Antitrust Bulletin* 35 (1990): 1009–36.
McGowan, Lee. *The Antitrust Revolution in Europe: Exploring the European Commission's Cartel Policy*. Cheltenham: Edward Elgar, 2010.
Motta, Massimo. *Competition Policy: Theory and Practice*. Cambridge: Cambridge University Press, 2004.
Nazzini, Renato. *The Foundations of European Union Competition Law: The Objective and Principles of Article 102*. Oxford: Oxford University Press, 2011.
Pérez, Sigfrido M. Ramírez, and Sebastian van de Scheur. 'The Evolution of the Law on Articles 85 and 86 EEC [Articles 101 and 102 TFEU]'. In *The Historical Foundations of EU Competition Law*, edited by Kiran Klaus Patel and Heike Schweitzer, 19–53. Oxford: Oxford University Press, 2013.
Posner, Richard A. *Antitrust Law*. 2nd ed. Chicago: University of Chicago Press, 2001.
Reich, Norbert, Annette Nordhausen Scholes, and Jeremy Scholes. *Understanding EU Internal Market Law*. 3rd ed. Cambridge: Intersentia, 2015.
Samkalden, I., and I. E. Druker. 'Legal Problems Relating to Article 86 of the Rome Treaty'. *Common Market Law Review* 3, no. 2 (1966): 158–83.
Wesseling, Rein. *The Modernisation of EC Antitrust Law*. Oxford: Hart Publishing, 2000.
Witt, Anne C. *The More Economic Approach to EU Antitrust Law*. Hart Studies in Competition Law, vol. 14. Oxford: Hart Publishing, 2016.
Yan, Xingyu, and Huaiwen He. 'Fine-Tuning the *Ex Ante* Approach to Regulating Data Combination Practices'. *Journal of Competition Law & Economics* 18, no. 4 (26 December 2022): 881–904. https://doi.org/10.1093/joclec/nhac005.
Yan, Xingyu, and Hans Vedder. 'Minimum Efficient Scale, Competition on the Merits, and the Special Responsibility of a Dominant Undertaking'. *Journal of Competition Law & Economics* 19, no. 1 (13 March 2023): 123–45. https://doi.org/10.1093/joclec/nhac012.

7 Development of theories of harm in the federated Chinese regime

The selection of cases

As discussed in Chapter 5, since the AML public enforcement agencies are largely free from judicial supervision, the enforcement agencies and the courts compete to a certain extent with each other in applying the AML. This chapter looks at how this competition has impacted the development of theories of harm under the AML. To that end, it selects cases from both the public and the private enforcement track and then critically describes the allegations of harms and elaboration of theories in these cases, with a focus on their internal logical consistency and the degree to which they make economic sense.

The cases are selected on the basis of three criteria: (1) whether a case decision or judgment is officially published or at least publicly accessible online, (2) whether its substance concerns abuse of dominance (Chapter 3 of the AML), and (3) whether it engages in substantive analyses and legal reasoning from which a theory of harm could be extracted. According to the third criterion, enforcement decisions that did not result in a finding of unlawful conduct (e.g., decisions that suspend or terminate investigations) are excluded, and court rulings that did not substantively review conduct illegality (e.g., adjudication decisions as opposed to judgments, and judgments that concluded on purely procedural or factual grounds) are also excluded.

I found 85 cases meeting these criteria by 31 December 2023 (see Appendix 2). They consist of 23 court-decided cases (all being civil-litigation cases) and 62 public-enforcement cases (including two NDRC cases, 21 SAIC cases, and 39 SAMR cases). These cases are analysed and grouped according to the abuse types they pertain to in the following sections. Three points should be noted before moving on to the next section. First, most of the cases contained two or more abuse offences, so these cases appear more than once in the following sections. Second, not all cases are individually analysed, due to this chapter's limited length and the fact that some cases add only marginal value to the theories of harm that this chapter focuses on. Third, there is no officially fixed pagination or paragraph numbering in the agency decisions and court judgments, so footnotes to these decisions and judgments are generally omitted; when necessary, the original sentences of the judgments will be quoted in the footnotes.

DOI: 10.4324/9781003479437-7

Defining relevant markets and finding dominance

The AML adopts the same two-tier analytical paradigm as Article 102 TFEU for assessing unilateral conduct that restricts competition: first defining the relevant markets and finding a dominant position, then examining the alleged abuses. Market definition and dominance finding is a prerequisite, even though it does not directly concern the development of theories of harm. The case record shows that the AML public enforcement agencies have generally approached market definition and dominance finding in a rather structured (albeit sometimes reductive) way, while the courts' approaches have been less consistent in comparison. In that light, this section spotlights two private enforcement cases: *Qihoo v Tencent* and *Yang Zhiyong v China Telecom*. They offer interesting insights on how the courts operationalized the AML in the early years.

The Guangdong High Court in **Qihoo v Tencent***: questionable application of the SSNIP test and an overly broad relevant market*

Qihoo v Tencent is the first AML case that reached the Supreme People's Court and the first AML case concerning digital platform markets. The dispute was between Qihoo, a security software provider, and Tencent, a conglomerate offering various Internet-related products. Qihoo accused Tencent of abusing its dominant position in the instant messaging ('IM') software market to exclude Qihoo in the security software market through a 'choose one from the two' requirement imposed on Tencent's IM users. There was an interesting background to this case: Tencent offered the popular IM product QQ, and it found in 2010 that Qihoo was offering computer users a security software product (QQ Bodyguard) that was targeting QQ and nudging users to disable QQ plug-ins. Tencent responded to the Qihoo software by changing QQ's coding and making QQ's software incompatible with Qihoo's security software on users' computers, thereby forcing users to choose between QQ and Qihoo's software. This incompatibility standoff lasted only one day before the sector regulator, the Ministry of Industry and Information Technology, called it off. Soon after, Qihoo filed an AML civil suit against Tencent. The High Court of Guangdong Province heard the case and issued the first-instance judgment in 2011, ruling in complete favour of Tencent. Qihoo appealed to the Supreme Court, which issued the final judgment in 2014, upholding the conclusion of the first instance judgment and most of the legal reasoning. The two judgments were both focused on defining the relevant IM market and examining whether Tencent's QQ had a dominant position; they never got to the abuse assessment part because neither court found dominance.

Defining the IM market at issue necessitated examining the substitutability of QQ with several other functionally adjacent products and services. To that end, the Guangdong High Court held that the SSNIP (small but significant non-transitory increase in price) test should be applied. In doing so, it dismissed Qihoo's argument that because IM products were normally free, the market competition lay not in price but in product quality, and therefore, the examination of product substitutability should follow the SSNDQ (small but significant non-transitory decrease in quality) test. However, the Court did not expand on the SSNIP test's applicability and the SSNDQ test's inapplicability nor did it explain how it intended to apply the SSNIP test against the fact that consumers usually paid zero monetary price to use IM products. After all, it would be difficult to implement a certain percent price increase when the baseline was zero, not to mention that an increase of service fee from zero to a positive figure might no longer be a 'small' increase to consumers. In that light, the Court's decision to apply the SSNIP test was apparently disputable.

Subsequently, the Court evaluated the demand-side substitutability of QQ with several products including (1) simplex IM products that offer only textual, audio, or visual communication service; (2) social network sites; (3) traditional communication products such as telephones and faxes; and (4) email products. It found the first two groups of products to be substitutes, mainly on the basis that they were all free. It also considered the supply-side substitutability of QQ with other internet service providers, including the plaintiff Qihoo. In that regard, the Court never drew a definitive conclusion, although it hinted at the existence of supply-side substitutability by highlighting the two-sidedness of platform markets: as it stated, although different platform operators might have different specialties to attract users, they could be engaging in the same competition of attracting advertisers and selling value-added services. This statement made sense, but it inadvertently displayed the Court's bias and selectivity in considering the two-sidedness of the IM market: on the one hand, the Court underscored the two-sidedness to find supply-side substitutability; but on the other hand, it disregarded the two-sidedness when assessing demand-side substitutability, as it failed to realize that advertisers and content providers were also customers to QQ and that their ability to switch mattered just as much as that of consumer users. Eventually, the High Court's definition of the relevant product was questionably broad. Its geographic market definition was unreasonable broad, too, as it defined the relevant geographic market as a global one, overlooking the high regulatory barriers that the Chinese government had raised in the consumer-internet sector against foreign companies. In this broadly defined relevant market, the Court unsurprisingly found no dominant position held by Tencent.

One could speculate that the Guangdong High Court's flawed judgment was likely motivated by local protectionism: at the time, Tencent was Guangdong Province's rising champion in the national digital platform sector; a judgment at the 'home turf' finding Tencent to be dominant in the IM market would likely have far-reaching negative legal implications for the company, so the Court tried to throw the case out as early stage as possible, even if that meant delivering a poorly reasoned judgment. This was unfortunate because had the Court adopted a more solid approach to defining the relevant market and finding dominance, Tencent's conduct would most likely have been exonerated at the abuse-assessment stage anyway for generating no anticompetitive effects.

The Supreme Court in* Qihoo v Tencent*: establishing the applicability of the SSNDQ test and the possibility to bypass market definition

In appeal, the Supreme Court continued the focus on market definition and dominance finding. It overruled a few aspects of the Guangdong High Court's market definition, such as the adoption of the SSNIP test and the geographic market definition, but it upheld the conclusion of no dominance.

First, the Supreme Court disapproved the High Court's application of the SSNIP test, holding that the SSNIP test was difficult to apply in cases where product differentiation was significant and undertakings competed intensively in non-price aspects. It observed that digital service providers usually adopted two-sided business models where they used revenues from the value-added services and advertisements to sustain the free services offered to consumers; it also observed that consumers were highly sensitive to price changes, in the sense that cancelling the free offering could result in significant user loss and jeopardize the whole two-sided business model. So it adopted the SSNDQ test instead and suggested that in this case, the test would have to be carried out in a qualitative manner because quantitative data was not available. The Supreme Court's SSNDQ analysis was rough, but it did break the ground for subsequent antitrust enforcement in digital markets. For instance, in 2020, the Shanghai AMR made the *Sherpa's* decision, in which it defined the relevant market—a regional online food ordering and delivery platform market—through a more quantitative and empirically robust use of the SSNIP and SSNDQ tests.

Second, the Supreme Court took a more nuanced look at the substitutability of the various groups of products with QQ. For example, it added the comparison of QQ with mobile IM apps with a view towards dynamic competition in the foreseeable future; also, regarding supply-side substitutability, the Supreme Court did not outright reject the High Court's reasoning, but it showed more caution by suggesting that empirical research was needed to draw a definitive conclusion.[1] Eventually, the Supreme Court defined a relevant product that was slightly narrower than the High Courts. It also narrowed the geographic market to the Chinese mainland. However, the Supreme Court did not question the High Court's dominance assessment, therefore leaving the biased and selective consideration of the two-sidedness of the market uncorrected.

Third, in light of the general difficulty of defining two-sided platform markets, the Supreme Court made the interesting ruling that a clearly defined market was not always necessary for assessing an abuse of dominance. It reasoned that defining the relevant markets was not an end in itself but rather a means to the goal of assessing the competitive effects of abuse conduct. The Supreme Court further suggested that when a relevant market could not be clearly defined, a court or agency could resort

1 The Supreme People's Court, *Qihoo v Tencent (appeal)* (中华人民共和国最高人民法院民事判决书[2013]民三终字第4号) ('其关键问题在于，网络平台之间为争夺用户注意力和广告主的相互竞争是否完全跨越了由产品或者服务特点所决定的界限，并给经营者施加了足够强大的竞争约束').

to 'direct evidence of competition elimination or impediment' to assess the market position of an undertaking and the competitive effects of the conduct. But it did not specify what would constitute such 'direct evidence'. This ruling corresponds to the one made by the ECJ in *United Brands*, where it stated that to find dominance, 'it may be advisable to take account if need be of the facts put forward as acts amounting to abuses without necessarily having to acknowledge that they are abuses'.[2] This ruling by the Supreme Court has proven to be impactful and controversial: in 2021, the SAMR published a draft Guidelines for Anti-Monopoly in the Field of Platform Economy, which contained a provision that embodied this ruling. But this provision was taken out in the adopted version of the Guidelines, possibly due to strong objections from the industry. It, therefore, remains to be seen how, if at all, this ruling would be upheld in future antitrust enforcement.

The Shanghai High Court in Yang Zhiyong v China Telecom*: assessing abuse without finding dominance*

In this case, Yang Zhiyong accused China Telecom of abusing its dominance through excessive pricing and imposing unreasonable trading conditions. The Shanghai High Court reviewed the case in appeal and issued the final judgment in 2015. It started by holding that the plaintiffs in AML civil suits assumed the burden of proving three aspects of facts: the defendant's dominant position, the existence of abusive conduct, and the anticompetitive effects resulting from that conduct. On that basis, the Court spent the remainder of the judgment to examine the third aspect, and it eventually ruled against the plaintiff on the grounds of insufficient evidence.

The most interesting part is that the Court approached the disputed conduct without examining whether the defendant had a dominant position, despite itself acknowledging the importance of finding dominance. This contradicted the Supreme Court's explicit holding in *Qihoo v Tencent* that finding dominance was a prerequisite for assessing the anticompetitiveness of conduct.[3] Arguably, in the event that the plaintiff could not meet the standard of proving the defendant's dominance, the Shanghai High Court should have dismissed the action or it should have exercised its inquisitional power to conduct the dominance assessment as the Supreme Court had done in *Qihoo v Tencent*.

Excessive pricing

Article 22(1)–(7) of the AML provides a non-exhaustive list of the prohibited types of abuse conduct, and the first type is excessive pricing, including unfairly high

2 Case 27/76 *United Brands Company and United Brands Continentaal BV v Commission of the European Communities* [1978] ECR 207, para 68.

3 The Supreme Court judgment on *Qihoo v Tencent* ('原则上，如果被诉经营者不具有市场支配地位，则无需对其是否滥用市场支配地位进行分析，可以直接认定其不构成反垄断法所禁止的滥用市场支配地位行为。不过，在相关市场边界较为模糊、被诉经营者是否具有市场支配地位不甚明确时，可以进一步分析被诉垄断行为对竞争的影响效果，以检验关于其是否具有市场支配地位的结论正确与否。').

prices offered by sellers and unfairly low prices offered by buyers. As this section shows, excessive pricing cases tend to take place either in public utilities (e.g., water and gas supplies) or markets where an undertaking had exclusive control over a product (e.g., intellectual property and pharmaceutical input).

The NDRC in Qualcomm

In the tripartite era, the NDRC was in charge of tackling price-related monopolistic conduct, so before 2018, only the NDRC had made public enforcement cases concerning excessive pricing. The first case is the 2015 *Qualcomm* case, in which the NDRC fined Qualcomm for abusing its dominance in the relevant markets through three types of practices: excessive pricing, tying, and imposing unreasonable trading conditions. *Qualcomm* is the first AML case involving intellectual property rights, and it resulted in the largest amount of fines in the tripartite era. The excessive pricing conduct by Qualcomm consisted of two aspects: (1) charging licensing fees for expired Standard Essential Patents ('SEPs') and (2) obliging certain licensees to grant reversely non-essential licenses or to grant licenses for free and prohibiting certain licensees from legally challenging Qualcomm's licenses.

The NDRC identified the primary harm to be monopolistic exploitation. Regarding the first aspect of the conduct, the NDRC held that it was unreasonable for Qualcomm to apply the same licensing fee standard without providing a list of the patents included in that package when there were constantly new patents entering and expired patents exiting the patent package; in this way, Qualcomm obscured the contract object to charge for expired patents. Regarding the second aspect, the NDRC held that those obligations were also unreasonable because they did not consider or compensate the values of those licensees' patents. Additionally, the NDRC alleged the harms of innovation inhibition and competition restriction, but it did not expand on them. As it stated briefly, the reverse-licensing obligation inhibited the innovation incentives of Qualcomm's licensees; that obligation also brought Qualcomm undue competitive advantages over other baseband chipset producers, therefore impairing competition in that market.

The second case is the *Zhejiang Second Pharmaceutical & Tianjin Handewei Pharmaceutical* case in 2017. The NDRC accused the two undertakings of abusing their collective dominant position in the isoniazid ingredient supply market through excessive pricing and refusal to deal. Regarding excessive pricing, the NDRC's reasoning was extremely brief: it found excessive pricing after describing the significant price increases and demonstrating their non-justifiability.

The SAMR and provincial AMRs

After consolidating the public enforcement powers in 2018 and before the end of 2023, the SAMR, along with the provincial AMRs it delegated, had produced nine cases involving excessive pricing. It is clear from the case record that the SAMR tends to take on excessive pricing cases in circumstances where a monopoly is inevitable. Most of the cases concern excessive pricing on irreplaceable pharmaceutical products. There are only two non-pharmaceutical-related cases: *Yixing Ganghua Gas* and *Tongfang CNKI*, in which the market structures were monopoly-prone due to regulatory barriers and network effects, respectively. The cases are listed in Table 7.1.

The SAMR and the provincial agencies applied a consistent theory of harm in these cases. First, it demonstrated the unfairness of the price in question by comparing the increase rate of a price with (1) the increase rate of the cost of producing the relevant product and (2), if any, the increase rates of the prices that competitors charged for the same product. Second, in some cases, the SAMR looked additionally at the case circumstances for measures that had helped implement the excessive pricing, e.g., deliberately downgrading the product/service quality to make the trading parties pay more (*Tongfang CNKI*), dividing labour between the collectively dominant firms to bypass regulatory price-control mechanisms and masquerade the price increase as production cost increase (*Shandong Kanghui Pharmaceutical, Shangyao First Pharmaceuticals & Wuhan Huihai Pharmaceutical*). Third, it summarized the harms caused by excessive pricing conduct as the distortion of the market-price mechanism and the reduction of consumer welfare.

In one case where the dominant firm was vertically integrated (*Northeast Pharmaceutical*), the handling agency also identified the harm of *downstream competition distortion* resulting from the firm's excessive prices charged to downstream competitors. It is debatable whether the handling AIC was right to lump this harm

Table 7.1 Excessive pricing cases of the SAMR and AMRs by 31 December 2023

Year	*Case name*	*Relevant product*	*Handling agency*
2019	*Hunan Er'kang & Henan Jiushi*	Chlorphenamine ingredient supply	The SAMR
2020	*Shandong Kanghui Pharmaceutical*	Calcium gluconate ingredient supply	The SAMR
2021	*Shangqiu Xinxianfeng Pharmaceutical*	Phenol ingredient supply	The AMR of Henan Province
2021	*Yixing Ganghua Gas*	Pipeline natural gas supply	The AMR of Jiangsu Province
2021	*Nanjiing Ningwei Pharmaceutical*	Pralidoxime chloride ingredient supply	The AMR of Shanghai Municipality
2022	*Tongfang CNKI*	Chinese academic literature online database service	The SAMR
2023	*Shangyao First Pharmaceuticals & Wuhan Huihai Pharmaceutical*	The supply of injectable polymyxin B sulphate	The AMR of Shanghai Municipality
2023	*Tianjin Jinyao Pharmaceutical*	The supply of injectable carmustine	The AMR of Tianjin Municipality
2023	*Northeast Pharmaceutical*	L-carnitine ingredient supply	The AMR of Liaoning Province

onto the excessive pricing conduct or it should have identified a separate abuse (i.e., margin squeeze or discriminatory treatment). Arguably, there could only be one of the two harms: the foreclosure of competition in the downstream drug manufacturing market or the exploitation of downstream drug manufacturers. After all, based on the single monopoly profit theorem, a monopolist would have no incentive to exclude a downstream undertaking when it wielded the power to price excessively since that would mean a loss of extractable monopoly rent. In that light, the theory of harm in this case was underdeveloped.

Regional courts and the Supreme Court

The Chinese judicial system has produced five AML civil cases involving excessive pricing by the end of 2023. They are listed in Table 7.2.

None of the courts in the first four cases found abuse in the form of excessive pricing. In *Damingxing v CAVCA*, the Kunming Intermediary Court held that the CAVCA (China Audio-Video Copyright Association) had a statutory monopoly in licensing audio-visual copyrights. To determine whether the CAVCA had abused its monopolistic position by charging excessive licensing fees, the Court proposed

Table 7.2 Court cases concerning excessive pricing by 31 December 2023

Year	*Case name*	*Relevant product*	*Adjudicating court*	*Conclusion*
2019	*Damingxing v CAVCA*	Audio-visual copyright licensing for karaoke television use	Yunnan Kunming Intermediary Court (first instance)	No abuse
2019	*Wu Zongqu v Yongfu Water Supply*	Municipal public water supply	Guangxi Nanning Intermediary Court (first instance)	No abuse
2020	*Haoyunlai v Xinzhonggang*	Pipeline steam supply	Zhejiang Ningbo Intermediary Court (first instance)	No abuse
2022	*Wang v Beijing Lianjia*	Real estate brokerage service	Beijing Intellectual Property Court (first instance); the Supreme Court (appeal)	No abuse
2023	*Yangmou v Hefei Yimou*	Desloratadine citrate disodium ingredient supply	Jiangsu Nanjing Intermediary Court (first instance); the Supreme Court (appeal)	Found abuse in first instance but reversed in appeal

to look at (1) whether the fees were devised in accordance with relevant regulations, (2) whether the adjustments of the fees were within a reasonable range, and (3) whether the fees in question had harmed the interests of the counterparty and consumers. Along the line, it found the disputed fees to be reasonable in the circumstances. In *Wu Zongqu v Yongfu Water Supply*, the Nanning Intermediary Court found the defendant to have abused its dominant position by tying water supply with water supply equipment and construction, but it did not find abusive excessive pricing because the disputed prices concerned the tied products, on which the defendant had no dominant position. In *Haoyunlai v Xinzhonggang*, the defendant was monopolistic as a public utility company, but the Ningbo Intermediary Court found the disputed price to be reasonable after comparing the prices of the defendant and two similar companies in other areas and considering the relatively high quality (i.e., greenness) of the defendant's product. In *Wang v Beijing Lianjia*, the first-instance and appeal courts consistently held that the plaintiff had failed to prove the excessiveness of the charged brokerage fees on the one hand and the fees could be potentially justified by the superiority of the brokerage service on the other.

In the first-instance judgment of *Yangmou v Hefei Yimou*, the Nanjing Intermediary Court ruled that the defendant had abused its dominance by excessively charging the plaintiff for the patented ingredient at issue. This ruling was based on two grounds: (1) the prices charged to the plaintiff were too high compared to the production costs and historically charged prices, and (2) the excessive prices had caused competition restriction effects in the downstream market where the plaintiff was a competitor of the defendant. But this ruling was quashed by the Supreme Court in appeal.

The Supreme Court in *Yangmou v Hefei Yimou* took a more nuanced look at the allegedly excessive prices from two aspects: (1) the prices' excessiveness and justifiability and (2) the prices' effects on competition and welfare. First, it examined whether the prices were indeed excessive and whether they were justifiable. To that end, it relied on the more lenient 'internal rate of return' criterion to assess the alleged excessiveness, rather than simply examining the amount of profits and comparing prices charged at different times; this criterion ultimately made the high prices more justifiable. The reason for adopting the criterion was because the Supreme Court found it necessary to give more room of profitability for companies that had been sinking heavy costs in R&D and had been granted pharmaceutical patents. In other words, the Supreme Court sought to balance between monopoly rent extraction and the legitimate exploitation of exclusive patents. Along the line, the Supreme Court also found that what the plaintiff paid to the defendant for the ingredient product constituted only 4% of the plaintiff's output selling price, suggesting that the figure was relatively small compared to how crucial the defendant's product was to the plaintiff's production. Admittedly, it found the defendant's price increase to be disproportionately significant compared to the cost increase, but it considered the defendant's excuse—the original price was set rather low for market-promotion purposes—to be a valid explanation.

Second, the Supreme Court examined the disputed prices' effects on competition and consumer welfare. Regarding the effects on competition, it referred to the concept of margin squeeze to explain that the defendant could have the incentive to exclude the plaintiff as a competitor in the downstream market by raising the plaintiff's production costs. Nevertheless, it found no concrete evidence suggesting that the plaintiff was being pushed out; instead, it found that the plaintiff's annual turnover and market share had been steadily rising. The Supreme Court acknowledged the hypothetical and counterfactual scenario where the plaintiff could have been even more successful if the input costs had been lower, but it found no evidence indicative of this hypothesis. With this reasoning, the Supreme Court conceptualized excessing price conduct as capable of causing the harm of downstream competition foreclosure. But this was done questionably, as the Supreme Court might have conflated two separate types of abuses: excessive pricing and margin squeeze. Regarding the effects on consumer welfare, the Supreme Court stressed that the price of the plaintiff's pharmaceutical product had not risen but had instead decreased over the years, suggesting that the disputed price increase had not negatively affected end consumers. Eventually, the Supreme Court found no abuse in the form of excessive pricing.

Tying and the imposition of unreasonable trading conditions

Tying and the imposition of unreasonable trading conditions are two types of abuse described in Article 22(5) of the 2022 amended AML (formerly Article 17(5) AML). In practice, these two types of abuse have been found capable of generating both exploitative harms towards consumers and exclusionary harms towards competitors, particularly when they were carried out by natural monopolists.

Notably, Article 22(4) identifies 'without justifiable reasons, requiring trading counterparties to deal exclusively with undertakings designated by the dominant undertaking' as an independent type of abuse, but a closer look at the provision and its application in practice would reveal that this is essentially a different description of the tying abuse: when a dominant firm designates the counterparty to trade with another firm, the traded product must be a complement to the dominant firm's product; it would not make sense for the dominant firm to require customers to trade with a firm supplying a substitute because that firm would essentially be a competitor. So this subsection also includes cases that invoked Article 22(4). Overall, tying as a type of abuse has the largest number of cases among all the abuse types listed in the AML.

The NDRC in **Qualcomm**

In *Qualcomm*, the NDRC found that besides excessive pricing, Qualcomm had committed two other abuses: (1) tying its SEPs with non-essential patents and (2) imposing unfair trading conditions in the sales of baseband chipsets.

The NDRC's reasoning on the tying conduct was brief, but it adhered to the four commonly established conditions for finding abusive tying: (1) whether there were two separate markets, (2) whether the undertaking had a dominant position in one of these markets, (3) whether the customers had no choice but to buy the tied product, and (4) whether this resulted in anticompetitive effects in the tied market. The NDRC implicitly identified the harm to be competition foreclosure, and it used 'limitation of customer choice' as a basis for presuming this harm had transpired, without engaging in a fact-intensive verification in light of the circumstances. As it stated, because non-essential patents were tied to SEPs, rational-thinking licensees would lose the incentive to spend additional costs to seek alternative patents in their product designs. Therefore, it considered Qualcomm's competitors in those non-essential patents to have been severely foreclosed.

Qualcomm was also accused of imposing unfair trading conditions, as it required chipset buyers not to challenge Qualcomm's patent-licensing agreements as a condition for Qualcomm's continued supply of baseband chipsets. The NDRC considered this conduct to be an exploitation of Qualcomm's dominance in the baseband chipset markets to force customers to comply with Qualcomm's unreasonable patent licensing contracts. The harm alleged by the NDRC was *competition restriction in the downstream markets* where the customers competed with each other. According to the NDRC, because the actual and potential customers were highly dependent upon Qualcomm's baseband chipset supplies, those who were disobedient to Qualcomm would be forced out of the various wireless communication terminal markets. No further analysis was provided. However, it is questionable whether this alleged harm was relevant to the conduct. First, according to the NDRC's description, the offense was that Qualcomm used its dominance in baseband chipset supplies to aggressively promote its patent-licensing business. In that sense, this offense could alternatively be characterized as a tying practice, so it would make more sense if the harm were alleged as competition foreclosure in the tied market, which, in this case, would be the market of non-essential patent licensing. Second, even if the NDRC chose to identify the harm from the perspective of the chipset customers, it would probably make more sense to phrase the harm as monopolistic exploitation instead of downstream competition restriction. This is because to assess downstream competition restriction, one has to prove the existence of differential treatment and its effect of competition distortion; in this case, the NDRC made no mention in that regard.

The SAIC in Tetra Pak

Tetra Pak was decided in 2016. It is the most time-consuming case in the tripartite era and the best-reasoned case of the SAIC. In this case, Tetra Pak was found dominant in three relevant markets: the market for paper-based aseptic packaging equipment, the market for technical services for paper-based aseptic packaging equipment, and the market for paper-based aseptic packaging materials. It was accused of committing three abusive practices: tying, exclusive dealing, and loyalty rebates. This subsection deals with the first one.

The SAIC found the packaging materials to be the tied product while the packaging equipment and technical services the tying products. In fact, according to the

SAIC's description, part of the conduct was similar to what Tetra Pak was fined for in the EU three decades ago.[4] The SAIC alleged the harm of competition restriction in the tied market. It applied the four conditions for finding abusive tying, and in this case, it looked closely at the severability of the tying and tied products, as well as the limitation of customer choice. In that sense, just like the NDRC in *Qualcomm*, the SAIC viewed the limitation of customer choice as a proxy for verifying the harm of competition restriction. In doing so, the SAIC refrained from engaging in a more contextualized exclusionary-effects examination. For example, it did not discuss to what extent, if at all, Tetra Pak's dominance in the tied product market—which the SAIC had found—contributed to the exclusionary effects of the tying. In that light, one could say that the SAIC's examination of anticompetitive effects in the tied market is largely presumptive. Given the case circumstances, it would have been relatively easy for the SAIC to expand on that, had it chosen to do so.

Overall, it seems that both the *Qualcomm* and the *Tetra Pak* decision were pioneering a presumptive theory of harm on tying, with their common approach of using customer choice limitation as a proxy to ascertain competition restriction in the tied market. This corresponds to the *quasi–per se* abusive test on tying in the EU context.[5]

The SAMR in three pharmaceutical cases

Not counting the provincial AMR cases it delegated, the SAMR has found infringement of Article 22(5) AML in three cases: the *Hunan Er'kang & Henan Jiushi* case in 2019, the *Shandong Kanghui Pharmaceutical* case in 2020, and the *Yuanda Pharmaceutical* case in 2023.

Hunan Er'kang & Henan Jiushi concerned the offense of tying. The undertaking in question was accused of leveraging its dominance in the market for chlorphenamine ingredient supply to the market for pharmaceutical excipients supply through tying. The SAMR adopted the four-condition analytical framework and the presumptive approach that its predecessors had established for assessing anticompetitive effects in the tied product. It highlighted the severability of the tying and tied products and the unjustifiability of the tying. On that basis, it concluded that anticompetitive effects had occurred.

The other two cases concerned the offense of imposing unfair trading conditions on the counterparties. In *Shandong Kanghui Pharmaceutical*, the imposed trading condition was that after buying the calcium gluconate ingredient from the dominant undertaking in question, the downstream drug manufacturers must (1) sell

4 Case C-333/94 P *Tetra Pak International SA v Commission of the European Communities* [1996] ECR I 5951, paras 34–8; Case T-83/91 *Tetra Pak International SA v Commission of the European Communities* [1994] ECR II 755, paras 134–41; Commission Decision 92/163/EEC of 24 July 1991 relating to a proceeding pursuant to Article 86 of the EEC Treaty (IV/31043—Tetra Pak II), para 146.

5 Nicholas Economides and Ioannis Lianos, 'The Elusive Antitrust Standard on Bundling in Europe and in the United States at the Aftermath of the Microsoft Cases', *Antitrust Law Journal* 76, no. 2 (2009): 536.

their products back to the dominant firm or (2) produce and sell calcium gluconate injection solutions at the dominant firm's request. The SAMR found that the downstream manufacturers were forced to accept these conditions because they could find no alternative ingredient supplies. It alleged the harm of competition restriction in the market for calcium gluconate injection solutions, presumably because other injection solution sellers were foreclosed of both input and output by these imposed conditions. To support its finding of abuse, the SAMR alleged additionally two exploitative harms: the harm to drug manufacturers' right to autonomous business operations and the harm to patient welfare and the public health fund.

In *Yuanda Pharmaceutical*, the undertaking was found dominant in the markets for norepinephrine ingredient and adrenaline ingredient supplies, and the trading conditions imposed on downstream drug manufacturers included (1) selling their products back to the dominant firm at low prices, (2) rebating the dominant firm through market promotion fee and research service fee payments, and (3) selling products only within the territories and at the prices determined by the dominant firm. The SAMR reasoned that the dominant firm's intention behind imposing these trading conditions was to undermine competitors in the downstream drug supply markets before extracting monopoly rents. Similar to the previous case, it alleged the harm of competition restriction in the downstream drug markets and additionally exploitative harms borne by the trading parties and patient consumers.

Provincial AICs and AMRs: two general observations

There have been a total of at least 41 cases concerning tying and imposing unfair trading conditions at the provincial level.[6] There were 15 cases made by AICs in the tripartite era, and the other 26 were made by provincial AMRs. The undertakings fined in these decisions were invariably monopolists. The relevant monopolies can be categorized into three groups. The first one is naturally monopoly-prone public utility supplies vis-à-vis water, natural gas, and heat. This group includes nine AIC cases and 21 AMR cases. The second group is monopolies resulting from high regulatory barriers, such as tobacco, salt, broadcast television, and cremation services. Four AIC cases and one AMR case fall under this group. The third group is monopolies resulting from exclusive control over a key product or service, such as essential pharmaceutical ingredients and exclusive dealership granted by another undertaking or the government. Two AIC cases and four AMR cases fall under this category.

Probably because the monopolistic positions and abusive conduct in these case circumstances were readily apparent, the handling agencies have kept the case decisions short and the legal reasoning brief. These decisions are not particularly informative on their own, but they offer some interesting insights as a collective.

6 This is a conservative counting based on the case decisions published by the SAIC and then the SAMR on their websites. It is possible that some cases were decided by provincial agencies but were not systemically published by the central agency in the earlier years.

First, by comparing the AMR and AIC cases, it can be seen that provincial agencies' enforcement expertise has been growing over the years, and there has been a more functional supervisor-delegate relationship between the SAMR and the AMRs than in the tripartite era. The AMR cases showed a high level of consistency with the secondary AML regulations and previous case decisions adopted by the SAMR. In comparison, the AIC cases were more erratic. For example, in the *Inner Mongolia Chifeng Tobacco* case, the monopolist tobacco company was accused of abusing its position by requiring retailers that wanted to purchase high-demand types of cigarettes to also purchase low-demand types of cigarettes. The handling AIC characterized the conduct as tying, but it did not delineate the tying and tied markets nor did it explain where and how competition foreclosure effects took place. After all, irrespective of high- or low-demand cigarettes, there was no competition encompassing the tobacco company due to strict regulatory control. Besides, as an industry that the government tightly controls, it is doubtful whether competition ought to be promoted in the production of any kind of cigarettes. So a more plausible approach to tackling this conduct would have been characterizing it as the imposition of unfair trading conditions causing exploitative harms. Another example was the *Sichuan Jiuyuan Yinhai Software* case, in which the AIC characterized the conduct in question as tying and alleged the harm of competition restriction in the tied market, but problematically, there was no mention, let alone examination, of the competitive situation in the tied product market. It is possible that the AIC used customer choice limitation as a proxy for ascertaining anticompetitive effects in the tied market, but this possibility could not be verified due to the lack of analysis.

Second, the sheer large number of cases concerning monopolists infringing Article 22(5) AML suggests a more systemic issue: the government had been contributing to the formation of monopolies. This inevitably resulted in the prevalence of monopolistic exploitation, making provincial antitrust enforcement preoccupied with exploitative abuses rather than exclusionary abuses. The harm of monopolistic exploitation was so obvious in these cases that sometimes the handling agencies did not even bother to explicitly allege it, as shown in the *Jingyang Water Supply* case. Had the central and local governments been more aware of competition neutrality in wielding administrative power, monopolistic exploitation would perhaps have been less of a common problem and the provincial agencies would have spent more resources on preserving competition where competition would actually be possible.

Regional courts and the Supreme Court

There have been eight private enforcement cases concerning tying and the imposition of unfair trading conditions (see Table 7.3). Three of these cases were closed with a finding of infringement of the AML: *Wu Xiaoqin v Shaanxi Broadcast, Wu Zongqu v Yongfu Water Supply*, and *Hongfu v Weihai Water Supply*. The most dramatic case is *Wu Xiaoqin v Shaanxi Broadcast*, which was closed with a retrial before the Supreme Court. The Shaanxi High Court found in the appeal that the defendant had been offering the tying product alone to a non-specific number of customers; based on this finding, it concluded that there had been a choice for the plaintiff, so there was no abusive tying. This was obviously a rushed conclusion on the part of the High Court: the fact that some customers could buy the tying product alone does not necessarily mean the choice was extended to the plaintiff. Subsequently, the High Court made a more serious mistake: after finding no abusive tying, it stated that because the defendant had not faithfully informed the plaintiff of the possible choice, the infringed legal interest was actually the plaintiff's right to information under consumer protection law; therefore, the plaintiff should have sought remedy under consumer law or contract law instead of the AML. This statement was wrong: by isolating the fact that the defendant concealed the possible choice from the plaintiff from the case circumstances, the High Court failed to see that this concealment served as a way to implement the coercive tying. Indeed, consumer protection law might also be applicable, but that could not preclude the applicability of the AML. Fortunately, the Supreme Court corrected the two flaws in the High Court's reasoning in the retrial judgment. The Supreme Court endorsed the first-instance judgment and found the tying abusive. It accentuated the limitation of consumer choice, which not only reflected the harm of monopolistic exploitation but also served as a proxy for ascertaining the harm of competition foreclosure. The Supreme Court also reversed the first-instance judgment in *Hongfu v Weihai Water Supply*, after taking a closer look at the case circumstances and found the element of implicit coercion. Then it followed the four-condition analytical framework to find abusive tying.

The other five cases were concluded without findings of abuse. The reasons given by the courts boiled down to the plaintiffs' failures to prove that the requisite conditions (e.g., the existence of coercion and two separate products) had been met for finding abuse. The two cases that engaged in deeper legal analysis were *Damingxing v CAVCA* and *Yangmou v Hefei Yimou*. In *Damingxing v CAVCA*, the court found that the defendant did force the plaintiff to buy the bundled products, but it reasoned that the bundle was justified by the defendant's mandate of protecting music creators' rights. In *Yangmou v Hefei Yimou*, the first-instance court found abuse in the forms of both tying and the imposition of unfair trading conditions, but the Supreme Court quashed these findings, as it took a closer look at the disputed conduct and reasoned that the first conduct was justified as a way to make up price difference and the second conduct had no evidence of coercion or anticompetitive harms.

Refusal to deal

Refusal to deal as a type of abuse is provided in Article 22(3) AML. By 31 December 2023, there have been five public enforcement cases concerning refusal to deal: one NDRC case, two AIC cases, and two SAMR cases.

The NDRC

In *Zhejiang Second Pharmaceutical & Tianjin Handewei Pharmaceutical*, the NDRC found abusive refusal to deal in addition to abusive excessive pricing.

Table 7.3 Court cases concerning tying and the imposition of unfair trading conditions by 31 December 2023

Year	*Case name*	*Disputed conduct*	*Adjudicating court*	*Conclusion*
2016	*Wu Xiaoqin v Shaanxi Broadcast*	Tying basic television programs with paid television programs	Shaanxi Xi'an Intermediary Court (first instance); Shaanxi High Court (appeal); the Supreme Court (retrial)	Found abuse in first instance; reversed in appeal; reversed again in retrial
2018	*Ding Qidong v China Unicom Beijing*	Universally terminating an old telecom service that the plaintiff wanted to continue using	Beijing Intellectual Property Court (first instance); Beijing High Court (appeal)	No abuse
2019	*Damingxing v CAVCA*	Licensing audio-visual copyrights of popular and unpopular songs in a bundle	Yunnan Kunming Intermediary Court (first instance)	No abuse
2019	*Wu Zongqu v Yongfu Water Supply*	Making tap water supply conditional on purchasing the defendant's supply equipment and construction service	Guangxi Nanning Intermediary Court (first instance)	Found abuse
2022	*Quanke v Chongqing Sanxia*	The defendant designating the plaintiff to contract a subsidiary company for construction service	Chongqing First Intermediary Court	No abuse
2022	*Hongfu v Weihai Water Supply*	Implicitly tying water supply with the construction of supply equipment	Shandong Qingdao Intermediary Court (first instance); the Supreme Court (appeal)	No abuse in first instance but reversed in appeal

(*Continued*)

Table 7.3 (Continued)

Year	*Case name*	*Disputed conduct*	*Adjudicating court*	*Conclusion*
2022	*Wang v Beijing Lianjia*	The defendant requiring the plaintiff to sign a transaction-guarantee contract when signing a real-estate brokerage contract	Beijing Intellectual Property Court (first instance); the Supreme Court (appeal)	No abuse
2023	*Yangmou v Hefei Yimou*	(1) charging for patent licensing fees after licensing contract had expired; (2) requesting the settlement of previous disputes when negotiating for continued supply	Jiangsu Nanjing Intermediary Court (first instance); the Supreme Court (appeal)	Found conduct (1) and (2) abusive in first instance but reversed in appeal

Regarding the refusal to deal, the NDRC found that the two collectively dominant undertakings had ceased supplying their previous customers after signing an exclusive distribution contract with a third party in 2014, without any objective justification. The NDRC alleged the harm of downstream competition distortion resulting from the input-foreclosure of those refused customers and the harm to consumer welfare resulting from the reduced number of drug producers and increased drug prices.

The AIC in Chongqing Qingyang Pharmaceutical *and* Chongqing Southwest Second Pharmaceutical

These two cases were handled by the AIC of Chongqing Municipality in 2015 and 2016, respectively. They had different relevant markets but the conduct in question was similar. In *Chongqing Qingyang Pharmaceutical*, the AIC accused Qingyang of abusing its monopolistic position in the market for allopurinol ingredients by cutting off supply to downstream allopurinol drug manufacturers. It found that Qingyang was trying to vertically integrate into the downstream allopurinol drug market and it had signed an exclusive distributor for its drug product before implementing the refusal in question. Based on this finding, the AIC reasoned that

Qingyang intended to input-foreclose competitors in the downstream market and reserve the allopurinol ingredient for the recently signed exclusive distributor. It considered the refusal had caused anticompetitive effects, as evidenced by the fact that drug producers had been forced out of the market due to ingredient shortage and that the price of allopurinol ingredient had more than doubled. The AIC alleged three harms arising from the refusal: distortion of the competitive order in the downstream market, capacity loss in allopurinol drug manufacturing, and the undermining of consumer welfare.

In *Chongqing Southwest Second Pharmaceutical*, the AIC found Southwest Second to be monopolistic in the market for phenol ingredients, considering its significant price increase in 2014 without any sales loss. It accused Southwest Second of abusing its monopolistic position by refusing to supply its old customers. It also found that Southwest Second stopped supplying those customers because it intended to reserve the supply to Xinxianfeng, the exclusive distributor it had just signed. This exclusive distribution contract essentially meant that an additional chain was to be inserted between the pre-existing supply-demand relationship between Southwest Second's monopolized phenol ingredient supply and downstream phenol drug manufacturers. According to the AIC's finding, the reason that Southwest Second would want to add another layer of monopoly (i.e., to share the monopoly rent with another firm) was because Xinxianfeng agreed to purchase another ingredient product, gastrodin, produced by Southwest Second. The AIC alleged four harms caused by the refusal in question: distortion of the competitive order in the downstream market, capacity loss in the phenol drug manufacturing, the injuring of the refused customers' interests, and the undermining of consumer welfare.

The case circumstances in *Chongqing Southwest Second Pharmaceutical* were relatively more complex. Based on the AIC's factual description, one could say that there were potentially more abuses in this case than a refusal to supply, including (1) the signing of the exclusive distribution contract in exchange for expansion in another product market and (2) the price-elevation when implementing the refusal after signing the contract. The first one could be characterized as tying and the second one as exploitative pricing. It is likely that when alleging the four harms, the AIC took into account these two potential abuses without expressly identifying them. A possible explanation for the AIC's not identifying these two abuses was the jurisdictional delimitation between the SAIC and the NDRC: the SAIC and local AICs were only supposed to handle non-price-related abuses. It was not until after the SAIC absorbed the NDRC's enforcement power and was renamed as the SAMR in 2018 that the exploitative pricing implied in this case was penalized—in the 2021 *Shangqiu Xinxianfeng Pharmaceutical* case.

The SAMR

In the 2019 *Hunan Er'kang & Henan Jiushi* case, the SAMR accused the two firms, Er'kang and Jiushi, of abusing their collective dominant position in the market for chlorphenamine ingredient supply in three ways: excessive pricing, refusal to supply, and tying. The SAMR's analysis of the refusal to supply conduct was brief: first, it described the conduct in question as including both outright refusal and implicit refusal (e.g., requiring the customers to deposit a too large amount of guarantee fees) and found no justification for the refusals; second, the SAMR described in a general manner the anticompetitive effects resulting from the refusals, including higher chlorphenamine drug prices to the detriment of patients' welfare and the restriction of competition in the downstream drug manufacturing market. Overall, the SAMR's brief theory of harm showed two flaws: first, although the indispensability of the accused firms' supply could be inferred from the near monopoly structure of the chlorphenamine ingredient market, the SAMR did not explicitly examine the element of indispensability; second, it did not explain why the collectively dominant firms would want to refuse to deal customers. Perhaps they intended to reserve the drug input to an affiliated downstream firm, but this was not clear from the decision.

The SAMR's analysis in the 2021 *Simcere Pharmaceutical* case was better. First, the SAMR established the accused firm's monopoly in the batroxobin ingredient supply market and examined the refusal in question. The SAMR's examination revealed that the refusal was unjustified for protecting its legitimate business interests on the one hand and that the accused firm was attempting to enter and monopolize the downstream drug manufacturing market on the other. The SAMR alleged two harms caused by the refusal: the restriction of downstream competition through input-foreclosing competitors and the harm to consumer welfare by disrupting the batroxobin drug supply.

Regional courts

By the end of 2023, there have been nine private enforcement cases in which regional courts substantively analysed refusal to deal under the AML. Four of these cases were about consumers suing an undertaking for not offering a product or service they wanted. They are as follows: *Gu Fang v China Southern Airlines, Ding Qidong v China Unicom Beijing, Tong Hua v China Mobile Shanghai,* and *Song Xin v China Railway Guangzhou*. None of these cases resulted in a finding of abusive refusal. This is understandable since generally speaking, a dominant or even monopolistic firm would have no anticompetitive incentive to turn away a transaction opportunity with a consumer. In other words, it is generally unlikely that a refusal to deal with a consumer as such would cause exclusionary or exploitative harms. This was acknowledged by the courts hearing these cases. Besides, as the courts in these cases had invariably found, the refusals tended to be objectively justified, either because they were triggered by the plaintiffs' violation of pre-established contractual obligations or because the defendant was universally discontinuing a product/service due to technical development or policy mandates.

The other five cases were disputes between undertakings or, in the case of *Xu Shuqing v Tencent*, between a business user and a platform operator. None of these cases resulted in a finding of abusive refusal to deal either. In *Xu Shuqing v*

Tencent, the defendant operated a messaging sticker platform on which end users could buy stickers designed by independent designers. The plaintiff was a sticker designer, and he accused the defendant of abusing its dominance in the sticker platform market by refusing to stock his stickers. The case was first tried before the Shenzhen Intermediary Court, which ruled against the plaintiff on the grounds that the defendant had no dominance in the relevant market for 'global Internet platform information service' and the plaintiff had no competitive relationship with the defendant. The case was appealed to the Guangdong High Court, which narrowed the geographic market to a Chinese one, but it still found no dominance. The High Court still went on assessing the disputed conduct, and it considered that the refusal to stock the plaintiff's stickers was justified by the plaintiff's pre-disclosed 'no solicitation' store policy and that the defendant's sticker platform was not an indispensable distribution channel to the plaintiff. So it found no abusive refusal to deal.

In *Damingxing v CAVCA*, the court found no exclusionary or exploitative motive for the defendant to refuse a deal with the plaintiff. This allowed it to conclude that the plaintiff could not obtain licensing from the defendant not because the defendant was determined to refuse to deal but because the two parties genuinely could not reach an agreement.

In *Panjin Dongxing v PetroChina and Beckbury*, the plaintiff accused one of the defendants, Beckbury, of abusing its dominant position by refusing to renew a contract with the plaintiff, as it had sunk significant costs in supplying the defendant. The Beijing Intellectual Property Court ruled against the plaintiff on two grounds. First, it found no dominance of the defendant in the defined relevant market. Second, it held that even if the defendant were dominant, the refusal would not constitute an abuse. There, the court showed an awareness of balancing the business interests of the refusing and refused undertakings. It held that the fact that the plaintiff had sunk costs in maintaining a business relationship with the defendant did not necessarily oblige the defendant to sign a contract since the plaintiff should have assessed the risk and return when negotiating the contract. Besides, it noted that by estimation, the plaintiff had already recouped the costs of building the facilities tailored for the defendant, and the fact that the facilities were still operable did not necessarily mean the defendant's freedom to contract should be compromised to benefit the plaintiff.

In *Hytera v Motorola Solutions*, the plaintiff accused the defendant of abusing its dominant position in the market for subway wireless telecommunications equipment, as the defendant had refused to open the APIs of its equipment, resulting in the plaintiff's inability to compete with the defendant in several bidding processes. The court redefined the relevant markets as each individual bidding constituting a separate relevant market, and it found the defendant dominant in three of them. It nonetheless found no abusive refusal on two grounds: first, there were other viable alternatives for accomplishing the functions that opening the APIs would have accomplished, meaning that the defendant's API access was not indispensable for the plaintiff; second, the court found that even if the defendant had provided API access, the plaintiff would not have been able to meet the tendering requirements, meaning that the plaintiff was not really a competitor in the bidding processes, and therefore, there were no effects of competition restriction.

In *Yunnan Yingding v Sinopec*, the plaintiff accused the defendant of abusing its dominance in the buyer market for biological diesel fuel by refusing to buy from the plaintiff. The case was initially heard in 2014 by the Yunnan Kunming Intermediary Court, which found abuse of dominance by the defendant but did not award any damages to the plaintiff. Both parties appealed to the Yunnan High Court, which quashed the first instance judgment and referred the case back on the grounds of misidentifications of facts. The Kunming Intermediary Court delivered a new judgment in 2016, this time ruling in favour of the defendant. The plaintiff appealed again to the Yunnan High Court, which issued a final judgment on 28 August 2017, upholding wholly the first instance judgment. In the retrial judgment, the Intermediary Court ruled that there was no abusive refusal on two grounds. First, it considered that although the defendant was dominant in the relevant buyer market and had a general statutory obligation under the Chinese Renewable Energy Law to purchase biodiesel fuel, this obligation was not yet operationalized since the State Council and provincial governments had not adopted secondary regulations to specify the quotas and prices of such purchases. Therefore, if the defendant did refuse to purchase, that refusal would be objectively justified. Second, the Intermediary Court held that there was no refusal to begin with. It reasoned from a contract law perspective that when the plaintiff sent a request to deal, the request contained no specific dealing conditions and should, therefore, be perceived only as an invitation to offer rather than an offer; consequently, the defendant was entitled not to respond with an offer to contract, and therefore, its non-responsiveness should not constitute a refusal to deal under the AML.

The second ground is questionable, as it implies that the conception of 'refusal to deal' under the AML context should be controlled by the much more rigid conception of 'deal' under contract law. One may dispute this reasoning by pointing out that an antitrust intervention against a refusal to deal comes inherently with a need to balance between the freedom of contract and the protection of competition. After all, the whole point of introducing the contractual notions of 'invitation to offer' and 'offer' was to emphasize an undertaking's freedom of contract, but this point should already be incorporated in the abuse analysis as one side of the to-be-balanced considerations. In that light, by borrowing notions from contract laws to interpret the AML concept of 'refusal to deal', the Intermediary Court in *Yunnan Yingding v Sinopec* unduly restricted the AML's applicability. In this way, it also questionably excused itself from assessing the disputed conduct's potential anticompetitive effects, in which it would have been expected to examine the indispensability of the defendant's distribution channel and the extent of output-foreclosure suffered by the plaintiff.

The Supreme Court

The Supreme Court has produced three appeal judgments concerning refusal to deal by the end of 2023. They are as follows: *Jinbi Dashijie v CAVCA, Ningbo Yongmou v Rimou,* and *Zhang v Quanzhou Crematorium*.

The *Jinbi Dashijie v CAVCA* case had similar circumstances to those in *Damingxing v CAVCA*. After confirming the finding of CAVCA's dominance, the Supreme Court laid down three general criteria for finding abusive refusal to deal: (1) whether the dominant undertaking could but refused to deal in the circumstances, (2) whether the refusal resulted in competition restriction to the detriment of consumer welfare, and (3) whether the refusal lacked objective justifications. Under these criteria, the Supreme Court concluded that there was no abusive refusal to license in this case because CAVCA had shown intention to deal by disclosing to the plaintiff the reasonably set licensing fee structure and charging procedures; the fact that the two parties did not strike a deal was because they could not reach an agreement regarding the licensing terms.

In *Ningbo Yongmou v Rimou*, the first-instance court found the defendant to have abused its dominant position in the market for essential patents for sintered NdFeB magnet production by refusing to license the plaintiff. The key basis of this finding was that in the court's opinion, the defendant's essential patents had constituted an essential facility for downstream production. But the Supreme Court reversed the finding of abuse after taking a closer look at the relevant market definition and the indispensability of the withheld product. It redefined the relevant market more widely as one for production technologies (rather than essential patents) for sintered NdFeB magnet production. Consequently, it found that the defendant's patents were not essential for the plaintiff's operations, as evidenced by the fact the plaintiff had been producing and selling the downstream product without actually infringing the defendant's patent rights.

Zhang v Quanzhou Crematorium is the only private enforcement case that was concluded with a finding of abusive refusal to deal. The plaintiff provided funeral intermediary services, and it accused the defendant of abusing its dominant position in the local cremation service market by refusing to deal with the plaintiff when the latter was acting on behalf of clients. In its judgment, the Supreme Court reversed the first-instance judgment and found the refusal abusive. First, it disapproved of the first-instance court's dismissal of the plaintiff's claims simply because they did not precisely identify the disputed conduct and the applicable rules. In the Supreme Court's opinion, due to the general complexity of AML cases, the first-instance court should have taken the initiative to exercise its inquisitional power to help clarify the disputed conduct and the applicable rules vis-à-vis the case circumstances. Second, the Supreme Court applied the three conditions it had established in *Jinbi Dashijie v CAVCA* for finding abusive refusal: the existence of refusal, the resulting anticompetitive effects, and a lack of justifications. Regarding the first condition, it found that the defendant had indeed refused to deal with the plaintiff by prohibiting Zhang, the legal representative of his funeral service company, from entering its premises. Regarding the second condition, the Supreme Court observed that the defendant was motivated to refuse because it had cultivated a hostile personal relationship with Zhang, who had been actively complaining to regulators about the defendant's illegal price charges. It also observed that the defendant held a monopolistic position in the local cremation service market and the defendant's cooperation was essential for the plaintiff to fulfil its clients' wishes. On that basis, it held that although the defendant was not competing with the plaintiff in the funeral intermediary service market, it nonetheless had caused competition restriction effects by targeting a less friendly downstream operator. Regarding the third condition, it found that the defendant's refusal to let Zhang into the premises was unjustified in light of the circumstances.

Exclusive dealing and loyalty rebates

Exclusive dealing and loyalty rebates have the common capability of causing exclusionary harm in the market dominated by the incumbent. As mentioned earlier, Article 22(4) describes two different types of abuses: exclusive dealing and tying. Cases invoking Article 22(4) but concerning tying are analysed in a previous section. This section analyses exclusive dealing cases, namely, cases where a dominant undertaking requires trading counterparties not to deal with its competitors. Additionally, this section covers loyalty rebates, which generate potentially anticompetitive effects in a way that is analogical to exclusive dealing.[7] There has only been one case in that regard: the 2016 *Tetra Pak* case. There, the SAIC described loyalty rebates as a separate type of abuse under Article 22(7), a catch-all provision concerning the prohibited types of abusive conduct. By the end of 2023, there have been seven public enforcement cases concerning exclusive dealing and loyalty rebates: one by the SAIC, three AMR cases, and three SAMR cases.

The SAIC *in* Tetra Pak

In this case, the SAIC found three abuses committed by Tetra Pak: tying, exclusive dealing, and loyalty rebates. The exclusive dealing conduct referred to the exclusive supply obligations that Tetra Pak imposed on Hong Ta, an upstream raw paper material producer. The SAIC considered this conduct an abuse of Tetra Pak's dominance in the market for paper-based aseptic packaging material to input-foreclose competitors. To begin with, the SAIC described the exclusive dealing conduct, noting that it took the form of contractually prohibiting Hong Ta from using information related to Tetra Pak's product parameters for purposes other than supplying Tetra Pak. The SAIC considered this prohibition to have effectively induced exclusive dealing because the inability to use such information would seriously undermine the quality of the raw paper materials produced by Hong Ta. On that basis, the SAIC alleged the harm of competition restriction in the aseptic packaging material market through input foreclosure.

Its theory of harm was three-fold. First, the SAIC examined the possibility of alternative supplies to the input-foreclosed competitors. It found no such possibilities on account of the heavy sunk costs and the lack of consistently large demand for the raw materials. To be sure, however, this examination was largely

7 Xingyu Yan, 'Whither Antitrust Regulation of Loyalty Rebates in China: The Tetra Pak Decision and Lessons from the EU', *World Competition* 40, no. 4 (2017): 623.

theoretical, as the SAIC did not further analyse to what extent the input-foreclosure had affected the competitors' performance nor did it empirically verify if there could indeed be no alternative suppliers.[8] Second, the SAIC examined whether the information restriction that Tetra Pak imposed on Hong Ta was justified. It found that the parameters of raw paper material production stemmed mainly from the technologies and knowledge possessed by the producers themselves, rather than information provided by the customers such as Tetra Pak. Therefore, Hong Ta was perfectly able to supply to other customers without compromising Tetra Pak's confidential information. The SAIC also found that much of the restricted information was publicly available, so it concluded that the information restriction was unjustified. Third, the SAIC underscored the link between adopting such publicly available information and the production of quality raw paper materials. It reasoned that by breaking that link, Tetra Pak effectively eliminated the possibility for Hong Ta to supply other customers, and this was enough evidence of competition restriction effects and the possibility of long-term impairment of the packaging material industry.

Loyalty rebates were the third offense in *Tetra Pak*. To begin with, the SAIC identified two types of loyalty rebates that Tetra Pak offered to customers when supplying paper-based aseptic packaging materials: (1) retroactively cumulative rebates, which included two subtypes, single retroactively cumulative rebates and compound retroactively cumulative rebates; and (2) individualized target rebates. Subsequently, the SAIC alleged the harm of competition restriction in the packaging material market, and its theory of harm was three-fold: First, it underscored the 'loyalty-inducing effects' inherent in the two types of loyalty rebates, which strongly motivated customers to buy as much as possible from Tetra Pak by making the price of their marginal units drop to zero or even negative. Second, the SAIC reasoned that under particular market circumstances, those loyalty-inducing effects could help the incumbent leverage market power from the non-contestable to the contestable share of demand, therefore yielding anticompetitive effects. The particular market circumstances considered by the SAIC included three factors that had reinforced the non-contestable share of demand: Tetra Pak's production capacity and product variety, the accompanying practice of tying, and the side-implementation of non-abusive discounts. Third, the SAIC ascertained the existence of anticompetitive effects in the dominated market, although only at the theoretical level. Overall, the SAIC in *Tetra Pak* established a theory of harm on loyalty rebates that was solidly effects-based, although it did not carry out a thoroughly circumstances-specific examination of the anticompetitive effects.[9] After *Tetra Pak*, there are no more enforcement decisions prohibiting loyalty rebates as a standalone type of abuse, but as exemplified by the following *Eastman* case, abusive loyalty rebates still exist; the enforcement agencies simply chose to prosecute them as exclusive dealing.

8 Yan, 'Whither Antitrust Regulation of Loyalty Rebates in China', 628.
9 Yan, 'Whither Antitrust Regulation of Loyalty Rebates in China', 624–7.

***Provincial AMRs:* Eastman, Sherpa's, *and* Yixing Ganghua Gas**

Two of the three AMR cases on exclusive dealing came from the AMR of Shanghai Municipality. They are the *Eastman* decision and the *Sherpa's* decision published in 2019 and 2021 respectively. The Shanghai AMR has risen to be a leading local agency in developing antitrust theories of harm. In *Eastman*, it developed a logically impeccable theory of harm on exclusive dealing; in *Sherpa's*, it produced arguably the most elaborate and economics-based market definition in the AML enforcement history to date.

In *Eastman*, the Shanghai AMR approached the exclusive dealing in five steps after establishing Eastman's dominance. First, it described the conduct as consisting of (1) contractually obliging six customers to purchase a minimum amount of products each year, which constituted 60%–80% of their annual demands, and (2) using rebates to financially incentivize a customer to lock in at least 75% of that customer's total demand. Second, the AMR examined the lock-in effect the two exclusive dealing schemes had on the customers. It reasoned that the minimum purchasing obligations and the rebate threshold were carefully designed by Eastman to lock in a large proportion of the customers' demands, and the lock-in effect was amplified by the customers' concerns for transaction costs, product compatibility, and stability. Third, the AMR examined the foreclosure effect that the exclusive dealing had on Eastman's competitors in the dominated market. In that regard, it observed that those locked-in customers were all direct-sales customers making up a large proportion of the total market demand, and they were highly sought-after by the competitors. So, because they were either contractually obliged or financially incentivized to buy mostly from Eastman, the competitors were significantly output-foreclosed. Fourth, the AMR discussed how the output-foreclosure of the competitors translated to anticompetitive effects in the relevant market. It reasoned that because the competitors could no longer obtain the more valuable direct-sales customers, they were forced to compete with Eastman only for dealership customers, whose demands were much fewer both individually and collectively. Consequently, the competitors lost the incentive to engage in price competition because they could not make up for the profit loss resulting from lower prices by selling more items. Furthermore, the AMR looked at the change of the Lerner index during the exclusive dealing conduct's existence and concluded that the conduct had indeed caused the reduction of competition. Fifth, the AMR held that although the exclusive dealing schemes could potentially help reduce transaction costs for Eastman and customers, this benefit was outweighed by the resulting anticompetitive effects, so these schemes were unjustified.

In *Sherpa's*, the conduct in question concerned the exclusivity obligations that Sherpa's, an operator dominant in the local food delivery platform service market, had imposed on its business users. The Shanghai AMR analysed the conduct in three steps. First, it described the conduct as comprising three aspects: the exclusive food-delivery clause between Sherpa's and restaurants, the requirement of closing shops on rival platforms, and the system for monitoring whether restaurants were adhering to the exclusivity requirement. Second, the Shanghai AMR identified two harms resulting from the conduct: *restriction of competition* and *impairment of business and consumer user interests*. It highlighted the role of platform network effects in amplifying the first harm: on the one hand, because the smaller rival platforms had not yet or just barely reached a critical user mass, they were more vulnerable than the dominant Sherpa's to the loss of restaurant users; on the other hand, because Sherpa's had harnessed the indirect network effects between restaurant and consumer users, it held an incumbency advantage whereby it could offer less or even no subsidies to restaurants and still win them over from rival platforms. The AMR presented empirical statistics showing that the rival platforms' numbers of restaurant users and daily orders had indeed declined significantly when the exclusive dealing was implemented; it therefore confirmed the harm of competition restriction. Regarding the harm to user interests, it briefly pointed to the reduction of restaurants' business venues and the increase of platform commission fees on the one hand and the limitation of consumer choice and the increase of delivery service fees on the other. Third, it examined the justification raised by Sherpa's that the exclusivity was to prevent restaurants from free-riding on Sherpa's careful curation of the restaurants' English menus, and it found that Sherpa's did not contribute much to the curation, so the justification was dismissed.

Yixing Ganghua Gas was relatively simple compared to the previous two cases. The Jiangsu AMR accused the undertaking of abusing its monopoly in the local pipeline natural gas supply market through excessive pricing, the imposition of exploitative trading conditions, and exclusive dealing. Regarding the exclusive dealing conduct, the Jiangsu AMR reasoned that it had significantly impeded users from switching to potential alternative suppliers—although it did not identify any alternative suppliers. The undertaking in question argued that the exclusivity requirement was to prevent users from reverting to the less clean fossil-fuel energy sources, which the local government had cracked down on. The AMR dismissed this argument, as it found that the government did not delegate the undertaking to restrict users' choices nor was the exclusive dealing aligned with the times of the regulatory crackdowns. Overall, the Jiangsu AMR's theory of harm was farfetched: it did not explain how the exclusive dealing had restricted competition when there were no realistically probable competitors in sight. In that light, it seems that the exclusive dealing conduct in this case was prosecuted more as a 'side offense' alongside the other two exploitative abuses.

The SAMR in *Alibaba, Meituan,* and *Tongfang CNKI*

Both *Alibaba* and *Meituan* concerned a subtype of exclusive dealing that is specific to the Chinese digital economy: forcing business users to choose one from two rival service providers. This specific subtype of exclusive dealing has been prevalent in Chinese digital platform markets because for over a decade, digital platform operators had faced little to no merger control, which allowed them to amass and entrench market power more easily through horizontal, vertical, and conglomerate mergers; besides, the government has been keeping the regulatory barriers high to keep out foreign platform operators. Eventually, Alibaba and Tencent emerged as two leading and rival digital platform corporations, with almost every top-tier firm in a specialized platform service market affiliated either to Alibaba or Tencent.[10] This backdrop explains why exclusive dealing in the Chinese digital markets often takes the form of 'choosing one from the two' instead of 'choosing one from multiple'.

In *Alibaba*, after establishing the undertaking's dominance in the market for online retail platform services, the SAMR first described the exclusive dealing conduct as comprising three aspects: prohibiting business users from opening stores on rival platforms, prohibiting business users from participating in promotional events organized by rival platforms, and applying various monitoring and punishment mechanisms to ensure the prohibitions were implemented. Second, it examined the unjustifiability of the conduct. Alibaba raised the excuse that the exclusivity requirements were to prevent users from free-riding on the promotional resources that Alibaba had invested in them, but the SAMR disagreed, stating that the exclusivity requirements were forced onto the users and they were not necessary for recouping the resources Alibaba had invested. Third, the SAMR identified four harms caused by the exclusive dealing: (1) restricting competition in the dominated market by foreclosing rival platforms of business users, (2) undermining the interests of business users (by limiting their freedom of choice and revenues) and distorting downstream market competition (i.e., competition among the different retail channels of a product brand), (3) impeding the proper allocation of market resources and the long-term development of the platform economy, and (4) undermining consumer welfare by reducing consumer choices.

The *Meituan* decision was issued only six months after *Alibaba*, and they concerned the same choosing-one-from-the-two conduct but in different markets. Here, the SAMR defined the relevant market as the national market for online food-delivery planform services and found Meituan dominant therein. It approached the exclusive dealing conduct the same way as it did in *Alibaba*: describing the various aspects of the conduct, examining its unjustifiability, and alleging and briefly explaining the four resulting harms. Overall, the SAMR's theories of harm in *Alibaba* and *Meituan* are sensible, but they are not as elaborate and well-reasoned as the Shanghai AMR's in *Sherpa's*. For example, when alleging that the exclusive dealing conduct had caused downstream competition distortion in these two cases, the SAMR never substantiated the allegations by looking at how the downstream competitive situations were before and after the conduct. The SAMR had likely rushed to conclude the two cases in 2021, as the top policymakers had just launched a campaign-style regulatory crackdown on homegrown tech giants and they expected to see antitrust results.

In *Tongfang CNKI*, the undertaking was accused of abusing its dominant position in the two-sided market for Chinese academic literature online database services by imposing exclusivity requirements on literature data producers (e.g., academic journals and universities). The SAMR approached the conduct the same

10 Xingyu Yan and Yang Feng, 'Mandating Interoperability of Interpersonal Communications Services in an Ecosystems Competition Context', *Computer Law & Security Review* 50 (September 2023): 12.

way as it did in the previous two cases: describing the conduct, examining its unjustifiability, and identifying the competitive harms. Regarding the unjustifiability, the SAMR pointed out that exclusive dealing was not a standard practice in the industry and that the exclusivity was not necessary for protecting the intellectual property rights of the dominant undertaking or its users. The SAMR identified the following harms: restricting competition in the relevant market through input foreclosure, undermining the legitimate interests of the literature data-producing and -consuming users in the two-sided relevant market, and impeding the dissemination of knowledge and the long-term development of the market.

The Supreme Court

By the end of 2023, there had been three private enforcement cases concerning exclusive dealing, and they all reached the Supreme Court. They are *Ma Lijie v China Mobile Henan, Yangmou v Hefei Yimou*, and *Tiyu v Chinese Super League*. In these cases, the Supreme Court showed a consistent emphasis on examining the justifiability of the conduct.

In *Ma Lijie v China Mobile Henan*, the plaintiff accused the defendant of abusing its dominance in the local mobile telecommunications service market by restricting him from porting his mobile phone number to another service provider. The first-instance court held that the plaintiff failed to prove the defendant's dominance so there was no abuse. The Supreme Court did not find abuse in the appeal judgment either, but it played a more active role in assessing the defendant's market position. It invoked the presumption of dominance provided by Article 24(3) of the AML (formerly Article 19(3) AML), after observing that there were only three undertakings in that market and their business operations showed a high level of consistency over the years. On that basis, the Supreme Court examined the restriction of portability in question, and it found no abuse because the restriction was justified in light of the contractual agreement between the two parties. There was no analysis of the restriction's effects on competition.

In *Yangmou v Hefei Yimou*, the Supreme Court reversed the first-instance court's finding of abusive exclusive dealing. The first-stance court assessed the disputed conduct in two steps: whether there was exclusive dealing and whether the exclusive dealing had resulted in anticompetitive effects. First, it observed that there was indeed exclusive dealing, as the defendant, which was the only supplier of *patented* desloratadine citrate disodium ingredient, had required to be the plaintiff's exclusive supplier of the ingredient product. Second, the first-instance court found that the exclusive dealing requirement had resulted in competition restriction effects in the ingredient market, as the requirement had effectively prevented the plaintiff from self-producing the *generic* desloratadine citrate disodium ingredient even though the plaintiff had obtained the license to do so. In appeal, the Supreme Court did not reject these two findings of the first-instance court; rather, it relied on them to further examine whether the competition-restricting conduct was justified. It ruled that in general, an exclusive dealing requirement resulting in competition restriction effects could still be justified if it was necessary for protecting intellectual property rights, data security, and investments that the undertaking had sunk specifically for the deal in question. Specific to this case, the Supreme Court found that although the defendant's exclusive dealing conduct had indeed resulted in competition restriction effects in the ingredient product market, it was nevertheless within the bounds and expiration date of the defendant's exclusive patent right, so it should not be considered an abuse. Overall, it is plausible that the Supreme Court nuanced the anticompetitive effects of exclusive dealing and the counterweighing objective justifications, but arguably, it could have made the theory of harm more convincing by, for example, discussing how protecting the defendant's exclusive patent right would result in more social welfare benefits than enabling the generic ingredient production. After all, the exercise of intellectual property rights does not enjoy a *per se* exemption from competition law.[11]

The Supreme Court's consideration of exclusive rights protection was better elaborated in *Tiyu v Chinese Super League*. In this case, the plaintiff accused the defendant of abusing its dominance in the market for Chinese Super League match pictures by licensing the use of official match pictures exclusively to a competitor of the plaintiff, thereby forcing users of such pictures to trade only with the licensed undertaking. The first-instance court ruled against the plaintiff on three grounds: the defendant had no dominant position, the exclusive dealing was justified as a legitimate exercise of the defendant's property rights, and there was no observable harm to competition. In appeal, the Supreme Court quashed the first-instance court's finding of no dominance, mainly because the defendant's monopolistic position in the market had triggered the presumption of dominance under Article 24(1) AML and the defendant had not proved otherwise. But it found no abuse. First, the Supreme Court held that in general, competition law did not *per se* prohibit private-law rights that came inherently with an element of exclusivity; rather, it only prohibited the misuse of such rights, and to that end, conduct exercising such rights must be examined regarding their justifiability. Second, the Supreme Court ruled that the defendant's exclusive licensing was justified as a common way to exercise its freedom of business operations. It reasoned that although the defendant was a monopolist in the relevant market, this monopoly was statutorily recognized, so the defendant should be free to pursue exclusive dealerships with counterparties just like any other undertakings. Third, it noted that the exclusive dealing in this case had multiple benefits such as the reduction of transaction costs, the prevention of free riding, and the management of brand reputation; besides, it considered that although the eventuality of the exclusive licensing was a monopoly, the bidding process for the exclusive licensing was very much competitive, so there were no effects of competition restriction.

Discriminatory treatment

Treating customers discriminatorily is a type of abuse written in Article 22(7) of the AML, which prohibits 'without justifiable reasons, applying differential prices

11 Tim Wu, 'Intellectual Property Experimentalism By Way of Competition Law', *Competition Policy International* 9, no. 2 (2013): 36.

and other transaction terms among their trading counterparties who are on an equal footing'. By the end of 2023, there have been a total of nine discriminatory treatment cases. They include three AIC cases, one AMR case, and five private enforcement cases.

Provincial AICs and AMR

The three AIC cases were *Jiangsu Pizhou Tobacco*, *Hubei Yinxingtuo Harbour*, and *Chifeng Salt Industry*. The one AMR case was *Huaneng Solar Heat*.

The *Jiangsu Pizhou Tobacco* case was decided by the Jiangsu AIC in 2014. Pizhou Tabacco held a statutory monopoly in the local tobacco wholesales, and it was accused by the AIC of abusing its dominance by treating retailers discriminatorily and causing the harm of downstream competition distortion. First, the AIC described the conduct as Pizhou Tabacco's discriminatory treatment of three retailers that were put into the same high-volume retailer category. Second, it reasoned that this discriminatory treatment was unjustified because these retailers were equal-footing customers, as evidenced by the fact that Pizhou Tabacco categorized them into the same group. Third, it alleged the harm of competition distortion at the retail level, after finding that the preferentially treated retail was affiliated to Pizhou Tobacco.

In the 2018 *Hubei Yinxingtuo Harbour* case, Hubei Yinxingtuo had a statutory monopoly in operating the Yinxingtuo Harbour, which included providing an intermediary service between truck companies (the customers) and the roll-on/roll-off shipping companies (the transportation providers). The Hubei AIC accused the monopolist of abusing its position in that intermediary service market by giving preferential treatment to an affiliated shipping company H. It described the conduct as including two aspects: prioritizing the ship-loading of H and assigning more lucrative truck transportation orders to H. Subsequently, the AIC alleged two competitive harms. The first one was the *disruption of competition encompassing the shipping companies*. To verify that harm, the AIC presented documentation evidence of Hubei Yinxingtuo being administratively sanctioned for committing the same offense in the past. The AIC observed that the undertaking had developed a pattern of discriminatory treatment so blatantly unfair that it resulted in physical altercations and local government intervention. It, therefore, considered that secondary-line competitive injury had transpired. The AIC supplemented the documentational evidence with its own investigation involving random retrievals of Hubei Yinxintuo's monthly dispatch records. This investigation confirmed that H had been consistently favoured. The second harm alleged by the AIC was the *undermining of the truck companies' benefits*. The AIC briefly mentioned that because of Hubei Yinxingtuo's preferential patronage of H, oftentimes, the truck companies would have to wait for an unnecessarily long time for the shipping service. In that light, this harm was essentially the first harm described from a different perspective.

While the previous two cases generated secondary-line competitive injury, the 2016 *Chifeng Salt Industry* case exemplifies how discriminatory treatment could also cause primary-line competitive injury. In this case, the Inner Mongolian AIC found Chifeng Salt to be a statutory monopoly in the local wholesale market for edible salt. It described the discrimination in question as Chifeng Salt's supplying certain types of salt to retailers located in counties adjoining other provinces while not to retailers located in counties not adjoining other provinces. Chifeng Salt defended itself by claiming that it, as an independent business entity, should be entitled to the freedom of selective trading. The AIC dismissed this defence, holding that Chifeng Salt's freedom of selective trading should only be understood as the right to selectively wholesale certain types of salt that were not under government-mandated supply obligations, rather than the right to select trading parties. Regarding the underlying harms, the AIC's decision revealed a key finding: Chifeng Salt implemented the discriminatory treatment because it wanted to prevent the 'invasion' of salt supplies from neighbouring provinces. But unfortunately, the AIC did not accentuate this finding or the potential primary-line competitive injury in its allegations of harm; it stressed the limitation of consumer choice in the non-adjoining areas instead.

The *Huaneng Solar Heat* case was handled by the Shandong AIC in 2023. The AIC found the undertaking in question to be a monopolist in the local heat supply market, and it fined the monopolist for committing two abuses: tying and discriminatory treatment. Interestingly, the AIC's rather brief analysis of the discrimination abuse revealed neither primary- or secondary-line competitive injury; instead, there was only monopolistic exploitation of certain users, as the conduct in question was essentially about charging a selected number of users that consumed heat periodically (e.g., schools) not by usage volume but by square meterage. The AIC found no justification for this discriminatory treatment, and it alleged the harms of overburdening those users and wasting heating resources. It is puzzling why the AIC chose to prosecute this exploitation-of-selected-users conduct as discriminatory treatment and not as excessively pricing or the imposition of unfair trading conditions. After all, discrimination is not condemnable *per se* under competition law even if it is discrimination of consumers; meanwhile, exploitative abuses by a monopolist are perfectly prosecutable even if the abuses are targeted only at certain customers. The theory of harm in this case is, therefore, questionable.

Regional courts and the Supreme Court

The four regional court cases are *Tong Hua v China Mobile Shanghai*, *Damingxing v CAVCA*, *Haoyunlai v Xinzhonggang*, and *Panjin Dongxing v PetroChina and Beckbury*. The case reviewed by the Supreme Court is *Ma Lijie v China Mobile Henan*. All five cases ended with the courts deciding against the plaintiffs on the grounds that there was no discrimination of equal-footing customers in the first place.

Both *Tong Hua v China Mobile Shanghai* and *Ma Lijie v China Mobile Henan* concerned consumers suing a telecommunications company for abusing its dominance by treating them discriminatorily. In the *Tong Hua* case, the plaintiff claimed that the defendant had infringed Article 17(6) (now Article 22(6)) of the AML by separating postpaid subscribers from prepaid subscribers and offering more favourable contractual terms to the former. Neither the first-instance nor the appeal court found the discriminatory treatment abusive. The appeal court held that there was no discrimination of equal-footing customers because the distinction between these two types of subscribers was pre-established. It held additionally that treating the two types of users discriminatorily had no negative impact on market competition or consumer choice. The *Ma Lijie* case had similar circumstances, and the Supreme Court reached the same conclusion: it held that there was no discriminatory treatment within the meaning of Article 17(6) AML to begin with since the pre-established distinction between 'standard' and 'special' phone number users meant that they were not 'trading counterparties who are on an equal footing'.

The other three cases concerned a downstream firm suing an upstream dominant firm for applying discriminatory trading conditions. Compared to the previous two cases, they were relatively more elaborate on why the plaintiffs and some other more favourably treated customers were not equal-footing counterparties. In *Damingxing v CAVCA*, the court advanced three conditions for establishing an abusive discriminatory treatment: (1) the disputed conduct had applied dissimilar trading conditions to equal-footing customers, (2) the discrimination had resulted in anticompetitive effects, and (3) the discrimination had no justification. It observed that although the defendant had indeed applied different licensing fees in different provinces, these dissimilar licensing fees were all below the regulatory cap and the defendant was legally given the discretion to set the fees variably across regions. On that basis, it ruled against the plaintiff for failing to prove that it was an equal-footing customer despite the regulatorily allowed fee variations. In *Haoyunlai v Xinzhonggang*, the plaintiff claimed that the defendant had abused its dominance by treating it less favourably compared to two other customers. The court concluded that the three undertakings were not on an equal footing, after comparing their demand volumes and transaction costs. In *Panjin Dongxing v PetroChina and Beckbury*, the plaintiff accused the defendants of abuse by buying the plaintiff's service at a price that was much lower than the price offered to another service provider. The court found that the plaintiff was not an equal-footing customer, as the plaintiff had shown a worse record in production safety and efficiency compared to the other service provider.

Notably, the plaintiffs in none of the three cases had made a solid claim that they were competitively disadvantaged by the discrimination in question. This may be an indication that they were indeed not equal-footing customers who had been discriminated against. So it seems that unless a plaintiff had produced convincing evidence of secondary- or primary-line competitive injury, a court would remain reluctant to recognize the existence of discriminatory treatment within the meaning of Article 22(6) AML.

Interim conclusions

The allegations of harms

By comparing the court judgments and administrative decisions, it can be observed that the enforcement agencies, particularly the SAIC and the succeeding SAMR, showed a better grasp of the anticompetitiveness of various abuse types in general compared to the courts. This observation can be explained from two aspects.

Limited harm allegations by the courts

The courts showed a palpable hesitation in articulating the potential competitive harms at issue when adjudicating private enforcement cases. For example, in *Qihoo v Tencent*, both the first instance judgment and the appeal judgment focused on defining the relevant market. It was only in the appeal judgment that the Supreme Court briefly identified the potential competitive harm arising from the disputed 'choose-one-from-two' practice as the leveraging of market power to a neighbouring market. This hesitation was more apparent in *Yang Zhiyong v China Telecom*, where the Shanghai High Court assessed the abusiveness of the conduct in question without a prior finding of dominance. It found no abuse at the end of the assessment, but instead of relying on this assessment conclusion, it invoked the ground that the plaintiff had failed to meet the standard of proof to dismiss the case.

In some other cases, a dominant position was clearly present, so the adjudicating court was confronted with the task of examining the abusive conduct in question. But even so, the adjudicating court tried to avoid making any allegation of harm by incorrectly denying the factual existence of an abuse. That was the case in *Wu Xiaoqin v Shaanxi Broadcast* and *Yunnan Yingding v Sinopec*. In the *Wu Xiaoqin* case, the Shanxi High Court made two logical mistakes in an attempt to deny the existence of a tying practice (although this ruling was quashed by the Supreme Court in the retrial); in the *Yunnan Yingding* case, the Kunming Intermediary Court denied the existence of a refusal to deal by subjecting the conception of 'deal' under the AML to the much more rigid conception of 'contract' under contract law.

Seemingly, it was only in cases where the circumstances indicated strongly a no-abuse-of-dominance conclusion that the courts showed more willingness to clarify the possible types of harm of the conduct in question. That was exemplified in *Gu Fang v China Southern Airlines* and *Xu Shuqing v Tencent*. Both cases were handled by the Guangdong High Court, and both were about a consumer suing an undertaking for refusing to deal. Precisely because the refused parties in both cases engaged in no market competition, the Guangdong High Court felt comfortable accentuating the harm of competition foreclosure of a refusal to deal. It suggested in the Gu Fang case that a consumer could be harmed only when the withheld product is public by nature.

Consistent harm allegations by the enforcement agencies

The administrative agencies made consistent efforts to allege the types of competitive harms in the cases they handled. This is well exemplified in the enforcement records of the SAIC and the SAMR. First, the SAIC consistently focused on the harm of competition restriction in its signature case, *Tetra Pak*, where three types of abuse (tying, exclusive dealing, and loyalty rebates) were involved. For the tying abuse, it used 'customer choice limitation' as a proxy for ascertaining whether the harm had transpired. For exclusive dealing, it advanced 'input foreclosure'. For loyalty rebates, it developed an effects-based analytical framework (despite the limited extent of effects analysis). Second, in *Alibaba* and *Meituan*, its two highest-profile cases, the SAMR unequivocally identified four harms stemming from abusive exclusive dealing: foreclosure of competition, downstream competition distortion, impeding long-term development of the platform economy, and reducing consumer choice and welfare. Third, in the 41 AIC and AMR cases concerning tying and the imposition of unfair trading conditions, the harm of monopolistic exploitation was commonly alleged. This is expected because these cases were invariably about monopolies. In some of the cases where there was a realistic prospect of competition despite the monopoly, the foreclosure harm was also advanced. The consistent harm allegations from the central to the local agencies are likely attributable to the secondary regulations that the SAIC and the SAMR had adopted to implement the AML.[12]

In its ten-year tenure, the NDRC had published far fewer AML enforcement cases compared to the SAIC. Its harm allegations were not as consistent and structured as the SAIC's but were nonetheless present. Acting as a price-control authority, it frequently emphasized the harm of unfairness or monopolistic exploitation that excessive prices had brought upon consumers. For instance, in its signature case, *Qualcomm*, the NDRC penalized three abuses: excessive pricing, tying, and the imposition of unreasonable trading conditions. Regarding the excessive pricing, the NDRC alleged the harm of unfairness in the sense of monopolistic exploitation; regarding the tying, it alleged the harm of competition foreclosure, using customer choice limitation as a proxy concern. Regarding the third abuse, however, it had a misplaced concern for downstream competition restriction, which resulted from an inaccurate characterization of the conduct in question. In *Zhejiang Second Pharmaceutical & Tianjin Handewei Pharmaceutical*, two abuses were identified: excessive pricing and refusal to deal. Regarding the first abuse, the NDRC briefly alleged the harm of unfairness; regarding the second abuse, it alleged the harm of downstream competition distortion resulting from the input-foreclosure of the customers and the impairment of consumer interests.

Comparing the courts and the agencies

By comparing the harm allegations of the courts and the agencies, we could observe a contrast between the courts' reluctance to show their comprehension of the competitive harms at hand and the agencies' consistent willingness and efforts therein. From an institutional perspective, one possible explanation for this

12 For example, Regulation on Prohibiting Abuses of Dominant Market Positions (《禁止滥用市场支配地位行为规定》), adopted by the SAMR on 10 March 2023, effective on 15 April 2023; the SAIC Regulation on the Prohibition of Conduct Abusing a Dominant Market Position (《工商行政管理机关禁止滥用市场支配地位行为的规定》), adopted by the SAIC on 31 December 2010, effective on 1 February 2011 (now invalidated).

contrast is that the courts operate only *reactively* whereas the agencies operate *proactively.*[13] While the enforcement agencies handle AML cases much more frequently by acting on their own initiatives, the courts have significantly fewer opportunities to accumulate antitrust expertise since litigations under the AML are yet to reach a scale allowing the courts to apply the law on a more regular basis. Consequently, the courts' grasp of the AML has remained largely at a generalist level, and their generalist perspectives have inhibited them to a large extent from accurately describing the types of competitive harm at stake in actual cases.

A consequence of the underdeveloped expertise is the court's increased susceptibility to judicial capture, particularly regional courts. Namely, a presiding court could inadvertently develop a distortive theory of harm that is plagued by information asymmetry and inadequate AML expertise to unduly favour a party. Even if we could neutralize the risk of judicial capture, there is still the possibility that a case-handling court invents a distortive theory of harm simply for the self-interest of enhancing its institutional role in the AML enterprise.

Admittedly, the enforcement agencies could also develop distortive theories of harm on account of regulatory capture and institutional self-interest. However, there is a slight difference between the agencies and the courts: the central and local agencies handle AML cases proactively and more regularly according to their legislatively entrusted or administratively delegated responsibilities. From an internal perspective, this makes it slightly more imperative for the agencies to normalize the case-handling procedures and more likely for them to gain expertise than the courts, and consequently, there will be more self-restraints in the agencies than the courts. From an external perspective, the more routinized enforcement activities make the agencies more exposed to public monitoring. These two factors help reduce, to a certain extent, the chances of distortive theories of harm being developed by the agencies.

Therefore, compared to an enforcement agency, a court is more likely to develop a distortive theory of harm in a scenario of judicial capture or a scenario where it is simply motivated to enhance its institutional role. The first scenario is yet to be verified in the collected cases due to the limited information disclosure, but there has been strong evidence suggesting the existence of the second scenario. This is discussed in the following subsection.

The elaboration of theories

A trend of judicial activism and its impact on the courts' reasoning

While the courts are less active than the enforcement agencies in making harm allegations, the case record shows that they are generally more engaged in elaborating their

13 Tom Ginsburg, 'Administrative Law and the Judicial Control of Agents in Authoritarian Regimes', in *Rule by Law: The Politics of Courts in Authoritarian Regimes*, ed. Tom Ginsburg and Tamir Moustafa (New York: Cambridge University Press, 2008), 64, 71.

'theories' of harm through legal reasoning. There is an apparent account for this observation: a court as an adjudicator is presented with the task of addressing the factual and legal disputes advanced by the parties; it has to be elaborate in its legal reasoning to fulfil its institutional mandate. This is exemplified by the fact that the court judgments analysed in this chapter are, on average, longer than the enforcement decisions, as they contain the parts describing and examining the disputes between the parties.

There is also a less apparent account: an observable trend of judicial activism in applying the AML, as demonstrated by the Supreme Court's control of local administrative monopolies.[14] This trend could be attributed to the dual-track institutional setting, which enabled a set of competitive dynamics between the courts and the enforcement agencies. As shown in the private enforcement cases, the courts went to great lengths to expand their scope of judicial review under the AML (e.g., exercising inquisitional power when the plaintiffs failed to meet the burden of proof, and proposing to examine abuse without first finding dominance in relevant markets), and at the same time, they showed a general lack of willingness or ability to engage in complex economic assessments (possibly due to their generalist background). The resulting problem is that they tended to produce questionable theories of harm in the cases they handled. In other words, the courts, while possessing limited competition law expertise, expanded their scope of judicial review at the expense of honouring the AML text and producing legal reasoning that is logically coherent and economically sensible. This problem is quite obvious in the following cases: *Qihoo v Tencent, Yang Zhiyong v China Telecom, Yunnan Yingding v Sinopec*, and *Yangmou v Hefei Yimou.*

The unsupervised agencies and the inadequate enforcement

The public enforcement agencies are less elaborate in their legal reasoning compared to the courts. To be sure, there are elaborate and well-reasoned enforcement decisions (e.g., the *Tetra Pak* case by the SAIC, the *Eastman* case, and the *Sherpa's* case by the Shanghai AMR), but the majority of decisions have relatively brief reasoning. An obvious explanation for this is that there is a steep learning curve for the enforcement agencies of a competition law regime that has been operationalized for less than two decades. This is corroborated by the fact that longer enforcement decisions have become more common as expertise accumulates over the years. From an institutional perspective, another explanation applicable to the tripartite era is that the jurisdictional delimitation had inhibited the optimization of performance of the NDRC and the SAIC: in cases where the two agencies had overlapping authority, the deciding agency had to be evasive (about the practices in question) or distort its theory of harm so as not to infringe the jurisdictional delimitation established between them.[15] Such cases include the following: the *Chongqing Southwest Second*

14 Eric C. Ip and Kelvin Hiu Fai Kwok, 'Judicial Control of Local Protectionism in China: Antitrust Enforcement against Administrative Monopoly on the Supreme People's Court', *Journal of Competition Law & Economics* 13, no. 3 (2017): 549–75, https://doi.org/10.1093/joclec/nhx018.

15 Xingyu Yan, 'The Jurisdictional Delimitation in the Chinese Anti-Monopoly Law Public Enforcement Regime: The Inevitable Overstepping of Authority and the Implications', *Journal of Antitrust Enforcement* 6, no. 1 (2018): 149.

Pharmaceutical case handled by the Chongqing AIC, the *Guangdong Dayawan Yiyuan Water Supply* case handled by the Guangdong AIC, and the *Wuhan Xinxing Pharmaceutical* case handled by the Hubei AIC. The latter two cases are not explicitly analysed in this chapter, but they concerned tying and the imposition of unreasonable trading conditions, respectively.

Nonetheless, these two explanations do not fully explain why the enforcement agencies were in general less elaborate on their theories of harm than the courts. In that regard, one possible account is the structurally induced selective enforcement. Namely, due to the lack of judicial supervision, the enforcement agencies enjoyed a high degree of discretionary power in the public enforcement sphere; this discretionary power, coupled with the agencies' susceptibility to political swaying, tends to make selective enforcement inevitable.[16] Consequently, the agencies were allowed to cherry-pick the cases they wanted to carry through. Those cases could either be easier to investigate (e.g., the regional tying cases with circumstances strongly implicating dominance and abuse) or they could be strategically or politically important to launch and close (e.g., the high-profile *Qualcomm* case when China was trying to promote 4G telecommunications technologies[17] and the exclusive dealing cases against digital platform operators circa 2021).

The conspicuous lack of predatory pricing cases

Predatory pricing is written in Article 22(2) as one of the seven types of abuses listed in Article 22 (including the catch-all provision), but this chapter fails to find either a public or private enforcement case concerning predatory pricing. This is likely due to the following reasons. First, there has been the Price Law that applies in parallel with the AML. Although much of the overlapping provisions have been taken out of the Price Law after the AML was adopted, predatory pricing could still be subject to Article 14(2) of the Price Law, which prohibits 'dumping commodities at prices lower than production cost in order to drive out rivals or monopolize the market'.[18] The enforcer of the Price Law had been the NDRC before it became the SAMR in 2018. So it is likely that the NDRC and the SAMR have dealt with predatory pricing cases, but they chose to apply Article 14(2) of the Price Law instead of Article 22(2) of the AML. Second, it is likely that on the one hand, the public enforcers have been more concerned with preserving competition in the short term rather than in the long term, meaning that they are more likely to appreciate the low prices resulting from predatory practices as welfare benefits brought

16 Yan, 'The Jurisdictional Delimitation in the Chinese Anti-Monopoly Law Public Enforcement Regime', 144.

17 Thomas K. Cheng, 'The PRC NDRC Case against Qualcomm: A Misguided Venture or Justified Enforcement of Competition Law?', *Journal of Antitrust Enforcement* 5, no. 1 (2017): 76–99, https://doi.org/10.1093/jaenfo/jnw005.

18 The Price Law of the People's Republic of China (《中华人民共和国价格法》), adopted by the Standing Committee of the National People's Congress on 29 December 1997, effective on 1 May 1998, http://english.www.gov.cn/services/doingbusiness/202102/24/content_WS6035f101c6d0719374af97b2.html (accessed 1 May 2024).

by vigorous competition; on the other hand, the enforcement agencies, particularly regional ones, have been busy with tackling abuses by natural and statutory monopolists, so they have perceived predatory pricing cases as a low priority due to the limited resources.

Reference list

Cheng, Thomas K. 'The PRC NDRC Case against Qualcomm: A Misguided Venture or Justified Enforcement of Competition Law?' *Journal of Antitrust Enforcement* 5, no. 1 (2017): 76–99. https://doi.org/10.1093/jaenfo/jnw005.

Economides, Nicholas, and Ioannis Lianos. 'The Elusive Antitrust Standard on Bundling in Europe and in the United States at the Aftermath of the Microsoft Cases'. *Antitrust Law Journal* 76, no. 2 (2009): 483–567.

Ginsburg, Tom. 'Administrative Law and the Judicial Control of Agents in Authoritarian Regimes'. In *Rule by Law: The Politics of Courts in Authoritarian Regimes*, edited by Tom Ginsburg and Tamir Moustafa, 58–72. New York: Cambridge University Press, 2008.

Ip, Eric C., and Kelvin Hiu Fai Kwok. 'Judicial Control of Local Protectionism in China: Antitrust Enforcement against Administrative Monopoly on the Supreme People's Court'. *Journal of Competition Law & Economics* 13, no. 3 (2017): 549–75. https://doi.org/10.1093/joclec/nhx018.

Wu, Tim. 'Intellectual Property Experimentalism By Way of Competition Law'. *Competition Policy International* 9, no. 2 (2013): 30–40.

Yan, Xingyu. 'The Jurisdictional Delimitation in the Chinese Anti-Monopoly Law Public Enforcement Regime: The Inevitable Overstepping of Authority and the Implications'. *Journal of Antitrust Enforcement* 6, no. 1 (2018): 123–49. https://doi.org/10.1093/jaenfo/jnx018.

Yan, Xingyu. 'Whither Antitrust Regulation of Loyalty Rebates in China: The Tetra Pak Decision and Lessons from the EU'. *World Competition* 40, no. 4 (2017): 613–36.

Yan, Xingyu, and Yang Feng. 'Mandating Interoperability of Interpersonal Communications Services in an Ecosystems Competition Context'. *Computer Law & Security Review* 50 (September 2023): 105850. https://doi.org/10.1016/j.clsr.2023.105850.

8 Comparisons and conclusions

Two modes of institutional dynamics

As shown in Chapters 4 and 5, the EU and Chinese laws on abuse of dominance have different institutional settings. On the one hand, EU competition law at the supranational level does not have private enforcement. The Commission monopolizes the law enforcement at the EU level, and the only way for the CJEU to get involved in private enforcement cases is through preliminary rulings.

On the other hand, the Chinese AML has a dual-track enforcement regime, where the courts are legislatively tasked with reviewing both private and public enforcement cases through civil and administrative litigations, respectively. However, as shown in Chapters 5 and 7, so far, there have been only 11 cases of administrative litigation under the AML; none of them ended with the court quashing the agency decision, and none concerned abuse of dominance. This near-absence of judicial supervision on administrative agencies is somewhat understandable: in the Chinese political context, administrative litigation is supposed to function as a third-party mechanism for the ruler (the principal) to rein in the administrative agencies (the agent) when carrying out their mandates; this is a cost-efficient mechanism for the ruler because the monitoring costs are paid by the private litigants.[1] It is, therefore, unsurprising that without sufficient independence, the Chinese courts exert limited constraints on administrative agencies.[2]

Consequently, different 'agency-court' dynamics flow in these two regimes. The EU regime embodies a supervisory mode, whereas the Chinese regime embodies a competitive mode of institutional dynamics vis-à-vis the application of competition law.

1 Tom Ginsburg, 'Administrative Law and the Judicial Control of Agents in Authoritarian Regimes', in *Rule by Law: The Politics of Courts in Authoritarian Regimes*, ed. Tom Ginsburg and Tamir Moustafa (New York: Cambridge University Press, 2008), 63.

2 Randall Peerenboom, *China's Long March Toward Rule of Law* (Cambridge: Cambridge University Press, 2002), 397, 420–4; Ji Li, 'The Leviathan's Rule by Law', *Journal of Empirical Legal Studies* 12, no. 4 (2015): 838; Haibo He, 'Litigations without a Ruling: The Predicament of Administrative Law in China', *Tsinghua China Law Review* 3 (2011): 271–4.

DOI: 10.4324/9781003479437-8

Within-regime and cross-regime differences in the development of theories of harm

The within-regime difference

In both the EU and Chinese regimes, the agencies and the courts within a regime display a difference in their development of theories of harm: the agencies are more adept at alleging the types of competitive harms at stake, while the courts are more comfortable at elaborating the theories of the harms. In the supervisory model of the EU, this difference entails an informal division of labour between the Commission and the CJEU since the CJEU plays only a reactive role in examining the 'draft theories of harm' advanced by the Commission in annulment cases and the Member State courts in preliminary ruling cases. In the competitive model of China, this difference is also present, but more because the courts are far less frequently exposed to competition law cases and thus have less expertise.

The cross-regime differences

Between the EU and Chinese regimes, there are two differences in their development of theories of harm. The first one pertains to their emphases on the types of harms. On most occasions, both regimes have shown a common concern for competition foreclosure, but other than that, they have made different emphases. The EU regime consistently advances the concern for market integration, which is the foundational policy mandate internalized in the objectives of EU competition law. Meanwhile, the Chinese regime frequently expresses concerns about monopolistic exploitation, which could be attributed to the fact that monopolies are still prevalent in the Chinese economy. Second, the EU regime generally produces more elaborate theories of harm than the Chinese regime. This could be explained by the much shorter time of the AML's existence. But to be sure, as the AML agencies and courts accumulate experience over the years, they are producing longer decisions. This is shown in Chapter 7.

An institutional account for the differences

Theory of harm development in the EU supervisory model

The Court's adherence to the legal text

In a supervisory 'court-agency' model, the judiciary displays a high level of loyalty to the legal text (including statutory law and decisional law). As shown in the case analyses in Chapter 6, as long as 'the verbal formulas'[3] of the law permitted it to reach a straightforward answer, the CJEU would be disinterested in adding

3 John J. Flynn, 'Antitrust Jurisprudence: A Symposium on the Economic, Political and Social Goals of Antitrust Policy: Introduction', *University of Pennsylvania Law Review* 125, no. 6 (1977): 1187.

more economic considerations to a theory-of-harm production. This is exemplified by the CJEU's presumptive rule of illegality on 'pricing below average variable costs' and 'rebates conditional on the customer's obtaining all, or most, or a given portion of their requirements exclusively from the manufacturer'. Even when a presumptive rule of illegality is considered inappropriate and proof of anticompetitive effects is required, the CJEU still shows a reluctance to engage in intensive economic assessments for the purpose of ascertaining the anticompetitiveness of an abuse. In such cases, it always refers to the ruling that facts-based predictions of potential anticompetitive effects would suffice and tends to use intermediaries, such as exclusionary intentions, to ascertain such potential anticompetitive effects.

This disinterest is institutionally supported, as the CJEU's individual decision-making faces no further scrutiny. The ensuing risk, however, is the making of Type I (false positive) errors under the premise that the CJEU takes the entrusted mandate of market integration seriously and that a powerful institution is inclined to prohibit things that threaten its core mandate.[4] In other words, when coupled with the 'market integration' mandate, the CJEU's rather strict adherence to the legal text increases the possibility of making false positive errors in its theory-of-harm production.

To be sure, such errors do not necessarily mean that the CJEU has done wrong in upholding the more value-loaded political and social objectives on top of economic objectives. But the problem is that unsubstantiated concerns for political and social objectives in individual cases negatively affect the quality of theories of harm, which in turn undermine the efforts to uphold such objectives. It is unfeasible to ascertain exactly how many false positive errors have been committed since there is no further way to challenge a judgment by the CJEU. Nonetheless, one could suspect that such errors existed in the commonly vague theories of harm of the ECJ cases in the 1970s.

The CJEU's change of attitude somewhere in the 1980s also indicated that there had indeed been such errors. As the integration mandate was achieved to a great extent (especially in the aspect of negative integrations), the mandate was becoming less dominant in the CJEU's theory-of-harm development in the 1980s and 1990s than it was in the 1970s.[5] This enabled the CJEU to become more receptive to economic thinking, as evidenced by the increasingly elaborate theories of harm from the 1980s onwards. Another possible enabler of this receptive attitude was that, by then, the CJEU might have become quite aware of the false positive risk. However, even with such valid reasons to be receptive, the CJEU needed and still needs to weigh the benefits of including more economic considerations in antitrust adjudication against the increased costs thereof.[6] Therefore, looking ahead,

4 Frank H. Easterbrook, 'Does Antitrust Have a Comparative Advantage?', *Harvard Journal of Law & Public Policy* 23, no. 1 (1999): 8–9.

5 Anne C. Witt, *The More Economic Approach to EU Antitrust Law*, Hart Studies in Competition Law, vol. 14 (Oxford: Hart Publishing, 2016), 10.

6 Thomas A. Lambert and Alden F. Abbott, 'Recognizing the Limits of Antitrust: The Roberts Court versus the Enforcement Agencies', *Journal of Competition Law & Economics* 11, no. 4 (2015): 796–8 (describing the various types of antitrust enforcement costs).

the extent of the CJEU's embrace of economics in the theory-of-harm development is likely to be limited.

The agency's use of economics as a counter-constraining mechanism

In the supervisory model, a public enforcement agency exerts its discretionary power under the constraint of the judiciary. Under the 'principal-agent' lens, this means that the judiciary functions as a third-party control mechanism on behalf of the legislators (the principal) to ensure that the enforcement agency (the agent) fulfils its delegated responsibilities.

Against this backdrop, the risk of making Type I (and Type II [false negative]) errors becomes the vantage point for the agency to bargain for more discretionary power in enforcement. This bargaining dynamic is observable in EU competition law: the Commission points out to the CJEU the constant risk of Type I errors when legal assessments contradict economics, thus persuading the CJEU to give out more discretion in enforcement decision-making. This dynamic is reflected in the established principle that the Commission is to be respected in terms of 'complex economic assessments'. Also, this dynamic puts into perspective the 'more economic approach' championed by the Commission.

In that light, the Commission possesses a counter-constraining mechanism against the CJEU: by using its proactive role as the public enforcer to pre-emptively add more economic 'inputs' in the development of theories of harm, it could make the CJEU more likely to defer to the Commission's contributions to the substantive law development. The effectiveness of this counter-constraining mechanism could be observed in the CJEU's preliminary ruling cases: these cases show a trend of the CJEU adopting, on its own initiative, certain economic rationales that were originally brought forward by the Commission. For example, in *TeliaSonera* and *Post Danmark I*, the CJEU employed the as-efficient-competitor rationale, which was introduced by the Commission in its Guidance Paper in 2009.

But to be sure, while benefiting from advocating a more economic approach to producing theories of harm, the Commission also needs to take into account the ensuing costs. For example, while reducing Type I and Type II errors, the increased use of economics could also induce expert-bias errors,[7] as well as the increased administrative costs that the Commission has to internalize. Besides, this counter-constraining mechanism could 'backfire' on the Commission in the sense that as the CJEU absorbs more economic thinking into the case law, the Commission will inevitably be held to a higher standard when its decisions are reviewed by the CJEU. This explains why the Commission has been pushing for *ex ante* sector regulation instead of *ex post* antitrust enforcement in the digital sector, where more economic considerations tend to advise against assertive intervention.

7 Jeffrey J. Rachlinski and Cynthia R. Farina, 'Cognitive Psychology and Optimal Government Design', *Cornell Law Review* 87, no. 2 (2002): 560.

Theory of harm development in the Chinese competitive model

Performance review as the key

A premise for discussing the competitive 'agency-court' dynamic is the concept of the principle-agent relationship, which informs us that the enforcement agencies and the courts could both be perceived as agents entrusted by the principal to achieve the desired outcomes of a law.[8] In that light, the AML's dual-track setting with little judicial supervision on public enforcement could be understood as the institutional choice that the policymakers and legislators currently have settled on for achieving the goal of competition protection.

There is a high level of judicial deference to administrative agencies, as exemplified by the fact that no plaintiffs have ever won in court in challenging an AML public enforcement decision. But to be sure, in the context of antitrust technocracy, judicial supervision of administrative agencies is not an end itself but rather a means to improving agency performance. So, the absence of judicial supervision does not necessarily render a competition law regime unworkable, as long as agency technocracy has been gaining expertise and verifiably transforming that expertise into better agency performance. Therefore, in a competitive 'agency-court' dynamic where the judiciary loses the supervisory role and behaves instead like a parallel-track enforcer, the key issue is assessing the performances of the agencies as well as the courts. One aspect of assessment is their development of theories of harm. This is done in Chapter 7. This assessment informs us on two issues: (1) whether the competitive dynamic has induced better performance of the agencies and the courts and (2) whether some other mechanisms have been functioning instead of judicial supervision.

The courts showing poorer performances

The case analyses in Chapter 7 reveal that the courts, in carrying out their private enforcement adjudication responsibilities, have not been very good 'agents' to their 'principal' in achieving the AML's goal of competition protection. Specifically, the courts have shown poorer performance compared to the agencies in the sense that they have produced problematic theories of harm at a higher rate and to a more serious extent. By producing inconsistent and distortive theories of harm, the courts are undermining instead of enhancing legal certainty. This is in contrast with the supervisory model of the EU, where the CJEU has been dutifully adhering to the Treaty provisions and the case law, even to a fault at times.

The dual-track setting and the competitive agency-court dynamic are behind the courts' poorer performance. First, being kept away from supervising the agencies, the courts lose the most important channel to grow competition law expertise. Secondly, being the competitors of the enforcement agencies, the courts are driven by

8 Suli Zhu, 'The Party and the Courts', in *Judicial Independence in China: Lessons for Global Rule of Law Promotion*, ed. Randall Peerenboom (Cambridge: Cambridge University Press, 2009), 56–7.

the common ambition of expanding judicial power in the AML enterprise. When coupled with inadequate expertise, this activist tendency generates questionable law-application outcomes.

The agencies' deeper problem: inadequate enforcement

Compared to the courts, the agencies (especially the SAIC and certain AMRs) produce higher-quality theories of harm. Their allegations of harm and elaborations of theories show more logical coherence and better use of economic theory and empirical methods than those of the courts. Nonetheless, there are also reasons to worry about the agencies' performance. First, the agencies' performance is just slightly better. Their theories of harm are not without problems. Besides, the agencies are expected to do better since they operate on a proactive basis and have processed much more cases than the courts. Second, the development of theories of harm is only 'the tip of the iceberg' in terms of assessing the agencies' overall performance. We must also recognize the cases and investigations that did not reach the decision-making stage and the other aspects of the decided cases (e.g., the severity of sanctions). In that light, the agencies have a deeper problem: inadequate enforcement.

Two institutional factors contribute to this problem. The first one is the capacity constraints. The AML agencies have been suffering from a manpower shortage since the beginning, and the shortage became worse after the three agencies consolidated in 2018, with anecdotal evidence suggesting that the SAMR had fewer employees than its three predecessors combined. The situation is slowly getting better, as now, the State Anti-Monopoly Bureau has been established under the SAMR, but the capacity constraint is likely to persist for a long time to come. The second factor is the setting of direct principal control: as the agencies become subject to administrative superior control instead of judicial supervision, they become more susceptible to policy influences that are not legally vetted. In that regard, the absence of judicial supervision represents the loss of institutional guarantee for independence. Had there been any judicial supervision, the agencies as more independent AML enforcers would probably have had a better chance of curing under-enforcement. This is an interesting contrast with the EU regime, where the Commission is in a sense 'battling for more discretion' with the CJEU and the concern is more about over- than under-enforcement. A lesson here is that direct principal control is an inferior substitute for third-party control for the 'ruler' of a young competition law regime seeking to rein in administrative agencies.

In light of this selective enforcement problem, the fact that the agencies produce higher-quality theories of harm is of limited value for the AML regime as a whole. First, the relatively better agency performance is achieved at the expense of inadequate enforcement. So one could always wonder if the agency performance would have been even better if more vigorous third-party supervision had been in place. Second, the production of higher-quality theories of harm is not sustainable, on account of the agencies' susceptibility to unchecked policy influences. The institutional safeguards preventing this from happening are severely limited, as exemplified by the campaign-style antitrust enforcement in digital markets.

Summary answers to the research questions

To the research questions posed in Chapter 1, this book draws the following conclusions. First, a theory of harm can be described as a narrative that demonstrates the anticompetitiveness or the competitive harm of a practice in question in the context of competition law. There are two essential components of a theory of harm: economic theories and the policy mandates of a legal regime. The quality of a theory of harm can be appraised with two basic criteria: internal consistency of logic and the degree to which it makes general economic sense.

Second, using the EU regime and the Chinese regime as research samples, this book observes that different institutions produce theories of harm differently. There are two levels of differences. Within a regime, the agencies appear to be better at alleging the types of harms at stake while the courts seem better at elaborating the theories. Across the regimes (of the EU and China), there are more nuanced differences, which could be characterized as two scenarios of 'agency-court' dynamics: the supervisory scenario of the EU regime and the competitive scenario of the Chinese regime. In the first scenario, the agency (the Commission) increases the use of economics in the development of theories of harm to loosen judicial constraints. The court (the CJEU) is less interested in the use of economics, mainly because of its institutional superiority and its responsibility to uphold the integration mandate. Nonetheless, the agency and the court have a common pursuit when developing theories of harm: reducing false positive and false negative outcomes, despite the different lengths to which they go for that pursuit. The second scenario shows more problems. There, the agencies struggle to overcome the persistent problem of inadequate enforcement. Meanwhile, the courts are more prone to producing distortive theories of harm due to two factors: the courts' lack of AML expertise on the one hand and their ambitions to expand the judicial power within the AML enterprise through adjudicating private enforcement cases on the other.

Third, the aforementioned findings have a crucial implication: the presence of judicial supervision, or the lack thereof, determines the type of institutional dynamics underpinning the development of theories of harm in a regime, so it has a definitive impact on the quality of the developed theories of harm. From a principal-agent perspective, judicial supervision serves as a third-party control mechanism fostering the development of higher-quality theories of harm. The lack of third-party control brings more problems than benefits, irrespective of whether the 'agent' is an administrative agency or a court. In that light, this book advises the AML legislators and policymakers to rethink the institutional structure, particularly the lack of third-party supervision on public enforcement. For example, an internal review mechanism could be established within the SAMR, like the one that exists in most (if not all) European competition authorities. Also, the SAMR and provincial AMRs should improve their procedural transparency and information disclosure. This would invite closer monitoring by peers in the antitrust community and the general public and thus would compensate, to a certain extent, the lack of third-party control.

A remark on further research

Based on the conclusions, this book identifies two areas where further studies would be appreciated. The first area is the study of the EU case law. Over the years, the Commission and the CJEU together have produced many landmark cases, including but not limited to the ones analysed in this book. The development of these theories of harm entails the formulation of legal concepts, standards, and analytical frameworks, so it is important to examine (1) to what extent, if at all, those legal concepts, legal standards, and analytical frameworks are compatible with each other and (2) to what extent, if at all, they can reinforce the more economic approach vis-à-vis the changing economic reality. There have been studies on these topics, and this book provides a basis for further research by analysing the theories of harm in landmark cases.

The second area is the study of the Chinese AML regime. Although this book has strived to cover as many AML cases as possible, most likely there are still cases left out. Besides, many other aspects of the AML necessitate problem-oriented research, which may go beyond the scope of law. For example, there is the observable problem of the AML's inconsistent enforcement against Chinese Internet giants. To study this problem, a legal doctrinal approach would not suffice; empirical analyses and political perspectives would probably be necessary. This book is a starting point for such problem-oriented research.

Reference list

Easterbrook, Frank H. 'Does Antitrust Have a Comparative Advantage?'. *Harvard Journal of Law & Public Policy* 23, no. 1 (1999): 5–10.

Flynn, John J. 'Antitrust Jurisprudence: A Symposium on the Economic, Political and Social Goals of Antitrust Policy: Introduction'. *University of Pennsylvania Law Review* 125, no. 6 (1977): 1182–90.

Ginsburg, Tom. 'Administrative Law and the Judicial Control of Agents in Authoritarian Regimes'. In *Rule by Law: The Politics of Courts in Authoritarian Regimes*, edited by Tom Ginsburg and Tamir Moustafa, 58–72. New York: Cambridge University Press, 2008.

He, Haibo. 'Litigations without a Ruling: The Predicament of Administrative Law in China'. *Tsinghua China Law Review* 3 (2011): 257–81.

Lambert, Thomas A., and Alden F. Abbott. 'Recognizing the Limits of Antitrust: The Roberts Court versus the Enforcement Agencies'. *Journal of Competition Law & Economics* 11, no. 4 (2015): 791–853.

Li, Ji. 'The Leviathan's Rule by Law'. *Journal of Empirical Legal Studies* 12, no. 4 (2015): 815–46.

Peerenboom, Randall. *China's Long March Toward Rule of Law*. Cambridge: Cambridge University Press, 2002.

Rachlinski, Jeffrey J., and Cynthia R. Farina. 'Cognitive Psychology and Optimal Government Design'. *Cornell Law Review* 87, no. 2 (2002): 549–615.

Witt, Anne C. *The More Economic Approach to EU Antitrust Law*. Hart Studies in Competition Law, vol. 14. Oxford: Hart Publishing, 2016.
Zhu, Suli. 'The Party and the Courts'. In *Judicial Independence in China: Lessons for Global Rule of Law Promotion*, edited by Randall Peerenboom, 52–68. Cambridge: Cambridge University Press, 2009.

Appendices

Appendix 1

List of EU cases

AKZO

- 85/609/EEC: Commission Decision of 14 December 1985 relating to a proceeding under Article 86 of the EEC Treaty (IV/30.698—ECS/AKZO), [31 December 1985] OJ L 374;
- Case 62/86 *AKZO Chemie BV v Commission of the European Communities* [1991] ECR I 3359.

AstraZeneca

- Commission Decision of 15 June 2005 relating to a proceeding under Article 82 of the EC Treaty and Article 54 of the EEA Agreement (Case COMP/A. 37.507/F3—AstraZeneca);
- Case T-321/05 *AstraZeneca AB and AstraZeneca plc v European Commission* [2010] ECR II 2805;
- Case C-457/10 P *AstraZeneca AB and AstraZeneca plc v European Commission*, ECLI:EU:C:2012:770.

BP

- 77/327/EEC: Commission Decision of 19 April 1977 relating to a proceeding under Article 86 of the EEC Treaty (IV/28.841—ABG/Oil companies operating in the Netherlands), [May 9, 1977] OJ L 117;
- Case 77/77 *Benzine en Petroleum Handelsmaatschappij BV and others v Commission of the European Communities* [1978] ECR 1513.

BPB Magill

- 89/205/EEC: Commission Decision of 21 December 1988 relating to a proceeding under Article 86 of the EEC Treaty (IV/31.851—Magill TV Guide/ITP, BBC and RTE), [March 21, 1989] OJ L 78;
- Case T-69/89 *Radio Telefis Eireann v Commission of the European Communities* [1991] ECR II 485;

- Joined Cases C-241/91 P and C-242/91 P *Radio Telefis Eireann (RTE) and Independent Television Publications Ltd (ITP) v Commission of the European Communities* [1995] ECR I 743.

Bronner

- Case C-7/97 *Oscar Bronner GmbH & Co. KG v Mediaprint Zeitungs- und Zeitschriftenverlag GmbH & Co. KG, Mediaprint Zeitungsvertriebsgesellschaft mbH & Co. KG and Mediaprint Anzeigengesellschaft mbH & Co. KG* [1998] ECR I 7791.

CBEM-Telemarketing

- Case 311/84 *Centre belge d'études de marché—Télémarketing (CBEM) v SA Compagnie luxembourgeoise de télédiffusion (CLT) and Information publicité Benelux (IPB)* [1985] ECR 3261.

Commercial Solvents

- 72/457/CEE: Décision de la Commission, du 14 décembre 1972, relative à une procédure d'application de l'article 86 du traité instituant la Communauté économique européenne (IV/26.911—ZOJA/CSC—ICI), [31 December 1972] OJ L 299;
- Joined Cases 6 and 7/73 *Istituto Chemioterapico Italiano S.p.A. and Commercial Solvents Corporation v Commission of the European Communities* [1974] ECR 223.

Continental Can

- 72/21/CEE: Décision de la Commission, du 9 décembre 1971, relative à une procédure d'application de l'article 86 du traité CEE (IV/26 811—Continental Can Company), [January 8, 1972] OJ L 7;
- Case 6/72, *Europemballage Corp and Continental Can Co Inc v Commission of the European Communities* [1973] ECR 215.

Deutsche Telekom

- 2003/707/EC: Commission Decision of 21 May 2003 relating to a proceeding under Article 82 of the EC Treaty (Case COMP/C-1/37.451, 37.578, 37.579—Deutsche Telekom AG), [14 October 2003] OJ L 263;
- Case T-271/03 *Deutsche Telekom AG v Commission of the European Communities* [2008] ECR II 477;
- Case C-280/08 P *Deutsche Telekom AG v European Commission* [2010] ECR I 9555.

DSD

- 2001/463/EC: Commission Decision of 20 April 2001 relating to a proceeding pursuant to Article 82 of the EC Treaty (Case COMP D3/34493—DSD), [21 June 2001] OJ L 166;
- Case T-151/01 *Der Grüne Punkt—Duales System Deutschland GmbH v Commission of the European Communities* [2007] ECR II 1607;
- Case C-385/07 P *Der Grüne Punkt—Duales System Deutschland GmbH v Commission of the European Communities* [2009] ECR I 6155.

France Télécom

- Case T-340/03 *France Télécom SA v Commission of the European Communities* [2007] ECR II 107;
- Case C-202/07 P *France Télécom SA v Commission of the European Communities* [2009] ECR I 2369.

General Motors

- 75/75/EEC: Commission Decision of 19 December 1974 relating to a proceeding under Article 86 of the EEC Treaty (IV/28.851—General Motors Continental), [3 February 1975] OJ L 29;
- Case 26/75 *General Motors Continental NV v Commission of the European Communities* [1975] ECR 1367.

Grundig-Consten

- 64/566/CEE: Décision de la Commission, du 23 septembre 1964, relative à une procédure au titre de l'article 85 du traité (IV-A/00004–03344 "Grundig-Consten"), [20 October 1964] OJ 161, 2545–2553;
- Joined Cases 56 and 58/64 *Établissements Consten S.à.R.L. and Grundig-Verkaufs-GmbH v Commission of the European Economic Community* [1966] ECR 299.

Hoffmann-La Roche

- 76/642/EEC: Commission Decision of 9 June 1976 relating to a proceeding under Article 86 of the Treaty establishing the European Economic Community (IV/29.020—Vitamins), [16 August 1976] OJ L 223;
- Case 85/76 *Hoffmann-La Roche & Co. AG v Commission of the European Communities* [1979] ECR 461.

IMS Health

- Case C-418/01 *IMS Health GmbH & Co. OHG v NDC Health GmbH & Co. KG* [2004] ECR I 5039.

Intel

- Commission Decision of 13 May 2009 relating to a proceeding under Article 82 of the EC Treaty and Article 54 of the EEA Agreement (COMP/C-3/37.990—Intel);
- Case T-286/09 *Intel Corp. v European Commission*, ECLI:EU:T:2014:547;
- Case C-413/14 P *Intel Corp. v European Commission*, ECLI:EU:C:2017:632.

Meta

- Case C-252/21 *Meta Platforms Inc and Others v Bundeskartellamt*, ECLI:EU:C:2023:537.

Michelin I

- 81/969/EEC: Commission Decision of 7 October 1981 relating to a proceeding under Article 86 of the EEC Treaty (IV.29.491—Bandengroothandel Frieschebrug BV/NV Nederlandsche Banden-Industrie Michelin), [9 December 1981] OJ L 353;
- Case 322/81 *NV Nederlandsche Banden Industrie Michelin v Commission of the European Communities* [1983] ECR 3461.

Michelin II

- 2002/405/EC: Commission Decision of 20 June 2001 relating to a proceeding pursuant to Article 82 of the EC Treaty (COMP/E-2/36.041/PO—Michelin), [May 31, 2002] OJ L 143;
- Case T-203/01 *Manufacture française des pneumatiques Michelin v Commission of the European Communities* [2003] ECR II 4071;

Microsoft

- Commission Decision of 24 March 2004 relating to a proceeding under Article 82 of the EC Treaty (Case COMP/C-3/37.792 Microsoft);
- Case T-201/04 *Microsoft Corp. v Commission of the European Communities* [2007] ECR II 3601.

Post Danmark I

- Case C-209/10 *Post Danmark A/S v Konkurrencerådet*, ECLI:EU:C:2012:172.

Post Danmark II

- Case C-23/14 *Post Danmark A/S v Konkurrencerådet*, ECLI:EU:C:2015:651.

SABAM

- Case C-372/19 *Belgische Vereniging van Auteurs, Componisten en Uitgevers CVBA (SABAM) v Weareone.World BVBA and Wecandance NV*, ECLI:EU:C:2020:959.

Société Technique Minière

- Case 56/65 *Société Technique Minière (L.T.M.) v Maschinenbau Ulm GmbH (M.B.U.)* [1966] ECR 235;

Sot Lélos

- Joined Cases C-468/06 to C-478/06 *Sot. Lélos kai Sia EE and Others v GlaxoSmithKline AEVE Farmakeftikon Proïonton, formerly Glaxowellcome AEVE* [2008] ECR I 7139.

Suiker Unie

- 73/109/EEC: Commission Decision of 2 January 1973 relating to proceedings under Articles 85 and 86 of the EEC Treaty (IV/26 918—European sugar industry), [May 26, 1973] OJ L 140;
- Joined Cases 40 to 48, 50, 54 to 56, 111, 113 and 114/73 *Coöperatieve Vereniging "Suiker Unie" UA and others v Commission of the European Communities* [1975] ECR 1663.

TeliaSonera

- Case C-52/09 *Konkurrensverket v TeliaSonera Sverige AB* [2011] ECR I 527.

Tetra Pak

- Case C-333/94 P *Tetra Pak International SA v Commission of the European Communities* [1996] ECR I 5951.

United Brands

- 76/353/EEC: Commission Decision of 17 December 1975 relating to a procedure under Article 86 of the EEC Treaty (IV/26699—Chiquita), [9 April 1976] OJ L 95;
- Case 27/76 *United Brands Company and United Brands Continentaal BV v Commission of the European Communities* [1978] ECR 207.

Appendix 2

List of Chinese cases

The NDRC cases

Qualcomm

- The NDRC, *The Qualcomm Decision* (中华人民共和国国家发展和改革委员会行政处罚决定书 发改办价监处罚[2015]1号), 9 February 2015, www.samr.gov.cn/zt/qhfldzf/art/2015/art_81812df2ad9f4ad4806bbe6a38bd46bc.html.

Zhejiang Second Pharmaceutical & Tianjin Handewei Pharmaceutical

- The NDRC, *The Zhejiang Second Pharmaceutical & Tianjin Handewei Pharmaceutical Decision* (国家发展和改革委员会行政处罚决定书[2017] 1–2号), 28 July 2017, www.samr.gov.cn/zt/qhfldzf/art/2017/art_e11bc136c01f4a43af706bf7a53570fe.html.

The SAIC and AIC cases

Alxa Left Banner Water Supply

- The SAIC, *The Alxa Left Banner Water Supply Case* (竞争执法公告2016年第4号内蒙古自治区阿拉善左旗城市给排水公司滥用市场支配地位案), 22 April 2016, www.samr.gov.cn/cms_files/filemanager/samr/www/samrnew/fldys/tzgg/xzcf/202204/t20220424_342037.html.

Chifeng Salt Industry

- The SAIC, *The Chifeng Salt Industry Case* (竞争执法公告2016年第7号 内蒙古赤峰市盐业公司滥用市场支配地位行为处罚决定), 16 August 2016, www.samr.gov.cn/cms_files/filemanager/samr/www/samrnew/fldys/tzgg/xzcf/202204/t20220424_342043.html.

Chongqing Natural Gas

- The SAIC, *The Chongqing Natural Gas Case* (竞争执法公告2014年第19号重庆燃气集团股份有限公司垄断行为案), 28 April 2014, www.samr.gov.cn/zt/qhfldzf/art/2014/art_bc80b8f8c35d46a48eda119b0584050a.html.

Chongqing Qingyang Pharmaceutical

- The SAIC, *The Chongqing Qingyang Pharmaceutical Case* (竞争执法公告2015年第12号 重庆青阳药业有限公司涉嫌滥用市场支配地位拒绝交易案), 28 October 2015, www.samr.gov.cn/cms_files/filemanager/samr/www/samrnew/fldys/tzgg/xzcf/202204/t20220424_342023.html.

Chongqing Southwest Second Pharmaceutical

- The SAIC, *The Chongqing Southwest Second Pharmaceutical Case* (竞争执法公告2016年12号 重庆西南制药二厂有限责任公司垄断行为案), 24 November 2016, www.samr.gov.cn/cms_files/filemanager/samr/www/samrnew/fldys/tzgg/xzcf/202204/t20220424_342053.html.

Guangdong Dayawan Yiyuan Water Supply

- The SAIC, *The Guangdong Dayawan Yiyuan Water Supply Case* (竞争执法公告2014年第13号 广东惠州大亚湾溢源净水有限公司滥用市场支配地位案), 16 December 2013, www.samr.gov.cn/cms_files/filemanager/samr/www/samrnew/fldys/tzgg/xzcf/202204/t20220424_341983.html.

Hainan Dongfang Tap Water

- The SAIC, *The Hainan Dongfang Tap Water Case* (竞争执法公告2015年第2号 海南省东方市自来水公司垄断案), 9 January 2015, www.samr.gov.cn/cms_files/filemanager/samr/www/samrnew/fldys/tzgg/xzcf/202204/t20220424_342003.html.

Hubei Yinxingtuo Harbor

- The SAIC, *The Hubei Yinxingtuo Harbor Case* (竞争执法公告2018年第5号湖北银杏沱港埠股份有限公司差别待遇案行政处罚决定书), 9 January 2018, www.samr.gov.cn/cms_files/filemanager/samr/www/samrnew/fldys/tzgg/xzcf/202204/t20220424_342093.html.

Inner Mongolia Chifeng Tobacco

- The SAIC, *The Inner Mongolia Chifeng Tobacco Case* (竞争执法公告2014年第16号 内蒙古自治区烟草公司赤峰市公司滥用市场支配地位案), 4 July 2014, www.samr.gov.cn/cms_files/filemanager/samr/www/samrnew/fldys/tzgg/xzcf/202204/t20220424_341989.html.

Jiangsu Pizhou Tobacco

- The SAIC, *The Jiangsu Pizhou Tobacco Case* (竞争执法公告2014年第18号 江苏徐州市烟草公司邳州分公司滥用市场支配地位案), September 2014, www.samr.gov.cn/zt/qhfldzf/art/2014/art_f1bd69c6171b41608a059ebdabd-f6e5d.html.

Liaoning Fushun Tobacco

- The SAIC, *The Liaoning Fushun Tobacco Case* (竞争执法公告2015年第7号 辽宁省烟草公司抚顺市公司滥用市场支配地位案), June 2015, www.samr.gov.cn/zt/qhfldzf/art/2015/art_5b38c9cbfd694b5a8ee3f577eedce8a9.html.

Qingdao Xin'ao Xincheng Natural Gas

- TheSAIC,*TheQingdaoXin'aoXinchengNaturalGasCase*(竞争执法公告2016年第2号 青岛新奥新城燃气有限公司滥用市场支配地位案), 21 March 2016, www.samr.gov.cn/cms_files/filemanager/samr/www/samrnew/fldys/tzgg/xzcf/202204/t20220424_342033.html.

Sichuan Jiuyuan Yinhai Software

- The SAIC, *The Sichuan Jiuyuan Yinhai Software Case* (竞争执法公告2017年12号 四川久远银海畅辉软件有限公司滥用市场支配地位案), 3 August 2017, www.samr.gov.cn/cms_files/filemanager/samr/www/samrnew/fldys/tzgg/xzcf/202204/t20220424_342081.html.

Suqian Kunlun Natural Gas

- The SAIC, *The Suqian Kunlun Natural Gas Case* (竞争执法公告2017年10号 宿迁中石油昆仑燃气有限公司滥用市场支配地位案), 30 December 2016, www.samr.gov.cn/cms_files/filemanager/samr/www/samrnew/fldys/tzgg/xzcf/202204/t20220424_342079.html.

Suqian Yinkong Water Supply

- The SAIC, *The Suqian Yinkong Water Supply Case* (竞争执法公告2016年13号 宿迁银控自来水有限公司垄断行为案), 28 November 2016, www.samr.gov.cn/zt/qhfldzf/art/2016/art_f841c1f881bb4db9ac3de00a89467989.html.

Tetra Pak

- The SAIC, *The Tetra Pak Decision* (国家工商行政管理总局行政处罚决定书 工商竞争案字[2016]1号), 9 November 2016, www.samr.gov.cn/cms_files/filemanager/samr/www/samrnew/fldys/tzgg/xzcf/202204/t20220424_342049.html.

Ürümqi Water Supply

- The SAIC, *The Ürümqi Water Supply Case* (竞争执法公告2016年11号乌鲁木齐水业集团有限公司滥用市场支配地位限定交易案), 12 October 2016, www.samr.gov.cn/zt/qhfldzf/art/2016/art_935c241e7b404e0188f365e4ca0222e9.html.

Wuhan Xinxing Pharmaceutical

- The SAIC, *The Wuhan Xinxing Pharmaceutical Case* (竞争执法公告2017年4号武汉新兴精英医药有限公司滥用市场支配地位案), 11 January 2017, www.samr.gov.cn/cms_files/filemanager/samr/www/samrnew/fldys/tzgg/xzcf/202204/t20220424_342067.html.

Wujiang Huayan Water Supply

- The SAIC, *The Wujiang Huayan Water Supply Case* (竞争执法公告2017年3号吴江华衍水务有限公司滥用市场支配地位案), 30 December 2016, www.samr.gov.cn/zt/qhfldzf/art/2017/art_0e3f5ac93b854d74baf585289249c615.html.

XilinGol League Broadcast Television

- The SAIC, *The XilinGol League Broadcast Television Case* (竞争执法公告2016年第5号　内蒙古广播电视网络集团有限公司锡林郭勒分公司滥用市场支配地位案), 7 June 2016, www.samr.gov.cn/cms_files/filemanager/samr/www/samrnew/fldys/tzgg/xzcf/202204/t20220424_342039.html.

Yongzhou Salt Industry

- The SAIC, *The Yongzhou Salt Industry Case* (竞争执法公告2016年14号　湖南盐业股份有限公司永州市分公司垄断行为案), 26 October 2016, www.samr.gov.cn/cms_files/filemanager/samr/www/samrnew/fldys/tzgg/xzcf/202204/t20220424_342057.html.

The SAMR and AMR cases

Alibaba

- The SAMR, *The Alibaba Case* (国家市场监督管理总局行政处罚决定书国市监处〔2021〕28号), 10 April 2021, www.samr.gov.cn/zt/qhfldzf/art/2021/art_74b2593fd32a432baf3dcbd163935167.html.

China Aviation Fuel Yunnan

- Yunnan AMR, *The China Aviation Fuel Yunnan Case* (云南省市场监督管理局行政处罚决定书云市监价处〔2021〕2 号), 30 June, 2021, www.samr.gov.cn/cms_files/filemanager/samr/www/samrnew/fldys/tzgg/xzcf/202204/t20220424_341613.html.

Chongqing Yongkang Gas

- Chongqing AMR, *The Chongqing Yongkang Gas Case* (重庆市市场监督管理局行政处罚决定书渝市监处字〔2022〕300号), 7 December 2022, www.samr.gov.cn/fldys/tzgg/xzcf/art/2023/art_ed05f218dbcd428da2a3067d98e9a236.html.

Eastman

- Shanghai AMR, *The Eastman Case* (上海市市场监督管理局行政处罚决定书沪市监案处字〔2019〕第 000201710047 号), 16 April 2019, www.samr.gov.cn/cms_files/filemanager/samr/www/samrnew/fldys/tzgg/xzcf/202204/t20220424_341759.html.

Fengyang Yimin Water

- Anhui AMR, *The Fengyang Yimin Water Case* (安徽省市场监督管理局 行政处罚决定书皖市监竞争处字〔2022〕1号), 17 January 2022, www.samr.gov.cn/zw/xzcfjd/art/2022/art_7b44e34d5f6f4fd8a1fcd5dd11862f81.html.

Guizhou Shuitou Water

- Guizhou AMR, *The Guizhou Shuitou Water Case* (贵州省市场监督管理局 行政处罚决定书黔市监价处〔2022〕9 号), 1 July 2022, www.samr.gov.cn/zw/xzcfjd/art/2022/art_113e2413bb084aa9b408fa80085b7101.html.

Guizhou Zhoufucheng Logistics

- Guizhou AMR, *The Guizhou Zhoufucheng Logistics Case* (贵州省市场监督管理局行政处罚决定书黔市监价处〔2022〕10号), 28 July 2022, www.samr.gov.cn/zt/qhfldzf/art/2022/art_865a524d707746468ae8eea91401020f.html.

Huaneng Solar Heat

- Shandong AMR, *The Huaneng Solar Heat Case* (山东省市场监督管理局行政处罚决定书鲁市监行处字〔2023〕5 号), 3 April 2023, www.samr.gov.cn/fldys/tzgg/xzcf/art/2023/art_24c190f8826e4c7a84f69d735e816894.html.

Hunan Er'kang & Henan Jiushi

- The SAMR, *The Hunan Er'kang & Henan Jiushi Case* (国家市场监督管理总局行政处罚决定书国市监处〔2018〕21–22号), 30 December 2018, www.samr.gov.cn/zt/qhfldzf/art/2019/art_5a07c9301dde4cf4a8b2276f88df09bf.html.

Jiangshan Crematorium

- Zhejiang AMR, *The Jiangshan Crematorium Case* (浙江省市场监督管理局行政处罚决定书浙市监案〔2020〕8号), 22 October 2020, www.samr.gov.cn/cms_files/filemanager/samr/www/samrnew/fldys/tzgg/xzcf/202204/t20220424_341859.html.

Jianke Gas Supply

- Shanxi AMR, *The Jianke Gas Supply Case* (山西省市场监督管理局行政处罚决定书晋市监价监罚字〔2020〕13号), 2 July 2020, www.samr.gov.cn/cms_files/filemanager/samr/www/samrnew/fldys/tzgg/xzcf/202204/t20220424_341843.html.

Jingyang Water Supply

- Shaanxi AMR, *The Jingyang Water Supply Case* (陕西省市场监督管理局行政处罚决定书陕市监反垄断处罚字〔2021〕1号), 12 August 2021, www.samr.gov.cn/cms_files/filemanager/samr/www/samrnew/fldys/tzgg/xzcf/202204/t20220424_341611.html.

Meituan

- The SAMR, *The Meituan Case* (国家市场监督管理总局行政处罚决定书国市监处罚〔2021〕74号), 8 October 2021, www.samr.gov.cn/zt/qhfldzf/art/2021/art_20d2233982c843f58681b40674441050.html.

Minhe Chuanzhong Gas

- Qinghai AMR, *The Minhe Chuanzhong Gas Case* (青海省市场监督管理局行政处罚决定书青市监垄断字〔2020〕02号), 14 May 2020, www.samr.gov.cn/cms_files/filemanager/samr/www/samrnew/fldys/tzgg/xzcf/202204/t20220424_341829.html.

Nanjiing Ningwei Pharmaceutical

- Shanghai AMR, *The Nanjing Ningwei Pharmaceutical Case* (上海市市场监督管理局行政处罚决定书沪市监反垄处〔2021〕3220190101511号), 17 November

2021, www.samr.gov.cn/cms_files/filemanager/samr/www/samrnew/fldys/tzgg/xzcf/202204/t20220424_341623.html.

Nanjing Water Supply

- Jiangsu AMR, *The Nanjing Water Supply Case* (江苏省市场监督管理局行政处罚决定书苏市监反垄断案〔2020〕7 号), 30 November 2020, www.samr.gov.cn/cms_files/filemanager/samr/www/samrnew/fldys/tzgg/xzcf/202204/t20220424_341875.html.

Nanjing Zhongran Gas

- Jiangsu AMR, *The Nanjing Zhongran Gas Case* (江苏省市场监督管理局行政处罚决定书苏市监反垄断案〔2023〕1号), 18 January 2023, www.samr.gov.cn/fldes/tzgg/xzcf/art/2023/art_c5ee795bea01476fab9a5246b70b9456.html.

Ningxia Changran Gas

- Ningxia AMR, *The Ningxia Changran Gas Case* (宁夏回族自治区市场监督管理厅行政处罚决定书宁市监处〔2022〕2号), 26 April 2022, www.samr.gov.cn/zw/xzcfjd/art/2022/art_199b001085924c37a76f192e18c2742e.html.

Northeast Pharmaceutical

- Liaoning AMR, *The Northeast Pharmaceutical Case* (辽宁省市场监督管理局行政处罚决定书辽市监反垄断处罚〔2023〕1号), 18 January 2023, www.samr.gov.cn/fldes/tzgg/xzcf/art/2023/art_2658f8c940c24a0e95bcbb7b9ccdb770.html.

Rizhao Water Supply

- Shandong AMR, *The Rizhao Water Supply Case* (山东省市场监督管理局行政处罚决定书鲁市监行处字〔2022〕120号), 15 December 2022, www.samr.gov.cn/cms_files/filemanager/samr/www/samrnew/fldys/tzgg/xzcf/202304/t20230407_354454.html.

Shandong Kanghui Pharmaceutical

- The SAMR, *The Shandong Kanghui Pharmaceutical Case* (国家市场监督管理总局行政处罚决定书国市监处〔2020〕8 号), 9 April 2020, www.samr.gov.cn/cms_files/filemanager/samr/www/samrnew/fldys/tzgg/xzcf/202204/t20220424_341823.html.

Shangqiu Xinxianfeng Pharmaceutical

- Henan AMR, *The Shangqiu Xinxianfeng Pharmaceutical Case* (河南省市场监督管理局行政处罚决定书豫市监处字〔2021〕1号), 27 September 2021, www.samr.gov.cn/cms_files/filemanager/samr/www/samrnew/fldys/tzgg/xzcf/202204/t20220424_341619.html.

Shangyao First Pharmaceuticals & Wuhan Huihai Pharmaceutical

- Shanghai AMR, *The Shangyao First Pharmaceuticals & Wuhan Huihai Pharmaceutical Case* (上海市市场监督管理局行政处罚决定书沪市监反垄处〔2023〕202301401–2号), 13 December 2023, www.samr.gov.cn/fldes/tzgg/xzcf/art/2023/art_b2d7e70f9c7c452e898fdeb85ef8ba34.html.

Shaoxing Keqiao Water

- Zhejiang AMR, *The Shaoxing Keqiao Water Case* (浙江省市场监督管理局行政处罚决定书浙市监案〔2022〕3 号), 2 June 2022, www.samr.gov.cn/zt/qhfldzf/art/2022/art_13d5d696b7b34f97b9c66578b5c34e0d.html.

Shaoxing Shangyu Water

- Zhejiang AMR, *The Shaoxing Shangyu Water Case* (浙江省市场监督管理局行政处罚决定书浙市监案〔2022〕4 号), 2 June 2022, www.samr.gov.cn/zw/xzcfjd/art/2022/art_e75637a7d055420fa127e49802977be1.html.

Sherpa's

- Shanghai AMR, *The Sherpa's Case* (上海市市场监督管理局行政处罚决定书沪市监反垄处〔2020〕06201901001号), 25 December 2020, www.samr.gov.cn/zt/qhfldzf/art/2021/art_3e376423f1cd486d89aa730d9e6bd47d.html.

Sichuan Fushun Gas

- Sichuan AMR, *The Sichuan Fushun Gas Case* (四川省市场监督管理局行政处罚决定书川市监处〔2021〕2号), 12 March 2021, www.samr.gov.cn/cms_files/filemanager/samr/www/samrnew/jzxts/tzgg/xzcf/202104/t20210401_327474.html.

Simcere Pharmaceutical

- The SAMR, *The Simcere Pharmaceutical Case* (国家市场监督管理总局行政处罚决定书国市监处〔2021〕1号), 22 January 2021, www.samr.gov.cn/zt/qhfldzf/art/2021/art_00da1837ccb940c89eeb0ace78b96576.html.

Sitong Taixing Water

- Yunnan AMR, *The Sitong Taixing Water Case* (云南省市场监督管理局行政处罚决定书云市监价处〔2021〕1号), 21 January 2021, www.samr.gov.cn/cms_files/filemanager/samr/www/samrnew/fldys/tzgg/xzcf/202204/t20220424_341895.html.

Suqian Zhengyuan Water Supply

- Jiangsu AMR, *The Suqian Zhengyuan Water Supply Case* (江苏省市场监督管理局行政处罚决定书苏市监案〔2019〕00027号), 12 October 2019, www.samr.gov.cn/cms_files/filemanager/samr/www/samrnew/jzxts/tzgg/xzcf/201911/t20191126_308830.html.

Tianjin Jinyao Pharmaceutical

- Tianjin AMR, *The Tianjin Jinyao Pharmaceutical Case* (天津市市场监督管理委员会行政处罚决定书津市监垄处〔2023〕1号), 14 March 2023, www.samr.gov.cn/cms_files/filemanager/samr/www/samrnew/fldys/tzgg/xzcf/202303/t20230322_354013.html.

Tianjin Water Supply

- Tianjin AMR, *The Tianjin Water Supply Case* (天津市市场监督管理委员会行政处罚决定书津市监稽罚字〔2019〕J1号), 23 May 2019, www.samr.gov.cn/cms_files/filemanager/samr/www/samrnew/fldys/tzgg/xzcf/202204/t20220424_341767.html.

Tongfang CNKI

- The SAMR, *The Tongfang CNKI Case* (国家市场监督管理总局行政处罚决定书国市监处罚〔2022〕87号), 26 December 2022, www.samr.gov.cn/fldes/tzgg/xzcf/art/2023/art_27cab7312a424e0ea46c6fa9e5044371.html.

Wanbangde Pharmaceutical

- Zhejiang AMR, *The Wanbangde Pharmaceutical Case* (浙江省市场监督管理局行政处罚决定书浙市监案字〔2020〕14号), 3 November 2020, www.samr.gov.cn/zt/qhfldzf/art/2020/art_83a23bdce17340a1b6a0b365c12ae9b9.html.

Wuhu Gas Supply

- Anhui AMR, *The Wuhu Gas Supply Case* (安徽省市场监督管理局行政处罚决定书皖市监竞争处字〔2022〕2号), 5 July 2022, www.samr.gov.cn/jzxts/tzgg/xzcf/art/2023/art_7fd12aaeb4854af982b25e7d991bcf92.html.

Xinzhou Gas Supply

- Shanxi AMR, *The Xinzhou Gas Supply Case* (山西省市场监督管理局行政处罚决定书晋市监价监罚字〔2020〕14号), 13 July 2020, www.samr.gov.cn/cms_files/filemanager/samr/www/samrnew/fldys/tzgg/xzcf/202204/t20220424_341845.html.

Yixing Ganghua Gas

- Jiangsu AMR, *The Yixing Ganghua Gas Case* (江苏省市场监督管理局行政处罚决定书苏市监反垄断案〔2021〕4号), 17 November 2021, www.samr.gov.cn/zt/qhfldzf/art/2021/art_78b30388d4094f5199e1866213269c99.html.

Yongfu Water Supply

- Guangxi AMR, *The Yongfu Water Supply Case* (广西壮族自治区市场监督管理局行政处罚决定书桂市监反垄断〔2022〕1号), 14 November 2022, www.samr.gov.cn/zt/qhfldzf/art/2022/art_459552098c85416395b073a0aaa23b9c.html.

Yuanda Pharmaceutical

- The SAMR, *The Yuanda Pharmaceutical Case* (国家市场监督管理总局行政处罚决定书国市监处罚〔2023〕9号), 21 May 2023, www.samr.gov.cn/fldys/tzgg/xzcf/art/2023/art_991d1d80a4a644aab4d15c8b998101de.html?eqid=d34060250002d4ab0000000664744626.

Court cases

Damingxing v CAVCA

- Kunming Intermediary People's Court, *Damingxing v CAVCA* (云南大明星欢乐园娱乐有限公司与中国音像著作权集体管理协会、云南天合世纪文化传播有限公司滥用市场支配地位纠纷一审民事判决书[2017]云01民初1782号), 7 May 2018.

Ding Qidong v China Unicom Beijing

- Beijing Intellectual Property Court, *Ding Qidong v China Unicom Beijing (first instance)* (丁啟东与中国联合网络通信有限公司北京市分公司拒绝交易纠纷一审民事判决书[2015] 京知民初字第339号), 29 December 2017;
- Beijing High People's Court, *Ding Qidong v China Unicom Beijing (appeal)* (中国联合网络通信有限公司北京市分公司等拒绝交易纠纷二审民事判决书[2018] 京民终440号), 17 September 2018.

Gu Fang v China Southern Airlines

- Guangdong High People's Court, *Gu Fang v China Southern Airlines (appeal)* (顾芳与中国南方航空股份有限公司拒绝交易纠纷二审民事判决书 [2014] 粤高法民三终字第1141号), 5 May 2015.

Haoyunlai v Xinzhonggang

- Ningbo Intermediary People's Court, *Haoyunlai v Xinzhonggang* (嵊州市好运来印染有限公司、浙江新中港清洁能源股份有限公司垄断定价纠纷一审民事判决书[2020] 浙02知民初182号), 30 October 2020.

Hongfu v Weihai Water Supply

- The Supreme People's Court, *Hongfu v Weihai Water Supply (appeal)* (威海宏福置业有限公司、威海市水务集团有限公司滥用市场支配地位纠纷民事二审民事判决书[2022] 最高法知民终395号), 23 June 2022.

Hytera v Motorola Solutions

- Beijing Intellectual Property Court, *Hytera v Motorola Solutions* (海能达通信股份有限公司与摩托罗拉系统(中国)有限公司北京分公司等滥用市场支配地位纠纷一审民事判决书[2017] 京73民初1671号), 31 December 2019.

Jinbi Dashijie v CAVCA

- The Supreme People's Court, *Jinbi Dashijie v CAVCA (appeal)* (广州市金碧大世界饮食娱乐有限公司、中国音像著作权集体管理协会滥用市场支配地位纠纷民事二审民事判决书[2020] 最高法知民终1519号), 28 March 2022.

Ma Lijie v China Mobile Henan

- The Supreme People's Court, *Ma Lijie v China Mobile Henan (appeal)* (马利杰、中国移动通信集团河南有限公司滥用市场支配地位纠纷民事二审民事判决书[2021] 最高法知民终1977号), 23 June 2022.

Ningbo Yongmou v Rimou

- The Supreme People's Court, *Ningbo Yongmou v Rimou (appeal)* (日某、宁波某公司滥用市场支配地位纠纷民事二审民事判决书[2021]　最高法知民终1449号), 14 December 2023.

Panjin Dongxing v PetroChina and Beckbury

- Beijing Intellectual Property Court, *Panjin Dongxing v PetroChina and Beckbury* (盘锦东兴油井措施服务有限公司与BECKBURY国际有限公司等滥用市场支配地位纠纷一审民事判决书), 28 August 2020.

Qihoo v Tencent

- Guangdong High People's Court, *Qihoo v Tencent (first instance)* (广东省高级人民法院民事判决书[2011] 粤高法民三初字第2号), 20 March 2013;
- The Supreme People's Court, *Qihoo v Tencent (appeal)* (中华人民共和国最高人民法院民事判决书[2013]民三终字第4号), 8 October 2014.

Quanke v Chongqing Sanxia

- Chongqing First Intermediary People's Court, *Quanke v Chongqing Sanxia* (重庆市全科房地产开发有限公司与重庆三峡水利供电有限公司重庆三

峡水利电力建设有限公司滥用市场支配地位纠纷一审民事判决书[2022] 渝01民初1875号), 24 October 2022.

Song Xin v China Railway Guangzhou

- Changsha Intermediary People's Court, *Song Xin v China Railway Guangzhou* (宋鑫与广州铁路(集团)公司、中国铁路信息技术中心等滥用市场支配地位纠纷一审民事判决书[2016] 湘01民初1460号), 28 August 2018.

Tiyu v Chinese Super League

- The Supreme People's Court, *Tiyu v Chinese Super League (appeal)* (体娱(北京)文化传媒股份有限公司、中超联赛有限责任公司等滥用市场支配地位纠纷民事二审民事判决书[2021] 最高法知民终1790号), 23 June 2022.

Tong Hua v China Mobile Shanghai

- Shanghai People's High Court, *Tong Hua v China Mobile Shanghai (appeal)* (童华与中国移动通信集团上海有限公司滥用市场支配地位纠纷二审民事判决书[2014] 沪高民三(知)终字第105号), 26 January 2015.

Wang v Beijing Lianjia

- Beijing Intellectual Property Court, *Wang v Beijing Lianjia (first instance)* (王林林与北京链家房地产经纪有限公司滥用市场支配地位纠纷一审民事判决书[2017] 京73民初561号), 28 June 2020;
- The Supreme People's Court, *Wang v Beijing Lianjia (appeal)* (王某某、北京链家房地产经纪有限公司等滥用市场支配地位纠纷民事二审民事判决书[2020] 最高法知民终1463号), 14 December 2022.

Wu Xiaoqin v Shaanxi Broadcast

- Shaanxi High People's Court, *Wu Xiaoqin v Shaanxi Broadcast (appeal)* (陕西广电网络传媒（集团）股份有限公司与吴小秦捆绑交易纠纷判决书[2013] 陕民三终字第00038号), 12 September 2013;
- The Supreme People's Court, *Wu Xiaoqin v Shaanxi Broadcast (retrial)* (吴小秦与陕西广电网络传媒（集团）股份有限公司捆绑交易纠纷申请再审民事判决书[2016] 最高法民再98号), 30 May 2016.

Wu Zongqu v Yongfu Water Supply

- Nanning Intermediary People's Court, *Wu Zongqu v Yongfu Water Supply* (吴宗区与永福县供水公司滥用市场支配地位纠纷一审民事判决书[2018] 桂01民初1190号), 8 October 2019.

Xu Shuqing v Tencent

- Guangdong High People's Court, *Xu Shuqing v Tencent (appeal)* (徐书青、深圳市腾讯计算机系统有限公司滥用市场支配地位纠纷二审民事判决书 [2016] 粤民终1938号), 2 June 2017.

Yang Zhiyong v China Telecom

- Shanghai High People's Court, *Yang Zhiyong v China Telecom (appeal)* (杨志勇与中国电信股份有限公司、中国电信股份有限公司上海分公司滥用市场支配地位纠纷二审民事判决书 [2015]沪高民三（知）终字第23号), 14 December 2015.

Yangmou v Hefei Yimou

- The Supreme People's Court, *Yangmou v Hefei Yimou (appeal)* (合肥某公司滥用市场支配地位纠纷二审民事判决书[2020] 最高法知民终1140号), 25 May 2023.

Yunnan Yingding v Sinopec

- Kunming Intermediary People's Court, *Yunnan Yingding v Sinopec (first instance)* (中石化、云南盈鼎反垄断诉讼重审一审判决书[2015]昆知民重字第3号), 8 October 2016;
- Yunnan High People's Court, *Yunnan Yingding v Sinopec (appeal)* (云南盈鼎生物能源股份有限公司、中国石化销售有限公司云南石油分公司拒绝交易纠纷二审民事判决书 [2017]云民终122号), 28 August 2017.

Zhang v Quanzhou Crematorium

- The Supreme People's Court, *Zhang v Quanzhou Crematorium (appeal)* (泉州某殡仪服务公司甲与泉州某殡仪服务公司乙拒绝交易纠纷二审民事判决书[2021] 最高法知民终242号), 16 June 2023.

Index

Note: Page numbers in *italic* indicate a figure and page numbers in **bold** indicate a table on the corresponding page.

abuse 105–7: assessing 107–9, 151; exploitative 120–1; *see also specific types*
activism, judicial 181–2
adherence to legal text 186–8
adjudicating courts 21–6
administrative actions 22, 74, 86–92
AEC test 137–140
agency technocracy 22–4
AICs 159–60, 176–7; *Chongqing Qingyang Pharmaceutical* 163–4; *Chongqing Southwest Second Pharmaceutical* 164
AKZO 113–17
Alibaba Case, The 172–4
'all circumstances' approach 117–18, 135–6
allegation of harms 123–4, 141, 178–81
AMRs 152–4, **153**, 159–60, 171–2, 176–7
anticompetitive effects 118–19
anticompetitive intent 113–15
Anti-Monopoly Commission (AMC) 73–4
Anti-Monopoly Law (AML): bygone tripartite public enforcement regime 73–83, **80**, **83**; judicial supervision of public enforcement 86–93, **89–91**; legal framework 70–3; new public enforcement regime led by SAMR 83–6, **85**; parallel track of private enforcement 93–6, **94**, *96*
antitrust concept: competitive harm 30–2; economic theories 36–48; framework for evaluation 48–9; theories of harm 32–6
antitrust institutional dynamics: adjudicating courts 21–6; enforcement agencies 17–21; impact factor on antitrust substantive law 11–14; political power game 14–17
Article 86 of EEC Treaty 57, 102, 104–15, 122–6, 133, 144–5
Article 101 TFEU 9, 33; and market integration 102–3; secondary legislation 55–7
Article 102 TFEU 33, 143–5; Chicago School 42–5; consideration for applying 46–8; Harvard School 40–2; and market integration 102–3; ordoliberalism 36–40; Post-Chicago School 45–6; secondary legislation 55–7; theories of harm 104–9
as-efficient-competitor approach 138
assessing: abuse 107–9; competition foreclosure 117–18; foreclosure harm 138
AstraZeneca 118–20

background premises 3–5
bases for judicial supervision 21–2
BP 121, 122–3, 124–6, 144–5
BPB Magill 121–3, 126–8, 143, 144
Bronner 121–3, 127–9, 1142

case law 5–7, 35, 57–60, 107–8, 121–7, 130–1, 137–43, 188–9; *see also specific cases*
case records 8, 87–8, 148, 152, 181
case-specific dimensions of theory of harm 34–5
CBEM-Telemarketing 121, 124–6, 128, 142
centralized EU regime: exploitative pricing 110–13; infringement of regulatory rules 118–21; institutional structure at the Union level 61–8, *67*; interim conclusions 141–5; legal framework 53–60; loyalty rebates 132–41; margin

squeeze 129–32; market integration mandate 99–109; predatory pricing 113–18; refusal to deal 121–9; restrictions of resale 109–10
Chicago School 42–5; calibrating 45
Chifeng Salt Industry Case, The 176
Chinese regime 147; bygone tripartite public enforcement regime 73–83, **80**, **83**; defining relevant markets and finding dominance 148–51; discriminatory treatment 175–8; excessive pricing 151–6, **153–4**; exclusive dealing and loyalty rebates 169–75; interim conclusions 178–84; judicial supervision of public enforcement 86–93, **89–91**; legal framework 70–3; new public enforcement regime led by SAMR 83–6, **85**; parallel track of private enforcement 93–6, **94**, *96*; refusal to deal 161–9, **162–3**; tying and the imposition of unreasonable trading conditions 156–61
Chinese competition law 1–3
Chinese competitive model 189–91
Chongqing Southwest Second Pharmaceutical Case, The 164
coherence, counterbalancing need for 35–6
Commercial Solvents 121, 122–3, 124–6, 128, 143–5
Commission, the *see* European Commission
competition, restriction of 32, 119, 165, 172
competition foreclosure 111, 112–13, 117–18, 134–5, 142–3
competition laws 1–3; institutional commitment to enforcing 15–16; and market integration 100–101
competition on the merits 119–20
competition protection 53–4
competition regulation before Anti-Monopoly Law 70–1
competitive harm 30–2, 109–10
competitive market structures 124–6
competitive model 189–91
composition: Court of Justice of the European Commission 66–8, *67*; European Commission 61–2
concrete administrative actions 86–92
conduct illegality 30
conduct-specific dimensions of theory of harm 34–5
Consten and Grundig v Commission 103
Continental Can 42, 57, 102, 105–7, 113, 142, 144
counterbalancing need for coherence 35–6
counter-constraining mechanism, economics as 188
Court of First Instance (CFI) 64–6, 126–7, 130–1, 135–6, 143–5
Court of Justice of the European Union (CJEU) 2, 143–5, 185–92; division of labour between the Commission and 141–2; as judicial supervisor 64–8, *67*; rulings 58–60
Court of Justice of the European Commission (ECJ) 109–10, 112–13; *AKZO* 115–18; AstraZeneca 119–20; *BP* 124–6; *Bronner* 127–9; *CBEM-Telemarketing* 124–6; *Commercial Solvents* 124–6; *Deutsche Telekom* 130–2; *Hoffmann-La Roche* 133–4; *IMS Health* 127–9; institutional hierarchy between GC and 66; *Magill* 127–9; Meta 120–1; *Michelin I* 135–6; *Post Danmark II* 137; *Sot Lélos* 127–9; *Suiker Unie* 133; *United Brands* 124–6

Damingxing v CAVCA 154, 161, 166, 168
decentralization reform 62–4
deference, judicial 22–4
Deutsche Telekom 129–30, 130–1, 143
Ding Qidong v China Unicom Beijing 165
discretionary power 18–19
discriminatory treatment 175–8
division of labour 141–2
dominance 148–56, **153–154**; activating abuse of dominance regulation for merger control 105–7; finding dominance 107–9
dormancy of Article 86 104–5
DSD 110–12, 143

Eastman Case, The 171–2
ECJ *see* Court of Justice of the European Commission (ECJ)
economics as counter-constraining mechanism 188
economic theories: Chicago School 42–5; consideration for applying 46–8; Harvard School 40–2; ordoliberalism 36–40; Post-Chicago School 45–6
EEC Treaty *see* Article 86 of EEC Treaty
elaboration of theories 141–2, 147, 181–4
enforcement 17–21; competition law 15–16; inadequate 182–3, 190–1; judicial supervision of AML public enforcement 86–93, **89–91**; parallel tracks 93–6, **94**, *96*; private enforcement

25–6, 93–6, **94**, *96*; supervising public enforcement 21–2; *see also* public enforcement regime; *and specific agencies*
entrenched centrality 62–4
equilibration 12–13
European Commission 61–4, 109, 111; *AKZO* 113–15; *AstraZeneca* 118–19; *BP* 122–4; and the CFI 126–7; *Commercial Solvents* 122–4; *Deutsche Telekom* 129–30; division of labour 141–2; *Hoffmann-La Roche* 133; *Intel* 138; *Magill* 122–4; *Michelin I* 134–5; *Michelin II* 134–5; *Suiker Unie* 132–3; *United Brands* 122–4
European Union (EU) competition law 1–3; and market integration 100–101; ordoliberal influence on 38–40
European Union (EU) regime, centralized: exploitative pricing 110–13; infringement of regulatory rules 118–21; institutional structure at the Union level 61–8, *67*; interim conclusions 141–5; legal framework 53–60; loyalty rebates 132–41; margin squeeze 129–32; market integration mandate 99–109; predatory pricing 113–18; refusal to deal 121–9; restrictions of resale 109–10
European Union (EU) supervisory model 186–8
evaluation of intent 119–20
excessive pricing 151–6, **153–4**
exclusionary purposes 118–19
exclusive dealing 169–75
exclusivity rebates 138–41
exploitation, monopolistic 112–13
exploitative abuse 120–1
exploitative pricing 110–13

facts, narratives to bridge law and 32–4
foreclosure: competition 111, 112–13, 117–18, 134–5, 142–3; harm 115–17, 137
form-based theory of harm 133–4
France Télécom 116–17
Freiburg School 36–8

General Court (GC): AstraZeneca 119–20; hierarchy 58–9, 66; Intel 138–41
General Data Protection Regulation (GDPR): infringement of 118, 120–1
General Motors 110–12, 141–2
Grundig-Consten see Consten and Grundig v Commission
Gu Fang v China Southern Airlines 165, 179
Guangdong High Court 148–50, 166, 179

Haoyunlai v Xinzhonggang 155, 177–8
harm: allegation of 123–4, 141, 178–81; competition foreclosure 134–5, 142–3; foreclosure 115–17, 137, 138; to market integration 133, 142; supplementary 143–5; *see also* harm, theories of; *and specific types*
harm, theories of 32–6; competitive harm 30–2; development in centralized EU regime 99–145; development in federated Chinese regime 145–84; differences in the development of 186–91; economic theories 36–48; elaboration of 181–4; form-based 133–4; framework for evaluation 48–9; primitive 122–3; structural 133–4
Harvard School 20, 40–2, 44
hierarchy: CJEU and General Court rulings 58–9; ECJ and GC 66
Hoffmann-La Roche 108, 113, 132–3, 133–4, 143, 145
Hongfu v Weihai Water Supply 160–1
Huaneng Solar Heat Case, The 176–7
Hunan Er'kang & Henan Jiushi Case, The 158, 164
Hytera v Motorola Solutions 166

ideological mindset 19–21
illegality, conduct 30
impact factor, institutional dynamics as 11–14
imposition of unreasonable trading conditions 156–61
IMS Health 122, 128–9, 142
incentive to take strategic actions for more power 16–17
indispensability test 127–9
Industrial Economics 42, 45–6
industrial organization 40–1
institutional actors 12–13, 54–5
institutional commitment to enforcing competition law 15–16
institutional dynamics 185; adjudicating courts 21–6; enforcement agencies 17–21; impact factor on antitrust substantive law 11–14; and parallel enforcement tracks 94–6, **94**, *96*; political power game 14–17
institutions, meaning of 11–12
Intel 132, 138–41, 143

intellectual property rights (IPR) 105, 119, 124, 126–8, 142, 174
intent: anticompetitive 113–15; evaluation of 119–20; intent-based AKZO formula 115–17
interdependence 12–13
inter-temporal change 35–6

Jiangsu Pizhou Tobacco Case, The 176
Jinbi Dashijie v CAVCA 167–8
judicial activism 181–2
judicial deference 22–4
judicial supervision 64–8, *67*, 86–93, **89–91**

law: Anti-Monopoly Law 70–96; antitrust law 13–14; antitrust substantive law 11–14; competition laws 1–3, 100–101; legal basis 57, 86–7, 93–4; legal frameworks 5, 7, 48, 53–60, 70–3; legal instruments 54–5; legislative process 71–2; narratives to bridge facts and 32–4; secondary legislation 54–7; soft law 57–8
limits/limitations 8, 21–2; limited harm analyses 109–10, 132–3
loyalty rebates 132–41, 169–75

Ma Lijie v China Mobile Henan 174, 177
Magill see BPB Magill
margin squeeze 129–32
markets 148–56, **153–154**; competitive market structures 124–6; market definition 150–1; market integration 99–103, 109–10, 111, 124–6, 142; market structure-oriented conception 137
Meituan Case, The 84, 172–4, 180
merger control 105–7; secondary legislation 57
Meta 118, 120–1
Michelin I 107–8, 117, 132, 134–5, 135–6, 143–5
Michelin II 132, 134–5, 135–6, 142–5
Microsoft 121, 123–4, 126–7, 143–4
Ministry of Commerce (MOFCOM) 2, 71–7; enforcement record 78–9
monopolistic exploitation 112–13
mission: CJEU 65–6

narratives to bridge law and facts 32–4
National Development and Reform Commission (NDRC) 2, 73–5, 77–9, 180–3; enforcement record 81–3, **83**; *Qualcomm* 152, 156–7; refusal to deal 161–3
Ningbo Yongmou v Rimou 168

ordoliberalism 36–40
organization, industrial 40–1

Panjin Dongxing v PetroChina and Beckbury 166, 178
parallel enforcement tracks 93–6, **94**, *96*
performance review 189
pharmaceutical cases 158–9
political power game 14–17
Post-Chicago School 45–6
Post Danmark I 113, 117–18
Post Danmark II 132, 137
power: discretionary 18–19; incentive and possibility to take strategic actions for 16–17; political power game 14–17
practical absence of judicial supervision 88–92
predatory pricing 113–18; lack of cases 183–4
presumptive: 'all circumstances' analytical framework on loyalty rebates 135–6; approach to exclusivity rebates 138–41; approach to protecting competitive market structures 124–6; as-efficient-competitor approach v presumptive approach 138; of the competition foreclosure harm 134–5; theory of foreclosure harm 115–17
pricing: exploitative 110–13, 151–6, **153–4**; predatory 113–18, 183–4
primitive theories of harm 122–3
private enforcement 25–6, 93–6, **94**, *96*
public enforcement: Anti-Monopoly Commission 73–8; consolidating agencies 83; enforcement record of MOFCOM 78–9; enforcement record of NDRC 81–3, **83**; enforcement record of SAIC 79–81, **80**; judicial supervision of AML 86–93, **89–91**; led by SAMR 83–6, **85**; supervising 21–2

Qihoo v Tencent: Guangdong High Court 148–9; Supreme Court 150–1
Qualcomm Decision, The 152, 156–8, 180, 183

reasoning of courts 181–2
rebates, loyalty 132–41

reform, decentralization 62–4
refusal to deal 121–9, 161–9, **162–3**
regional courts 154–6, **154**, 160–1, 165–7, 177–8
resale, restriction of 109–10, 142, 144
research methods 5–6
research questions 3–5; summary answers to 191–2
responsibilities of the Commission 61–2
restriction of competition 32, 119, 165, 172
restriction of resale 09–10, 142, 144

SABAM 110, 112–13
SAIC *see* State Administration for Industry and Commerce (SAIC)
SAMR *see* State Administration of Market Regulation (SAMR)
S-C-P paradigm *see* structure-conduct-performance (S-C-P) paradigm
secondary legislation 1, 54–7
Shandong Kanghui Pharmaceutical Case, The 153, 158
Shanghai High Court 151, 179
Shangyao First Pharmaceuticals & Wuhan Huihai Pharmaceutical Case, The 153
Sherpa's Case, The 150, 171–3, 182
Sichuan Jiuyuan Yinhai Software Case, The 160
Simcere Pharmaceutical Case, The 165
Société Technique Minière 102
soft law 57–8
Song Xin v China Railway Guangzhou 165
Sot Lélos 121–2, 127–9, 142
SSNDQ (small but significant non-transitory decrease in quality) test 149–51
SSNIP (small but significant non-transitory increase in price) test 148–50
standard harm allegations 123–4
State Administration for Industry and Commerce (SAIC) 2, 73, 75–7; enforcement record 79–81, **80**; *Tetra Pak* 157–8, 169–70
State Administration of Market Regulation (SAMR) 7, 152–4, **153**, 172–4; pharmaceutical cases 158–9; public enforcement led by 83–6, **85**; refusal to deal 164–5
State Anti-Monopoly Bureau 83–4, 190
strategic actions for more power 16–17
structural competition foreclosure 142–3
structural theory of harm 133–4
structure-conduct-performance (S-C-P) paradigm 40–1, 42–4
substantive law 11–14
Suiker Unie 109–10, 132–3, 133–4, 142, 144–5
supervising public enforcement 21–2
supervisory model, EU 186–9
supplementary harms 143–5
supranational regime, EU: institutional structure at the Union level 61–8, *67*; legal framework 53–60
Supreme Court 150–1, 154–6, **154**, 160–1, 167–9, 174–5, 177–8

technocracy, agency 22–4
TeliaSonera 117, 129, 131–2, 188
terminology 8–9
Tetra Pak Decision, The 157–8, 169–70
text of Anti-Monopoly Law 72–3
theories, economic: Chicago School 42–5; consideration for applying 46–8; Harvard School 40–2; ordoliberalism 36–40; Post-Chicago School 45–6
theories of harm 32–6; competitive harm 30–2; development in centralized EU regime 99–145; development in federated Chinese regime 147–84; differences in the development of 186–91; economic theories 36–48; elaboration of 181–4; form-based 133–4; framework for evaluation 48–9; primitive 122–3; structural 133–4
Tiyu v Chinese Super League 174–5
Tong Hua v China Mobile Shanghai 165, 177
Tongfang CNKI Case, The 153, 172–4
trading conditions, unreasonable 156–61
Treaty of Lisbon 53, 57, 65
Treaty on the European Union (TEU) 53–4, 58, 60, 65, 100
Treaty on the Functioning of the European Union (TFEU) 7–9, 30, 33, 36–48, 53–63, 65–7, 99–110, 118–21, 142–3, 148
tripartite public enforcement regime: Anti-Monopoly Commission 73–8; consolidating agencies 83; enforcement record of MOFCOM 78–9; enforcement

record of NDRC 81–3, **83**; enforcement record of SAIC 79–81, **80**
tying 156–61

United Brands 108–12, 122–3, 124–6, 141–2, 144, 151
unreasonable trading conditions, imposition of 156–61
unsupervised agencies 182–3

Wang v Beijing Lianjia 155
workable competition 40
Wu Xiaoqin v Shaanxi Broadcast 160
Wu Zongqu v Yongfu Water Supply 155

Xu Shuqing v Tencent 179

Yang Zhiyong v China Telecom 151, 179, 182
Yangmou v Hefei Yimou 155, 161, 174
Yixing Ganghua Gas Case, The 153, 171–2
Yuanda Pharmaceutical 159
Yunnan Yingding v Sinopec 167, 179, 182

Zhang v Quanzhou Crematorium 167–8
Zhejiang Second Pharmaceutical & Tianjin Handewei Pharmaceutical Decision, The 161–3

Kolibri 360 GmbH
Ferdinand-Jühlke-Straße 7
99095 Erfurt, Deutschland
produktsicherheit@kolibri360.de